POLICING PROBLEM PLACES

POLICING PROBLEM PLACES

Crime Hot Spots and Effective Prevention

Anthony A. Braga
David L. Weisburd

UNIVERSITY PRESS

2010

OXFORD
UNIVERSITY PRESS

Oxford University Press, Inc., publishes works that further
Oxford University's objective of excellence
in research, scholarship, and education.

Oxford   New York
Auckland   Cape Town   Dar es Salaam   Hong Kong   Karachi
Kuala Lumpur   Madrid   Melbourne   Mexico City   Nairobi
New Delhi   Shanghai   Taipei   Toronto

With offices in
Argentina   Austria   Brazil   Chile   Czech Republic   France   Greece
Guatemala   Hungary   Italy   Japan   Poland   Portugal   Singapore
South Korea   Switzerland   Thailand   Turkey   Ukraine   Vietnam

Copyright © 2010 by Oxford University Press, Inc.

Published by Oxford University Press, Inc.
198 Madison Avenue, New York, New York 10016

www.oup.com

Oxford is a registered trademark of Oxford University Press

Library of Congress Cataloging-in-Publication Data
Braga, Anthony Allan, 1969–
Policing problem places ; crime hot spots and effective prevention /
Anthony A. Braga, David Weisburd.
     p.   cm. — (Studies in crime and public policy)
Includes bibliographical references and index.
ISBN 978-0-19-534196-6
1. Problem-oriented policing.   2. Crime prevention.
I. Weisburd, David.   II. Title.
HV7936.P75B73 2009
363.2'3—dc22   2009044078

9 8 7 6 5 4 3 2 1

Printed in the United States of America
on acid-free paper

ACKNOWLEDGMENTS

This book was developed from an ongoing and collaborative research enterprise examining strategic crime prevention, hot spots policing, the nature of high-activity crime places, and criminological theory. The primary contribution of this book lies in assembling, updating, and synthesizing these separate bodies of work. This book builds on material originally developed with colleagues in the following publications: A. A. Braga. (2001). "The Effects of Hot Spots Policing on Crime." *Annals of the American Academy of Political and Social Science* 578:104–25; A. A. Braga. (2005). "Hot Spots Policing and Crime Prevention: A Systematic Review of Randomized Controlled Trials." *Journal of Experimental Criminology* 1:317–42; A. A. Braga. (2008). "Preventing Crime at Problem Places." Chapter 3 in *Problem-Oriented Policing and Crime Prevention*. 2nd ed. Monsey, N.Y.: Criminal Justice Press; J. Eck and D. Weisburd. (1995). "Crime Places in Crime Theory." In: J. Eck and D. Weisburd (eds.), *Crime and Place*. Monsey, N.Y.: Criminal Justice Press; D. Weisburd. (2008). *Place-Based Policing*. Ideas in American Policing Series 9. Washington, D.C.: Police Foundation; D. Weisburd and A. A. Braga. (2006). "Understanding Police Innovation." In: D. Weisburd and A. A. Braga (eds.), *Police Innovation: Contrasting Perspectives*. New York: Cambridge University Press; D. Weisburd and A. A. Braga. (2006).

"Hot Spots Policing as a Model for Police Innovation." In: D. Weisburd and A. A. Braga (eds.), *Police Innovation: Contrasting Perspectives*. New York: Cambridge University Press; D. Weisburd, S. Bushway, C. Lum, and S. Yang. (2004). "Trajectories of Crime at Places: A Longitudinal Study of Street Segments in Seattle." *Criminology* 42:283–322; and D. Weisburd, L. Wyckoff, J. Ready, J. Eck, J. Hinkle, and F. Gajewski. (2006). "Does Crime Just Move Around the Corner? A Controlled Study of Spatial Displacement and Diffusion of Crime Control Benefits." *Criminology* 44:549–92.

CONTENTS

TABLES

FIGURES

POLICING PROBLEM PLACES

Introduction

On Valentine's Day 1989, in the capital of the U. S., 14 people were hit by gunshots. Four of them were shot on one block of Drake Place, S.E. One of the wounded, age 26, died; another, a 15-year-old girl, was found in her apartment with 11 firearms, including a machine gun, a shotgun and five bullet-proof vests...This one small block of Drake Place and its adjacent public housing complex had witnessed five murders in 1988. That was bad enough. But in the first seven weeks of 1989, Drake Place was the site of 4 murders and 14 bullet woundings.

Drake Place was a "hot spot" of crime. It was so hot that the police said they stayed away from it as much as possible, unless they got a call....It was so hot that every night after dark, one officer claimed there were gun shots all night long....It was so hot that after the St. Valentine's Day Massacre, the Washington, D.C. police assigned a special patrol car to guard the block 24 hours a day/...Drake Place may have been one of the hottest spots of crime in the U.S. in 1989.

—Sherman, 1995: 35–36

Crime hot spots, such as Drake Place in Washington, D.C., during the late 1980s, have long been serious concerns to the police and the public. Local newspapers often include stories of community concern over drinking establishments, sex shops, or twenty-four-hour convenience stores that are seen as magnets for crime and criminals.

Community advocates suggest taking legal action against the owners of places that disrupt neighborhoods and demand increased police attention to specific locations that generate a disproportionate amount of crime and disorder. Unfortunately, there are no easy answers when dealing with crime hot spots. The problems of high-activity crime places can seem chronic, intractable, and very difficult to manage. Over the last two decades, American police departments have increasingly taken on the challenge of dealing with problem places by engaging a strategic approach that seems to be generating noteworthy crime prevention gains. This approach is generally known as "hot spots policing."

The locations of crime are natural targets for police intervention. Indeed, police officers are deployed to deal with specific crime incidents reported at particular addresses, and police managers typically allocate additional officers to districts and beats suffering from elevated levels of crime. Unfortunately, these traditional responses do not strategically focus on crime hot spots, such as street-intersection areas, mass-transit stations, or bars, in a sustained manner or attempt to address any under-lying conditions that cause crime and criminals to cluster at particular places. Hot spots policing is an innovation that attempts to refocus the strategic approaches of policing so that crime hot spots are a central concern.

In this book, we make the case that hot spots policing is an effective approach to crime prevention that should be engaged in by police departments in the United States and other countries. There is a strong and growing body of rigorous scientific evidence that the police can con-trol crime hot spots without simply displacing crime problems to other places. Putting police officers in high-crime locations may be an old and well-established idea. However, the age and popularity of an idea does not necessarily mean that it is being done properly. We believe that how police address crime hot spots matters. Police officers should strive to use problem-oriented policing and situational crime prevention tech-niques to address the place dynamics, situations, and characteristics that cause a "spot" to be "hot." We also make the point that the strategies used to police problem places can have more or less desirable effects on police-community relations. Particularly in minority neighborhoods where residents have long suffered from elevated crime problems and historically poor police service, police officers should make an effort to develop positive and collaborative relationships with residents and not engage in strategies that will undermine the legitimacy of police agencies, such as indiscriminant enforcement tactics.

In this introductory chapter we introduce the idea of hot spots policing by tracing its origins to two key studies in the development of modern police strategies. In 1974, the Kansas City Preventive Patrol Experiment challenged the ability of police patrol as a crime prevention approach (Kelling et al., 1974). In 1995, the Minneapolis Hot Spots Experiment showed that police could prevent crime if they focused on high crime hot spots (Sherman and Weisburd, 1995). The Minneapolis study led to a series of hot spots studies that we describe in chapter 4. We also introduce a key objection to hot spots policing, that it will simply displace crime to other areas. Focusing on the Jersey City Drug Market Analysis Experiment (Weisburd and Green, 1995) and the Jersey City Displacement and Diffusion study (Weisburd et al., 2006) we show why this argument has not hindered the development of hot spots approaches. Adding to the argument for hot spots policing we also show that crime hot spots evidence stability over time, making them an efficient focus for crime prevention. Finally, we examine the diffusion of hot spots policing as a concept in American policing. In concluding, we lay out the chapters that follow and their importance for making the case for hot spots policing.

Preventive Patrol and Crime Prevention

In 1974 the Police Foundation published a study that was to shatter the traditional assumptions behind the major crime prevention strategy of American policing. At least since the Second World War, the bedrock of American policing's efforts to prevent crime was found in preventive patrol by a motorized police force. The strategy was reinforced by a simple and persuasive logic that was advocated no less by scholars than by police professionals. A visible police presence across urban centers would be a powerful deterrent to criminals. Random preventive patrol across American cities was seen as the key strategy of police for doing something about crime.

The strategy was not an inexpensive one. Estimates at the time placed the price tag for preventive patrol at more than 2 billion dollars per year (Kelling et al., 1974). In today's dollars that would mean that the police were spending slightly more than 13 billion dollars per year on preventive patrol in the 1970s.[1] But it should be kept in mind that the strategy was very much fit to the overall obligations of American police agencies, which is one reason why preventive patrol is such an enduring approach to do something about crime in the United States. With the development of emergency calls for service systems in the 1930s, Americans had become accustomed to the police being there when they call (Walker, 1992). First developed in 1968, the 911 system of emergency calls for police service was a popular innovation in American policing, and by the 1970s Americans had begun to expect that the police would respond rapidly to public requests for emergency service (Sparrow, Moore, and Kennedy, 1990). Of course, for the police to respond quickly they must be out on the street. Random preventive patrol provided an efficient solution to the question of what to do with the police when they were not responding to emergency calls. If they could simply continue to patrol in the areas that they were assigned, the public would not only gain the advantage of police that could be dispatched to them quickly, but also the benefit of preventing future crimes.

The logic behind preventive patrol was simple and persuasive. A potential offender looking to commit crime in the community would be deterred by the visible presence of the police. That visible presence, of course, was multiplied many times by the constant movement of police cars throughout a city. Random preventive patrol in this sense was not only a natural extension of the popular emergency-response system; it was also a way to maximize the possible deterrent value of police visibility through the omnipresence of the police throughout a community. And the extent of visibility was likely to represent in a very general way the concentration of crime in the city. Most American police agencies did not simply dispatch patrol cars serendipitously across the city landscape. They often used data about the distribution of crime across precincts or beats, so that there were more cars available in geographic areas that had more crime, and during periods of higher activity.[2] In this regard, again, the link between the emergency-call system and preventive patrol aided in concentrating resources where they were assumed to be most needed.

But the same logic that supported the salience of random preventive patrol as a crime prevention tactic, also suggested that it would be a mistake to ignore major areas of a city in designing a strategy of preventive patrol. Offenders in this context were assumed to be highly motivated to commit crime. While they would be deterred by the visual presence of the police, the blocking of an opportunity for crime in one place was assumed likely to lead to the commission of crime in another. Thomas Repetto (1976) was among the first to coin the term "displacement" for this phenomenon, focusing on the fact that crime prevention in one locale would lead to offenders moving to another to commit crime. If offenders would react to police presence by displacing to other areas, then it made sense for the police to spread preventive patrol as widely as possible. Preventive patrol focused in small areas was assumed to simply shift crime around. The police sought to balance this idea of displacement, with the fact that certain areas had more crime (Wilson, 1963). But the overall result was that effective preventive patrol was seen to require a very broad spread of police resources in areas across the city. For this reason, preventive patrol was termed "random" preventive patrol in many places (Larson, 1972; Wilson, 1963).

When the Police Foundation set out to assess the benefits of preventive patrol there had been few rigorous studies evaluating what the police did and what impacts that they had on crime (Kelling et al., 1974). Indeed, the Police Foundation study was seen as a major experiment in policing that would lead to other rigorous tests of policing strategies such as rapid response to calls for service and follow-up criminal investigations (Greenwood, Chaiken, and Petersilia, 1977; Kansas City Police Department,

1978). Patrick Murphy, the distinguished former commissioner of the New York City Police Department, and then president of the Police Foundation, noted in the foreword to the report on the Kansas City Preventive Patrol study that the "experiment was unique in that never before had there been an attempt to determine through such extensive scientific evaluation the value of visible police patrol" (Kelling et al., 1974: i). The study was conducted in a city with an innovative police chief, Clarence Kelly, who was later to become head of the Federal Bureau of Investigation. The study itself was led by George L. Kelling, who later was to play a central role in the development of police innovation in the United States (e.g., Kelling and Coles, 1996; Wilson and Kelling, 1982).

The study design was straightforward, dividing Kansas City into police beats that received a "normal level" of preventive patrol, beats that received heightened patrol, and beats that did not receive any preventive patrol beyond that which would have naturally occurred because of responses to emergency calls for service. The study included a host of different data sources including surveys, analysis of crime calls and crime incidents, and represented perhaps the most extensive data collection ever conducted on the police. The findings, which were unambiguous, challenged the continued reliance on preventive patrol as a core crime prevention strategy in American policing. The researchers found that preventive patrol had no measurable effect on crime or citizen feelings of security.

The findings of the Kansas City study had strong impact on a generation of police scholars and practitioners. While a few other studies included more promising findings (e.g., Schnelle et al., 1977), the sheer scope of the Kansas City experiment, and its unambiguous conclusions, led to an assumption, at least by scholars, that random preventive police patrol had no impact on crime (e.g., see Bayley, 1994; Gottfredson and Hirschi, 1990; Klockars, 1985). And the skepticism regarding preventive patrol was to extend more generally to the ability of the police to prevent crime. By the early 1990s there was a broad consensus among criminologists and police scholars that crime was a product of larger social forces, and the police could do little if anything to impact upon crime or crime rates (Bayley, 1994; Gottfredson and Hirschi, 1990). The police as crime fighters might have been a popular idea in the media and among the public, but the idea that the police could do something about crime had little credence in the universities or research institutes that were concerned with policing.

For police practitioners the story was more complex. Whatever the benefits of preventive patrol, it was as we have already noted very much consistent with the emergency response systems that had come to dominate the work of American policing (Sparrow, Moore, and Kennedy, 1990; Walker, 1992). Moreover, many police executives were not convinced by the study's findings. The logic of preventive patrol was still very much accepted in America's police agencies if not among American police scholars (Hale, 1982). The idea that visible police presence would prevent crime not only made common sense, it was consistent with the experiences of police practitioners. What was the logic underlying the failures of preventive patrol, as evidenced in the Kansas City experiment? While scholars had come quickly to assume that random preventive patrol did not achieve its goals, they did not provide to the police a clear explanation for why the logic it relied upon was flawed. Whatever the broad social trends responsible for overall fluctuations in crime in society, criminologists had long recognized that differential guardianship will impact upon crime (e.g., see Sutherland, 1947). What explains the fact that variation in such guardianship in Kansas City appeared to have little impact upon crime? Could it simply be that the police could not have an impact upon crime irrespective of what strategies they employed, as some scholars had begun to assume? Or was there a fundamental disjuncture between the understanding that scholars and the police had about crime in the city and the patrol strategies that the police used?

The Emergence of Hot Spots Policing

This latter question was at the heart of the development of what has come to be called hot spots policing. Simply defined, hot spots policing is the application of police interventions at very small geographic units of analysis. It does not sound like a very radical innovation, but indeed it represents a major reform not only in how the police organize to do something about crime, but also in how scholars define and understand the crime problem.

The approach developed from a collaboration between Lawrence Sherman and David Weisburd that began in the late 1980s. Sherman had recently collected data on crime at addresses in Minneapolis, Minnesota, for a study of problem-oriented policing (Buerger, 1992, 1993; Sherman, 1987; Sherman, Buerger, and Gartin, 1989). The data were startling, in that they suggested a tremendous concentration of crime at certain street addresses. Table 1.1 presents the distribution of emergency crime calls to

Table 1.1. Distribution of All Dispatched Calls for Police Service in Minneapolis, by Frequency at Each Address and Intersection, December 15, 1985–December 15, 1986

No. of Calls	Observed No. of Places	Expected No. of Places	Cumulative % of Places	Cumulative % of Calls
0	45,561	6,854	100%	—
1	35,858	19,328	60.4	100
2	11,318	27,253	29.2	88.9
3	5,683	25,618	19.4	81.9
4	3,508	18,060	14.4	76.7
5	2,299	10,186	11.4	72.4
6	1,678	4,787	9.4	68.8
7	1,250	1,929	7.9	65.7
8	963	680	6.8	63.0
9	814	213	6.0	60.6
10	652	60	5.3	58.4
11	506	15	4.7	56.3
12	415	4	4.3	54.6
13	357	1	3.9	53.1
14	297	0	3.6	51.7
15=>	3,841	0	3.3	50.4

Mean = 2.82 X^2 = 301,376   df = 14   p < .0001
Source: Sherman, Gartin, and Buerger (1989): 38.

the police for one year in the city of Minneapolis arranged by street addresses with the highest crime totals (Sherman, Gartin and Buerger, 1989). What is apparent from the table is that most addresses in the city experienced no crime at all, while fully 50 percent of the crime in Minneapolis occurred at just 3.5 percent of the street addresses.[3]

This distribution of crime in the city suggested much greater concentration of crime at specific places than criminologists or the police had assumed. As we have already noted, the police had long recognized that the demands of police service varied by neighborhoods and beats. Random preventive patrol was never random, in the sense that some neighborhoods, police precincts, or police beats were given greater priority. But the idea that the concentration of crime was found not in beats or precincts but across discrete places in a city, such as addresses, challenged the traditional organization of police patrol, and indeed more general understandings of crime.

Sherman and Weisburd, both police scholars, began to consider how these findings impacted upon the conclusions reached regarding the effectiveness of police patrol, and the ability of the police to do something about crime more generally. They believed that the study offered a potential direct answer to the failures of the Kansas City Preventive Patrol Experiment:

> The premise of organizing patrol by beats is that crime could happen anywhere and that the entire beat must be patrolled. Computer-age data, however, have given new support to Henry Fielding's ([1751] 1977) proposal that police pay special attention to a small number of locations at high risk of crime. If only 3 percent of the addresses in a city produce more than half of all the requests for police response, if no police are dispatched to 40 percent of the addresses and intersections in a city over one year, and, if among the 60 percent with any requests the majority register only one request a year (Sherman, Gartin, and Buerger, 1989), then concentrating police in a few locations makes more sense that

spreading them evenly through a beat. (Sherman and
Weisburd, 1995: 629)

Sherman and Weisburd sought to design a study to test their conjecture that would be as persuasive as the Kansas City Preventive Patrol Experiment to scholars and practitioners, and that would be a fair test of this new idea about allocation of police resources across a city. They were able to gain significant funding, more than $800,000, from the National Institute of Justice, for the development of a Minneapolis Hot Spots Patrol Experiment. The first problem however was to define what was meant by hot spots of crime. The Minneapolis data had identified the concentration of crime at street addresses. But was it reasonable to assume that crime was clustered at "street addresses" or a higher level of geographic aggregation? Examination of the Minneapolis data suggested that some high-rate crime addresses were actually different entrances to the same building (Buerger, Cohn, and Petrosino, 1995). More generally, it seemed reasonable to assume that many high-rate addresses would cluster together into larger crime hot spots.

Sherman and Weisburd (1995) began by identifying 5,538 street addresses and intersections in the city that had more than three "hard crime" calls, excluding calls for such disorderly events as street fights, alarms, vandalism and disorderly persons. They then used computerized crime mapping to identify the location of these high-crime addresses. Having linked the addresses one to another, 420 high crime clusters of addresses with 20 or more hard crime calls were identified for visual inspections by research staff in the study.

To limit the sample to places where crime "occurred in public and could reasonably be deterred by police presence," Sherman and Weisburd (1995: 631) excluded all residential and large commercial buildings. Parking garages, indoor malls, hospitals, and public schools were also excluded, as were "magnet phone" locations from which events occurring elsewhere were reported. Sherman and Weisburd (1995) limited each hot spot to an area that could be easily viewed from some central location which they defined as an "epicenter." The computer maps and observations suggested that most of the crime clusters were concentrated on street blocks from intersection to intersection. Working from a revised group of 268 crime hot spots, they then identified hot spots that evidenced long-term crime problems from year to year. The final step in their identification of the hot spots was to ensure that there was enough distance one to another to avoid obvious contamination of what would become control sites by the "treatment" hot spots. After these efforts, and negotiation with the police on the number of hot spots that could receive adequate "dosage" of police presence, the experiment was begun with 110 hot spots of crime that were randomly assigned in equal numbers to a control group that would receive normal emergency response service, and an experimental group that would receive two to three times that "dosage" of patrol each day.

One of the criticisms of the earlier Kansas City study was that there was no measurement of how much dosage the different patrol areas actually received. In Minneapolis, Sherman and Weisburd (1995) measured dosage of police patrol at the experimental and control hot spots through 7,542 hour-long observations by a group of 19 observers and supervisors. The observed ratio of police presence in the treatment as opposed to control sites varied a good deal across the intervention period, but was maintained at a ratio of at least 2:1 for the first eight months of the experiment. However, the data suggested that the experiment was disrupted during the summer months when the call load for the department peaked (and vacation time for the police was highest).

The results of the Minneapolis Hot Spots Patrol Experiment stood in sharp distinction to those of the earlier Kansas City study. For the eight months in which the study was properly implemented, Sherman and Weisburd (1995) found a significant relative improvement in the experimental as compared to control hot spots both in terms of crime calls to the police and observations of disorder. Indeed, the effects of the program on crime, as measured by the difference between crime calls in the pre-experimental and experimental years, was found to be stable across the eight month period in which the program was properly implemented (see figure 1.1). Sherman and Weisburd (1995: 645) concluded

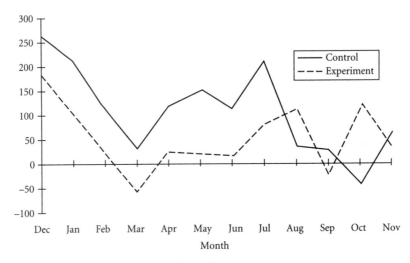

Figure 1.1. The Minneapolis Hot Spots Experiment

Note: Lines represent absolute differences between baseline and experimental years in total crime calls per month.

Source: Sherman and Weisburd (1995).

that their results show "clear, if modest, general deterrent effects of substantial increases in police presence in crime hot spots." They noted that it was time for "criminologists to stop saying 'there is no evidence' that police patrol can affect crime" (1995: 647).

The Threat of Crime Displacement

The Minneapolis Hot Spots Patrol Experiment established the importance of crime hot spots for policing, and challenged the conventional logic that had assumed that police patrol could not be effective. But the case for hot spots policing that it presented was shadowed by a key question that was not addressed by the Minneapolis data or the patrol experiment. Sherman and Weisburd raised the issue at the time:

> The main argument against directing extra resources to the hot spots is that it would simply displace crime problems from one

Displacement

address to another without achieving any overall or lasting reduction in crime. The premise of this argument is that a fixed supply of criminals is seeking outlets for the fixed number of crimes they are predestined to commit. Although that argument may fit some public drug markets, it does not fit all crime or even all vice.... In any case, displacement is merely a rival theory explaining *why* crime declines at a specific hot spot, if it declines. The first step is to see whether crime can be reduced at those spots at all, with a research design capable of giving a fair answer to that question. (1995: 629)

Having established that crime can be reduced at hot spots, the question remained whether concentrating on such places would merely shift crime from place to place. The prevailing assumption of criminologists and the police was voiced by Thomas Repetto in the 1970s:

The police...cannot be everywhere; all houses and commercial establishments cannot be secured with attack-proof doors and windows, and all neighborhood environments cannot be altered. A differential level of protection between various potential targets, both human and nonhuman, will always exist. Given the differential and no reduction in the offender population, will not the foreclosure of one type of criminal opportunity simply shift the incidence of crime to different forms, times and locales? (Repetto 1976: 167)

Would the hot spots policing approach simply lead to a shifting of crime from street to street in a city? While there might be very short crime prevention gains from such an approach, it suggested that hot spots policing would lead to the police "chasing" criminals around the city. The first hot spots study to examine the problem of displacement directly was the 1995 Jersey City Drug Market Analysis Experiment conducted by David Weisburd and Lorraine Green (Mazerolle). The study identified 56 drug hot spots of varying sizes, from a group of addresses, to a group of street segments evidencing similar drug activities, and then randomly allocated them to a treatment group that received a systematic problem-oriented response to drug crime, and a control group that received the normal reactive responses typical of drug enforcement at the time. The study again showed a strong crime prevention benefit for the hot spots policing approach. We describe this study and other hot spots policing experiments, as well as the crime displacement phenomena, in more detail in chapter 4. At this point, we want to focus specifically on the efforts of Weisburd and Green (1995) to examine crime displacement.

They identified a "displacement catchment area" of two blocks around each drug hot spot identified (Weisburd and Green, 1995). They then examined crime calls to the police not only in the study areas but also in the catchment areas. The results supported a developing idea about crime at place that was advanced by Ronald V. Clarke and David Weisburd (1994). They coined the term "diffusion of crime prevention benefits" to describe the "reverse" of displacement of crime. Clarke and Weisburd argued that crime prevention programs led often not to "displacement" as had been assumed by Repetto, but rather to crime reductions outside the areas that are targeted by crime prevention programs. This is precisely what Weisburd and Green (1995) found in the Jersey City Drug Market Analysis Experiment. For both public morals and narcotics crime calls there was a significant decrease in the catchment areas in the experimental sites as compared with the control sites. Looking at newly emerging drug hot spots, they also found support for the idea that the treatment did not lead to displacement of crime. There was almost twice as many new drug hot spots found after the experiment near the control areas as contrasted with the treatment areas.

As we describe in more detail in chapter 4, the findings of the Jersey City study were replicated in a number of other settings. The simple assumption that crime will displace to nearby areas as a result of focused crime prevention efforts at hot spots is not consistent with what experiments in hot spots policing have shown. Indeed, there is much stronger evidence that hot spots policing will lead to a diffusion of crime prevention benefits than that it will lead to displacement of such benefits.

Given the common assumption of spatial displacement, it is worthwhile to note a recent Police Foundation Study that focused specifically on this question and offers important data on "why" hot spots policing does not lead to a displacement of crime from the targeted locations (Weisburd et al., 2006). Unlike earlier studies, the Jersey City Displacement and Diffusion Project was not designed to assess the impacts of particular police interventions. Rather it was singularly focused on examining to what extent there was immediate spatial displacement or diffusion as a result of hot spot policing strategies and why displacement or diffusion occurred or did not occur. Two sites with substantial street-level crime and disorder were selected to be targeted and were carefully monitored during an experimental period. Two neighboring areas were selected to serve as catchment areas in order to assess immediate spatial displacement or diffusion. Intensive police interventions were applied to each target site but not applied to the catchment areas. More than three thousand twenty-minute social observations were conducted in the target and catchment areas during the study period. These data were supplemented by interviews and ethnographic field observations. The study supported the position that the most likely outcome of such focused crime prevention efforts is a diffusion of crime-control benefits to nearby areas.

Importantly, the study provided rich qualitative data for understanding why police interventions focused on hot spots would lead to diffusion of crime prevention benefits and not displacement of those benefits. Though the focus of the study was specifically on crime hot spots of prostitution, and drugs and violent crime, the data collected provided important insights into why crime does not simply move around the corner.

While traditional theoretical perspectives have predicted significant displacement outcomes in place-based crime prevention (Weisburd, 2002), recent theorizing in the area of rational choice (Cornish and Clarke, 1986) and routine activities (Cohen and Felson, 1979) suggest that displacement outcomes are likely to be limited. The main assumptions of these perspectives are that specific characteristics of places such as the nature of guardianship, the presence of motivated offenders, and the availability of suitable targets will strongly influence the likelihood of criminal events (see also Felson, 1994). Studies examining the factors that predict crime at microcrime places such as street segments or facilities (e.g., bars and taverns) generally confirm this relationship (see Roncek and Bell, 1981; Roncek and Meier, 1991; Smith, Frazee, and Davison, 2000).

These perspectives provide a context for understanding why offenders may not simply move around the corner, or possibly to other areas, in response to police intervention. Rational choice theories emphasize the importance of the balancing of effort, risks, and opportunities with the benefits that will be gained from criminal activities (Cornish and Clarke, 1986, 1987). Qualitative data from the Jersey City study suggest that spatial movement from crime sites involves substantial effort and risk by offenders (Weisburd et al., 2006).

A number of the offenders they spoke to complained about the time and effort it would take to reestablish their activities in other areas as a reaction to the police intervention. One respondent arrested at the drug-crime site, for example, explained that it is difficult to move because the "money won't be the same," that he "would have to start from scratch," and that it "takes time to build up customers" (Weisburd et al., 2006: 578). Respondents in the study repeatedly focused on the importance of regular customers. In fact, in the drug crime site, they were told that if a buyer was new they would have to be recommended by a regular customer. Even buyers they spoke to said they go to the same dealers because they know them and trust their product is good. The focus on the efforts required to move elsewhere is also evident in interviews at the prostitution hot spot, where prostitutes argued that such a move would be difficult for their regular customers.

Fear of victimization was also an important factor in preventing spatial displacement. One prostitute explained:

If they aren't regulars, I try to feel them out. I use precautions. I never will get into a car with two men. I always check the doors to make sure I can get out if I need to, like if an emergency arises, like a guy trying to hurt me. I will always go into an area I know. This way, if I need help, I know that somehow I can find someone or get someone's attention. But, in the same way, I don't go into an area that would give away what I am doing and get me arrested. I basically don't let the guys take me where they want to go. If they insist on this, then I make them pay me up front, before the zipper goes down. (Weisburd et al., 2006: 578)

This concern certainly applied to the prostitution site. Unlike the target site, which had few occupied buildings, one of the catchment areas included many residential addresses and thus places where citizens were much more likely to call the police. Moreover, some prostitutes who lived in the public housing projects in that area told the researchers that they did not feel comfortable soliciting near their homes where friends or relatives might see them.

Another respondent explained that going to a different area of town was difficult because other prostitutes got angry and told her "this is our turf, stay away" (Weisburd et al., 2006: 578). Similar resistance to displacement was evident in interviews with offenders arrested in the drug crime site. The drug dealers' intimacy with the area in which they work was one of the primary mechanisms preventing spatial displacement. A number of dealers explained that you work near where you live because that is your "turf." One arrestee elaborated, "you really can't deal in areas you aren't living in, it ain't your turf. That's how people get themselves killed" (Weisburd et al., 2006: 578).

Another emphasis of rational choice theorists is that the factors influencing offender choices are often very similar to those of nonoffenders (Cornish and Clarke, 1986). This insight has been part of a number of important criminological perspectives (e.g., see Akers, 1973; Sutherland, 1947), but it is sometimes lost in the identification of individuals as criminals and the criminological focus on what distinguishes them from noncriminals (Weisburd and Waring, 2001). One important explanation for the resistance to spatial displacement is simply that offenders, like non-offenders, come to feel comfortable with their home turf and the people that they encounter. As with non-offenders, moving jobs or homes can be seen as an important and difficult change in life circumstances. One prostitute noted, for example:

> I walked over (to the graveyard cemetery) and I didn't think I'd make money. It was unfamiliar to me. It was like, It was like…unfamiliar to me. I didn't know the guys (clients). On Cornelison you recognize the guys. I know from being out there every day (on Cornelison), the cars, the faces. It's different. In my area, I know the people. Up on "the hill"—I don't really know the people at that end of town. (Brisgone, 2004: 199)

The prostitutes interviewed were comfortable with the atmosphere of the prostitution hot spot. One prostitute explained that people work in the area because it is quiet and spaced out enough so that they can work alone or meet up and talk for a few minutes. Moving to another market may have meant challenging this comfort and would have required extra effort to acclimate. Another prostitute, explaining why she did not move to another central prostitution area in Jersey City, said she was uncomfortable there because it was "faster," with hotel rooms, fewer regulars, and not as many drugs.

While these data reinforce routine activities and rational choice perspectives, and help us to understand why crime does not simply move around the corner as a response to hot spots interventions, they do not explain why researchers found a significant diffusion of crime-control benefits both in the prostitution and drug-crime sites. Even if there is good reason not to move to other sites either because they do not offer similar opportunities, or increase the risks for offenders, why should observed crime and disorder go down in targeted hot spots? One simple explanation for this might be that crime in areas near to hot spots is due at least in part to the activities of offenders in the targeted sites. If many offenders are arrested and taken off the streets in hot spots interventions we would expect a decline in activity in nearby areas as well. It is also important to note that offenders in the Jersey City study did not assume that "things would be better elsewhere." They acted in a context of what rational choice theorists call "bounded rationality" (Johnson and Payne, 1986) in which they made assumptions about police behavior that were based on limited or incorrect information. In this context, they often assumed that the crackdowns at the hot spots were not limited to the target areas but were part of a more general increase in police activities. We suspect moreover, that such considerations apply more generally in hot spots policing studies.

Moreover, the Jersey City study suggests that spatial displacement is a much more difficult adaptation to focused crime prevention at hot spots than had been assumed. In some ways this finding is not at all surprising. For non-offenders, moving jobs or homes is considered a difficult life event that causes significant stress (Holmes and Rahe, 1967). Losing work and business readjustments rank close to a death in a family for stress-creating events in one's life (Holmes and Rahe, 1967). Why should we assume, in this context, that moving offending locations is an easy affair for offenders? In Jersey City, researchers found that other forms of adaptation to police strategies were likely to come before spatial displacement:

> The most dramatic shift during this period was in the incidence of method displacement.... Narratives suggest that this occurred as research subjects became more aware of what the intervention entailed and began engaging in different tactics to avoid being detected and arrested by police. Research subjects began pre-arranging dates by means of phone or beepers and working from home (combining spatial and method displacement); quizzing potential clients to ensure they were not police officers; disguising their looks and engaging in stealthy solicitation. Also at this time, research subjects began talking about (and some actually followed up) converting street clients into full-time customers—including

one woman who agreed to be locked inside the man's house every day while he went to work to avoid working on the street. (Brisgone, 2004: 200)

While these adaptations suggest that the crime prevention benefits of focused-enforcement efforts are to some extent limited, it is important to recognize that method displacement often means that the level or intensity of criminal behavior has been reduced. For example, when prostitutes have to make "dates," they are likely to have fewer customers than they would normally have if they were free to solicit on the street. The same is true for the adaptations of drug dealers. Importantly, as well, from the perspective of the police and the community, even if such crime continues indoors or in other settings, the interventions have significantly reduced the problematic street-level disorder associated with such crimes.

It is also important to note that desistence is likely an important component of the diffusion of crime prevention benefits observed in hot spots studies. Indeed, nine of forty-nine prostitutes interviewed by Brisgone (2004) in the Jersey City Displacement and Diffusion Study claimed that they had decided to stop criminal activities altogether. As one prostitute explained:

> I was tired of being tired. Sick of running. Then it started to scare me. It seemed like there would be stings (police roundups) constantly. I got scared of going to jail. I got tired of hurting my mother—letting her watch me do the things I did. She hated the fact that I worked the street. I got tired of hurting my family in general. I started to dislike myself. I started getting scared. I had a fear in my heart that I was going to die. I felt someone was going to kill me or I would do something terrible to get locked up for a long time . . . I was at the point. I was over the edge. I didn't know how I was doing this job. I had been told that I had a warrant. I didn't want to do it (prostitution) anymore. Or my drug habit anymore. (Brisgone, 2004: 205)

Do Hot Spots Make Stable Targets for Crime Prevention?

The finding that crime is concentrated at hot spots has now been repli-cated in a number of other studies (see, e.g., Brantingham and Branting-ham, 1999; Eck, Gersh, and Taylor, 2000; Spelman, 1995; Weisburd and Green, 1994, 2000; Weisburd, Maher, and Sherman, 1992; Weisburd et al., 2004). With the development of powerful computerized crime-mapping and database technologies, identifying crime hot spots has become a common exercise in understanding the nature of urban crime problems. For instance, Braga, Hureau, and Winship (2008) found that gun-vio-lence hot spots covered only 5 percent of Boston's 48.4 square miles, but generated nearly 53 percent of fatal and nonfatal shootings in 2006 (figure 1.2). But if the logic of hot spots policing is to be accepted, it is necessary to show not only that crime is concentrated at crime hot spots and that crime prevention benefits will not be simply displaced, but also that concentration of crime at hot spots evidences stability over time. What would be the point of the police investing large-scale crime pre-vention resources on crime hot spots if the location of such hot spots shifted year to year irrespective of police activities?

This question was not fully addressed for more than a decade after the Minneapolis Experiment. In the early years of this new century, a research team from the University of Maryland was able to gain a long series of data on crime from the Seattle Police Department (Weisburd et al., 2004). These data not only reinforced the early findings in Minneapolis, they illustrated that crime hot spots have a surprising degree of stability of offending rates over time. Looking at crime incidents at street segments in Seattle over a fourteen-year period, they found that year to year about 50 percent of the crime was found in approximately 4.5 percent of street segments (see figure 1.3). This finding is remarkable not only because it is so close to those reported in the Minneapolis study (Sherman, Gartin, and Buerger, 1989) but also because it now established the stability of such crime concentrations year to year.

Of course, the concentration of crime year to year does not preclude the possibility that each year different crime hot spots would develop, or

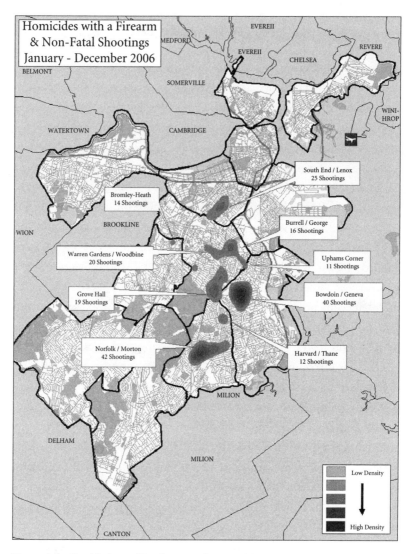

Figure 1.2. Gun Violence Hot Spots in Boston, 2006
Source: Braga, Hureau, and Winship (2008): 151.

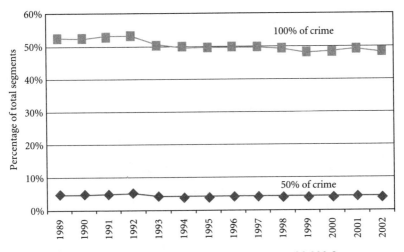

Figure 1.3. The Concentration of Crime Incidents Across 30,000 Street Segments in Seattle, Washington

Source: Weisburd, Bushway, Lum, and Yang (2004): 294.

that hot spots in one year would naturally become cool the next. Such "regression to the mean" is common in social phenomena, and a key concern for the idea of hot spots in policing was that the same places would evidence high crime activity year to year. Only very strong continuity in crime hot spots would support a large-scale commitment to hot spots as a focus of police operations.

For this reason, the Seattle study also looked at the developmental trends of street segments in Seattle over the fourteen-year period studied. Using a recently developed technique for identifying crime trends over time (see Nagin, 1999), the approximately 30,000 street segments in Seattle were grouped into "trajectories" with similar developmental trends over time. Figure 1.4 presents the eighteen trajectories and the number of street segments found in each. Important to the application of hot spots policing, there is a group high crime street segments at the top of the figure. Only about 1 percent of the street segments in Seattle fall in this group, but they consistently account for a very large share of reported crime between 1989 and 2002. Though overall, the high rate

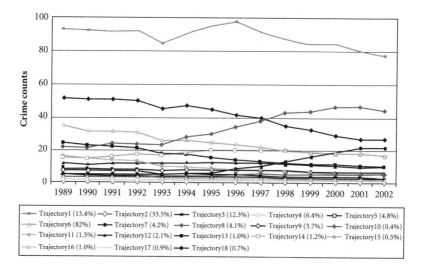

Figure 1.4. Trajectories of Crime for Street Segments in Seattle, 1989–2002
Source: Weisburd, Bushway, Lum, and Yang (2004): 299.

segments show a crime decline during this period, reflecting the national crime drop (Blumstein, 2000; Cook and Laub, 2002), they remain distinct from other street segments throughout the observation period. While there are developmental trends with some trajectory groups increasing or decreasing, hot spots of crime evidence a remarkable degree of stability, at least over the time period examined in the Seattle study. This is true not only for the hot spots, but also for the vast majority of places in the city that show very low and stable crime rates over time.

Several other studies have come to similar conclusions about the stability of crime at specific places over time. Spelman (1995) analyzed calls-for-service at high schools, housing projects, subway stations, and parks in Boston, and found that the risks at these public places remained fairly constant over time. Taylor (1999) also reports evidence of a high degree of stability of crime at place over time, examining crime and fear of crime at ninety street blocks in Baltimore, Maryland, using a panel design with data collected in 1981 and 1994 (see Robinson et al., 2003; Taylor, 2001). Data included not only official crime statistics, but also measures of citizen perceptions of crime and observations of physical conditions at the sites. Although Taylor and his colleagues observed significant deterioration in physical conditions at the blocks studied, they found that neither fear of crime nor crime showed significant or consistent differences across the two time periods.

The stability of crime at hot spots reinforces the logic that underlay the Minneapolis Hot Spots Experiment. Without police intervention, crime hot spots are not likely to disappear in short time periods. Concentrating police resources on such places makes very good sense both for short-term and long-term gains.

The Link between Research and Practice

Hot spots policing not only makes sense as a policing strategy, it has also become widely diffused in American policing. In a 2001 Police Foundation study more than seven in ten police departments with more than one hundred sworn officers reported using crime mapping to identify "crime hot spots" (Weisburd, Mastrofski, et al., 2001). A 2007 Police Executive Research Forum study found that 74 percent of police departments surveyed in 192 jurisdictions used "hot spots enforcement" as a strategy to address violent crime (Police Executive Research Forum, 2008). And there is wide recognition that hot spots policing is an evidence-based strategy. The Committee on Police Strategies and Practices of the National Research Council of the National Academy of Sciences concluded "...studies that focused police resources on crime hot spots provide the strongest collective evidence of police effectiveness that is now available." (Skogan and Frydl, 2004: 250). But the fact that the research literature is supportive of hot spots policing and that police have implemented this approach widely, does not necessarily mean that research strongly impacted police practice. For example, it may be that the police adopted hot spots policing independently and later evidence simply confirmed that the strategy was useful.

While the Minneapolis Hot Spots Experiment is the first example we know of a successful program in which microlevel crime hot spots were systematically identified on a large scale for the purpose of police intervention, it is not the first example of police use of crime mapping to identify crime problems. Hand-developed pin maps have been widely used in police agencies for over half a century (Weisburd and McEwen, 1997). And one can find isolated examples of what today we would define as hot spots policing in earlier periods (e.g., see Weiss, 2001). Moreover, during the 1970s, crime analysts looked for patterns in crime by plotting the locations and times at which crimes were committed to direct patrol officers to the most likely targets (Reinier, 1977), and cutting-edge crime analysts were experimenting with computerized crime mapping before the hot spots studies were well known (Weisburd and Lum, 2005). The widespread adoption of the Compstat management and accountability model can also be credited with the increasing interest in crime mapping and hot spots policing (Weisburd et al., 2001).

Nonetheless, a recent study by Weisburd and Lum (2005) suggests that the timing of the wide-scale implementation of hot spots policing follows very closely the basic and applied research we have reviewed. The study examined the diffusion of computerized crime mapping in police agencies using data from the National Institute of Justice Crime Mapping Laboratory (Mamalian, LaVigne, and Groff, 1999), and a small pilot study of ninety-two police agencies of more than one hundred sworn officers conducted by the researchers. They found that computerized crime mapping in larger police agencies first began to emerge in policing in the late 1980s, early 1990s. Adoption began to grow steeply in the mid-1990s with the number of adopters increasing at a large rate after 1995 (see figure 1.5).

Weisburd and Lum (2005) make a direct link between the diffusion of innovation in crime mapping and the adoption of hot spots policing in their survey. When they asked why departments developed a crime-mapping capability, nearly half of those surveyed responded that crime mapping was adopted to facilitate hot spots policing. Of other categories of responses, many were likely related to hot spots approaches though respondents gave more general replies such as "crime mapping was initially developed in response to a specific police strategy." Moreover they found that 80 percent of the departments in their sample that have a

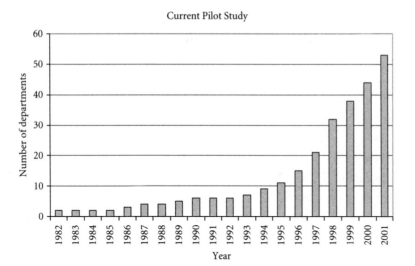

Current Pilot Study

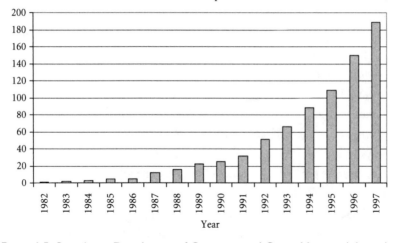

1997 CMRC Adoption Curve

Figure 1.5. Cumulative Distribution of Computerized Crime Mapping Adopted from the Weisburd et al. Pilot Study and the CMRC Study

Source: Weisburd and Lum (2005).

computerized crime-mapping capability conduct computerized hot spots analysis, and two thirds of departments that have computerized crime-mapping capabilities use hot spots policing as a policing tactic.

If we can make the link between hot spots policing and computerized crime mapping suggested by Weisburd and Lum, then the data suggest that hot spots policing emerged as an important police strategy precisely during the period that evaluation findings were being widely disseminated. Results of the Minneapolis Hot Spots Experiment, for example, though first published in an academic journal in 1995, was the focus of a plenary panel at the Academy of Criminal Justice Sciences in 1990 that was chaired by the then Director of the National Institute of Justice, James K. Stewart. Overall, the emergence of crime mapping and hot spots policing follow closely the development of strong research evidence regarding the hot spots approach. Of course, these data do not confirm with certainty a causal link between research and practice in the adoption of hot spots policing, but they suggest that hot spots policing approaches began to be widely implemented after research studies began to show their effectiveness.

While we are making a strong claim that scientific research drove police interest in hot spots policing, it is also true that the police were "primed" for the science and improvements in crime mapping. In many ways, these developments fell on the policing profession like seeds on damp fertile ground. The police did not blindly follow the science. Rather they were ready for it. Indeed, the 1976 Police Foundation study, "Three Approaches to Criminal Apprehension in Kansas City," documents strong police interest in rudimentary forms of hot spots policing (termed "location-oriented patrol") and a willingness to collaborate with social scientists to determine more effective crime control approaches (Pate, Bowers, and Parks, 1976). All the field research cited here and in the chapters that follow involved the active cooperation of police agencies at no little sacrifice on their part. Hot spots policing studies were possible because some police executives shared an interest in developing a line of research that would lead to more focused and effective crime prevention policies. Just as a small number of criminologists invested their time and creativity in this substantive area, a small number of police managers and agencies worked to coproduce the science discussed here.

The concept of hot spots policing has been influential in American policing. However, the police have not really taken full advantage of this approach in reforming the way they work or the organization of policing. Research accordingly suggests that it is time for police to shift from person-based policing to place-based policing. While such a shift is largely an evolution in trends that have begun over the last few decades, it will nonetheless demand radical changes in data collection in policing, in the organization of police activities, and particularly in the overall world view of the police. It remains true today that police officers see the key work of policing as catching criminals. It is time to change that world view so that police understand that the key to crime prevention is in ameliorating crime at place.

What Follows

Given the widespread adoption of hot spots policing, and the growing empirical evidence of its effectiveness as a strategy for policing, we thought it important to bring together what is known about this approach both in terms of its application by police and research evidence in a comprehensive way. Our goal was both to summarize what is known and also to raise questions about what we need to know to improve our knowledge and to improve policing.

In the chapter that follows we frame the origins of hot spots policing in the crisis of legitimacy and effectiveness of American policing of the 1970s and 1980s. Other major police innovations, such as community and problem-oriented policing, contributed to and complemented the development of hot spots policing as these approaches challenged the police to focus on local crime and disorder problems which often were manifested at very specific places within communities. However, as we describe in chapter 2, a major difference between other police innovations in this period and hot spots policing can be found in the use of innovations in crime theory and research in the development of the approach. Chapter 3 reviews theoretical perspectives and basic research on crime and criminal offenders that support taking a place-oriented approach to crime problems. Understanding the underlying conditions, dynamics, and situations that create and sustain high-activity crime places is important in justifying hot spots policing and thinking about the types of police actions that might best be used to control problem places.

Chapter 4 presents the empirical evidence on the crime prevention effectiveness of hot spots policing. We begin the chapter by briefly describing the strengths and weaknesses of different types of evaluations that researchers use to determine whether crime prevention programs "work" in preventing crime. We then present the findings of three rigorous reviews of hot spots policing evaluations that conclude the approach is effective in preventing crime without simply displacing criminals to other locations. Several evaluations observe the opposite of crime displacement and suggest that hot spots policing can diffuse local crime prevention benefits into areas immediately surrounding targeted areas. In chapter 5, we consider the methods police can use to address the problems of crime hot spots. Given the complex problems at crime hot spots, the police need to go beyond one-dimensional enforcement strategies. We argue that the problem-oriented policing approach, even when not fully implemented, seems to be best positioned to generate strong crime prevention gains in crime hot spots. Problem-oriented policing challenges police officers to understand the underlying conditions that give rise to crime hot spots and to implement an array of tailored responses to the problems of crime places.

Crime hot spots tend to cluster in disadvantaged, minority neighborhoods where police-community relationships can often be characterized by distrust and suspicion. If the police are not viewed as legitimate authorities in such neighborhoods, they will be challenged in developing the community cooperation necessary to deal with serious crime problems. In chapter 6, we suggest that hot spots policing programs infused with community policing principles hold great promise in improving police legitimacy in the eyes of community members living in places suffering from crime and disorder problems. Police actions that seek to prevent crime by changing places are better positioned to generate positive community perceptions of the police relative to simply increasing presence and arresting large numbers of offenders. Community engagement and treating citizens with respect and dignity need to accompany heightened levels of police activity in small places. Our concluding thoughts on the prospects of hot spots policing as a central police crime prevention strategy are presented in chapter 7.

Putting Hot Spots Policing in Context   **2**

Police officers have long recognized the importance of place in crime problems (Weisburd and McEwen, 1997). Police officers know the locations within their beats that tend to be trouble spots and are often very sensitive to signs of potential crimes across the places that comprise their beats. As Bittner (1970: 90) suggests in his classic study of police work, some officers know "the shops, stores, warehouses, restaurants, hotels, schools, playgrounds, and other public places in such a way that they can recognize at a glance whether what is going on within them is within the range of normalcy." Police managers have also long recognized that certain high-activity areas generate repeated crime incidents. As Carolyn Block (1997) has noted in discussing interest in crime mapping among police, "Crime maps are nothing new. Pin maps have graced walls behind police chiefs' desks since pins were invented." The traditional response to such trouble spots typically included heightened levels of patrol and increased opportunistic arrests and investigations. Until recently, however, police crime prevention strategies did not focus systematically on crime hot spots and did not seek to address the underlying conditions that give rise to high-activity crime places.

Recent police interest in hot spots policing is part of a larger set of changes and innovations that have occurred in policing over the last three decades (Weisburd and Braga, 2006). Some have described the period of change and innovation that began in the policing industry during the 1980s as the most dramatic in the history of policing (e.g., see Bayley, 1994). This claim does not perhaps do justice to the radical reforms that led to the creation of modern police forces in the nineteenth century, or even the wide-scale innovations in tactics or approaches to policing that emerged after the Second World War. However, observers of the police today are inevitably struck by the pace and variety of innovation in the last few decades. Whether this period of change is greater than those of previous generations is difficult to know since systematic observation of police practices is a relatively modern phenomenon. But there is broad consensus among police scholars that the last three decades have "witnessed a remarkable degree of innovation in policing" (Skogan and Frydl, 2004: 82).

The focus of this book is on one important innovation—hot spots policing. It is not the only recent innovation that has been concerned with the concentration of crime at place. Indeed, dealing with crime hot spots has been a key component of many recent police innovations such as Compstat (Silverman, 1999), community policing (Skogan, 2006), and problem-oriented policing (Eck, 2006). However, to understand the emergence of hot spots policing, it is necessary to understand the crisis in American policing that required the police to innovate. It is also important to understand the relationship of hot spots policing to other strategic innovations such as community policing and problem-oriented policing. This chapter examines crisis and change in American policing, reviews several key strategic police innovations, and then traces the theoretical and empirical insights that led to the emergence of hot spots policing.

Crisis and Change in American Policing

The police developed as a mechanism to do justice by apprehending offenders and holding them accountable (Wilson and McLaren, 1977). Since their primary practical goal was to reduce crime victimization, police long believed that they were in the business of crime prevention (U.S. President's Commission on Law Enforcement and Administration of Criminal Justice, 1967a, 1967b). Police strategists relied upon two ideas to prevent crimes: deterrence and incapacitation. The imminent threat of arrest was their main strategy to generate general deterrence to dissuade the general public from contemplating crimes. The police attempted to generate specific deterrence by apprehending criminals with the intent to discourage them from committing crimes in the future. The police also believed that arrests would prevent crime by incapacitating criminals, through their removal from the street and subsequent placement in jail or prison. In particular, the police sought to prevent repeat offenders from continuing their careers through specific deterrence, incapacitation, and, to some degree, rehabilitation (as part of their subsequent incarceration or community supervision). The police were reliant on the other parts of the criminal justice system to pursue these goals, but they could at least start the process by arresting offenders and building credible cases against them. As many observers have pointed out, these police crime prevention efforts were, in reality, reactive (see, e.g., Goldstein, 1979); they only began after a crime was committed.

In addition to preventing crime through deterrence and incapacitation, prevention, in policing circles prior to 1965, also conjured up the work of a unit handling juvenile cases (often referred to as the "crime prevention unit") or a unit of officers assigned to conducting educational "out-reach" programs in the schools. These programs were neither department-wide nor large in size, but were significant in that they were often seen as segregating and compartmentalizing the "prevention" work of the police.

Since the early 1990s, the police have become much more interested in a broader idea of prevention and the use of a wide range of crime prevention tactics (Roth et al., 2000). The search for greater citizen satisfaction, increased legitimacy, and more effective crime prevention alternatives to the traditional tactics used by most police departments led to the development of innovative police crime prevention strategies. The operational paradigms of many modern police departments have steadily evolved from a "professional" model of policing to a community-oriented, problem-solving model (Roth et al., 2000; Greene, 2000).

Growing community dissatisfaction, rising crime rates, and a series of research studies that questioned the effectiveness of the professional model's basic tenets served as catalysts for the shift.

Professional policing was itself a reform of the deplorable policing practices before the 1930s during the so-called "political era." Corruption, widespread abuse of authority, scandals, and a lack of professional standards were pervasive problems; these considerable shortcomings resulted in public outcry for better policing. Criminologists such as August Vollmer—the reform-minded chief in Berkeley, California, from 1905 to 1932—and O. W. Wilson—the Chicago police chief in the post–World War II period—were pivotal figures in the development of "professional," also known as "reform" or more recently termed the "standard model of policing" (Braga, 2008; Skogan and Frydl, 2004; Weisburd and Eck, 2004). These police leaders were the architects of the dominant paradigm, between the 1940s and 1960s, which remained influential through the 1980s and continues to be followed in many police agencies. The professional model emphasized military discipline and structure, separating the police from political influence, and the adoption of technological innovations ranging from strategic-management techniques to scientific advances such as two-way radios and fingerprinting. This model relies generally on a "one size fits all" application of reactive strategies to suppress crime, and continues to be the dominant form of police practices in the United States (Weisburd and Eck, 2004). The standard model is based on the assumption that generic strategies for crime reduction can be applied throughout a jurisdiction regardless of the level of crime, the nature of crime, or other variations.

The corrupt policing practices of the "political era" were slowly eliminated during the 1940s and 1950s as departments changed operational strategies to the reform model. The more rigorous standards and professionalism of the reform model successfully controlled much misbehavior and maintained policing as a viable profession. During the post–World War II period, the police role as "crime fighter" was solidified (Walker, 1992). Policing focused itself on preventing serious crimes and advanced three operational strategies to achieve this goal: preventive patrol, rapid response, and investigation of more serious cases by specialized detective units.

During the 1970s, researchers sought to determine how effective these policing strategies were in controlling crime. Preventive patrol in radio cars was thought by most police executives to serve as a deterrent to criminal behavior. Contrary to this consensus, an early British experiment concluded that crime increases when police patrol is completely removed from beats, but the level of patrolling in beats makes little difference in crime rates (Bright, 1969). The well-known Kansas City Patrol Experiment, discussed in our introduction, further examined the effectiveness of varying levels of random preventive patrol in reducing crime. The study revealed that crime rates and citizen satisfaction remained the same no matter what the level of radio car patrol—whether it was absent, doubled, or tripled (Kelling et al., 1974). Replications followed and obtained similar results. In Nashville, Tennessee, a level of thirty times the normal amount of patrol for selected districts was found to be successful in reducing crime at night, but not during the day (Schnelle et al., 1977). However, permanent long-term increased preventive patrol of an entire district is neither cost effective, economically feasible, nor practical for a department's operations. Others studies revealed that preventive patrol's inefficiency might be due to the fact that many serious crimes occur in locations (homes, alleys, businesses) not easily visible from a passing radio car (see Eck and Spelman, 1987; Skogan and Antunes, 1979).

In addition, police departments have placed a great emphasis on reducing response time in the belief that it would increase the probability of arrest. However, several studies found that rapid response has little effect on clearance rates (e.g., Spelman and Brown, 1984; Kansas City Police Department, 1978). Only about 3 percent of crimes are reported in progress; thus rapid response to most calls does not increase the probability of arrest (Spelman and Brown, 1984). The problem is that police departments have no control over two key elements between the time a crime is committed and the time a police officer arrives on the scene: the interval between the commission of a crime and the time it is discovered; and the interval between discovery and the time the citizen calls the police (Walker, 1992). Most crimes are discovered after the fact and for most "involvement" crimes—where the victim is present (e.g., assault)—there is some delay between victimization and the subsequent call to the police.

The third component of the professional "crime fighter" model—successful investigations—rests on the reputation of detectives as possessing special skills and crime solving abilities. However, this image is largely perpetuated and romanticized by the media. Several researchers have described the reality that criminal investigations largely consist of routine, unspecialized work that is often unfruitful (Walker, 1992). Studies by the RAND Corporation (Greenwood, Chaiken, and Petersilia, 1977) and the Police Executive Research Forum (Eck, 1983) documented that investigations involve mostly paperwork, phone calls, and the interviewing of victims and witnesses. Only 21 percent of all "index crimes" are cleared, and patrol officers at the scene of the crime usually make these arrests. In fact, most crimes are solved through the random circumstances of the crime scene, such as availability of witnesses or the presence of evidence such as fingerprints, rather than by any special follow-up investigations by detectives.

The research on preventive patrol, response time, and the efficacy of investigations were not the only studies to "debunk" the predominant police practices of the professional or standard model of policing. James Levine, for example, analyzed national crime data on the effectiveness of increasing the number of police in an article published in 1975. His title sums up his findings: "The Ineffectiveness of Adding Police to Prevent Crime." Levine begins by noting the broad consensus for the principal that adding more police will make cities safer. He then goes on to note that "(s)ensible as intensified policing may sound on the surface, its effectiveness in combating crime has yet to be demonstrated" (Levine, 1975: 523). Finally, drawing upon simple tabular data on police strength and crime rates over time, he concludes:

> It is tempting for politicians and government leaders to add
> more police: it is an intuitively sensible and symbolically

satisfying solution to the unrelenting problem of criminal violence.... The sad fact is, however, that they receive a false sense of security; in most situations they are just as vulnerable with these extra police as without them. (Levine, 1975: 544)

This series of studies, conducted in the 1970s and 1980s, challenged the three basic tenets of the standard policing model and raised many questions about proper crime-control methods. This view of the ineffectiveness of policing strategies was reinforced by official crime statistics. These statistics, widely available to the public, suggested that the police were losing the "war on crime." In particular, in America's largest cities, with their well-established professional police forces, crime rates and especially violent crime rates were rising at alarming rates. Between 1973 and 1990 violent crime in cities doubled (Reiss and Roth, 1993). It did not take a statistician to understand that the trends were dramatic. For example, in Figure 2.1 we report the trends in violent crime rates per 100,000 U.S. population between 1970 and 1990. Clearly crime was on the rise, and the trend had been fairly consistent over a long period. Thus, not only were scholars showing that police strategies did little to impact upon crime, but the overall crime statistics commonly used by the government and community to define police effectiveness were providing a similar message.

An additional harbinger of change was the growing community dissatisfaction with the activities of the police departments that served them. The decade of the 1970s began with a host of challenges to the police as well as the criminal justice system more generally (U.S. President's Commission on Law Enforcement and Administration of Criminal Justice, 1967a, 1967b). This was the case in part because of the tremendous social unrest that characterized the end of the previous decade. Race riots in American cities, and growing opposition, especially among younger Americans, to the Vietnam War often placed the police in conflict with the young and minorities. But American fears of a failing criminal justice system were also to play a role in a growing sense of crisis for American policing. In 1967, a presidential commission report on the

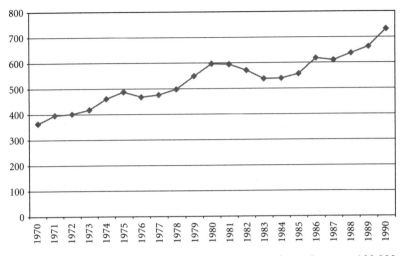

Figure 2.1. FBI Uniform Crime Reports Violent Index Crime Rate per 100,000 U.S. Population, 1970–1990

Source: http://bjsdata.ojp.usdoj.gov/dataonline/Search/Crime/State/
RunCrimeStatebyState.cfm.

Challenge of Crime in a Free Society reinforced doubts about the effectiveness of criminal justice in combating crime in the United States:

> In sum, America's system of criminal justice is overcrowded and overworked, undermanned, underfinanced, and very often misunderstood. It needs more information and more knowledge. It needs more technical resources. It needs more coordination among its many parts. It needs more public support. It needs the help of community programs and institutions in dealing with offenders and potential offenders. It needs, above all, the willingness to reexamine old ways of doing things, to reform itself, to experiment, to run risks, to date. It needs vision. (President's Commission, 1967a: 80–81)

Shortly after the presidential report on the Challenge of Crime in a Free Society was published, the Kerner Commission on Civil Disorders was established, and it too was to raise significant questions about the nature of criminal justice in the United States, and the organization of American policing (U.S. National Advisory Commission on Civil Disorders, 1968). However, in this case it was the question of race and the relationship between police and minority communities that was to have central stage. The challenges to patterns of American discrimination against African Americans were not focused primarily on the police, but the police, as other criminal justice agencies, were seen as "part of the problem" and not necessarily working to help in producing a solution to difficult social issues:

> In Newark, Detroit, Watts and Harlem, in practically every city that has experienced racial disruption since the summer of 1964, abrasive relationships between police and Negroes and other minority groups have been a major source of grievance, tension and ultimately disorder. (Commission on Civil Disorders, 1968: 157)

The concerns of the commission reports in the 1960s and the sense of growing alienation between the police and the public in the later half of that decade led policymakers, the police,and scholars to question the nature of American policing, and in particular the strategies that were dominant in policing since World War II. The police were viewed as part of the problem and not a solution (Weisburd and Uchida, 1993). The responding tactics of the police were viewed as draconian, and there was public outcry over a force that resembled and acted like "occupying armies" rather than civil servants (Kelling and Moore, 1988). As the crime rate soared and public satisfaction with the police decreased, the legitimacy of the police was deeply questioned (Kelling and Moore, 1988).

As the United States entered the decade of the 1990s there appeared to be a general consensus that traditional police practices did not work in preventing or controlling crime. As Michael Gottfredson and Travis Hirschi wrote in their classic book *A General Theory of Crime* in 1990: "No evidence exists that augmentation of patrol forces or equipment, differential patrol strategies, or differential intensities of surveillance have an effect on crime rates" (Gottfredson and Hirschi, 1990: 270). The distinguished police scholar David Bayley wrote even more strongly in 1994:

> The Police do not prevent crime. This is one of the best-kept
> secrets of modern life. Experts know it, the police know it, but
> the public does not know it. Yet the police pretend that they
> are society's best defence against crime.... This is a myth. First,
> repeated analysis has consistently failed to find any connection
> between the number of police officers and crime rates.
> Secondly, the primary strategies adopted by modern police
> have been shown to have little or no effect on crime. (1994: 3)

Police Innovation as a Response to the Crisis in Policing

The crisis we have outlined was to have a deep effect on police and police scholars, and was to lead to a significant period of innovation in American policing (Weisburd and Braga, 2006). Those innovations tended to take two main directions, which represented two very different types of solutions to the crisis of confidence and legitimacy that police agencies faced. One solution was simply to redefine the role of the police in urban areas. In the standard model of policing, the primary and most important role of police was as crime fighters. In fact, this image of policing was never a full one of the work of the police, and indeed a series of studies of policing at that time showed that most police work had little to do with crime (Reiss, 1971). A major part of the police function was always in order maintenance and could be described more easily as elements of service to the public than crime fighting per se. However, whatever the reality in the standard model of policing, crime fighting was a central task in legitimizing the police.

A series of innovations in policing in the 1980s and 1990s sought to overcome the critique of American policing brought in earlier decades by reorienting, or at least adding new tasks, to the police function. For example, innovations like community policing and "broken windows" policing argued that the police should take on a wider set of problems.

Importantly, these problems were believed to be "solvable" by the police. In some sense then, this adaptation to the crisis we have described "solves the problem" of the failures of the standard model of policing by arguing that the police are important not only as crime fighters (or in some cases not primarily as crime fighters) but also because they play an important role in dealing with other community problems. In many cases, this is not described as taking on a new set of tasks, but rather as returning to a mode of policing that was popular in the distant past (Kelling and Coles, 1996; Kelling and Moore, 1988; Wilson and Kelling, 1982).

Research in the 1970s and 1980s pointed the police in promising directions not only in developing strategies to deal with these new police responsibilities, but also in justifying a reorientation of the police task. The Newark Foot Patrol Experiment, for example, revealed that although foot patrol did not affect the rate of serious crime, citizens perceived their environments as safer and their opinions about the police improved (Police Foundation, 1981). In Houston, a multifaceted fear-reduction project was implemented. The components of this project included community stations, citizen-contact foot patrol, community organizing teams, and a victim re-contact program. The evaluation of the program found generally positive results. Although serious crime did not decrease, communication between police and citizens increased and fear of crime was reduced (Pate et al., 1986).

Another important finding of these projects was that a large gap existed between the serious crime problems that professional departments attacked and the day-to-day concerns of citizens. Frequently, the police officers who staffed these programs were called upon to deal with less serious complaints, such as abandoned cars, raucous neighborhood youth, and barking dogs (Trojanowicz, 1983). Disorder in the community was more of an ongoing concern for the average citizen than the risk of being the victim of a serious crime. Police agencies soon learned that social incivilities (such as unsavory loiterers, loud music, public drinking, and public urination) and physical incivilities (such as trash, vacant lots, graffiti, and abandoned buildings) had a definite impact on the quality of life in communities (Skogan, 1990).

Community policing was one of the most widely diffused and earliest of these approaches to solving the crisis in policing we have described (Roth et al., 2000). The approach was even to give its name to a large federal agency—The Office of Community Oriented Policing Services—created by the Violent Crime Control and Law Enforcement Act of 1994. Police strategies associated with community policing have been diverse and have often changed over time. However, a central innovation in community policing was that it sought to expand the problems that police addressed. For decades a professional model of policing had been encouraged in which the main task of policing was to fight crime, and the police were seen as experts who like other professionals at the time such as doctors, would be best left alone to do their job. But the research evidence on policing suggested that the police were not doing a very good job on their own. One central element of the community policing movement was that the community should play a central role in defining the problems the police address, and that these problems should extend much beyond conventional law enforcement. As Kelling and Moore (1988: 4) argue, "during the 1950s and 1960s, police thought they were law enforcement agencies primarily fighting crime."

In the "community era" or community policing era, the police function broadens and includes "order maintenance, conflict resolution, provision of services through problem solving, as well as other activities" (Kelling and Moore, 1988: 2). The justification for these new activities was drawn either from the fact that historically the police had indeed carried such functions, or that the community from which the police gained legitimacy saw these as important functions of the police. David Bayley notes that this approach "creates a new role for police with new criteria for performance:"

> If police can not reduce crime and apprehend more offenders,
> they can at least decrease fear of crime, make the public feel
> less powerless, lessen distrust between minority groups and the
> police, mediate quarrels, overcome the isolation of marginal
> groups, organize social services, and generally assist in

developing "community." These are certainly worthwhile objectives. But are they what the police should be doing? They are a far cry from what the police were originally created to do. (Bayley, 1988: 228)

One way to understand the impetus toward community policing is to recognize that it responds to the question of what is the importance of policing if the police cannot do something about crime problems. Community policing, at least in its earliest stages when crime fighting was much less a central component, finds a set of new tasks for the police with which they can perhaps be more successful.

By listening to the concerns of residents, community policing orients the police to tackle problems that are often manifested at specific places within neighborhoods. As such, community policing implicitly encourages the police to pay attention to local crime-and-disorder hot spot locations. In their description of an early community policing program in Detroit, Skolnick and Bayley (1986: 67) note:

A crime prevention block captain from a working-class neighborhood of single-family houses talks at a [community] meeting about a vacant house, recently sold, where heavy auto traffic disturbs neighbors throughout the night. The neighbors suspect the property is being used as a drug house. The [community policing] officer agrees with this assessment and alerts narcotics officers. He also calls the realtor and learns that keys to the house had been loaned out but would be returned that day. The block captain is instructed to inform police if occupancy continues.

Other innovations in policing also look to redefine the role of the police in one way or another. Like community policing, these innovations encourage the police to pay more attention to neighborhood conditions and the places within neighborhoods that generate problems. Broken windows policing, for instance, also seeks to direct the police to problems that had often been ignored in standard police practices. The idea of broken windows policing developed out of the Newark Foot Patrol Experiment. From that study James Q. Wilson and George Kelling (1982) identified a link between social disorder and crime which suggested the importance of police paying attention to many problems that were seen in earlier decades as peripheral to the police function. Wilson and Kelling were impressed by the activities of the police officers who walked patrol in the Police Foundation study, and thought that what might be seen in traditional policing as inappropriate behavior actually held the key to public safety and crime reduction. Kelling and Coles (1996: 18) write:

> Most New Jersey police chiefs were dismayed when they learned from program evaluators what (anonymous) officers, who were supposed to be "fighting crime," were actually doing while on foot patrol. For example, after being called a second time during the same evening to end brawls in the same bar, one foot patrol officer had had enough: although the "bar time" was some hours away, he ordered the bar closed for business as usual. The bartender grumbled, closed up, and opened the next day for business as usual. When this incident was recounted to the chief of the department in which it occurred....he responded, "that wouldn't happen in my department, the officer would be fired."

Wilson and Kelling argued that concern with disorder was an essential ingredient for doing something about crime problems. Indeed, the broken windows thesis was that serious crime developed because the police and citizens did not work together to prevent urban decay and social disorder:

> (A)t the community level, disorder and crime are usually inextricably linked, in a kind of developmental sequence. Social psychologists and police officers tend to agree that if a window in a building is broken *and is left unrepaired*, all of the rest of the windows will soon be broken. (Wilson and Kelling, 1982: 31)

In the context of crime, Wilson and Kelling argued "that 'untended' behavior also leads to the breakdown of community controls:

> A stable neighborhood of families who care for their homes, mind each other's children, and confidently frown on unwanted intruders can change in a few years or even a few months, to an inhospitable and frightening jungle. A piece of property is abandoned, weeds grow up, a window is smashed. Adults stop scolding rowdy children; the children, emboldened, become more rowdy. Families move out, unattached adults move in....Such an area is vulnerable to criminal invasion. Though it is not inevitable, it is more likely here, rather than in places where people are confident they can regulate public behavior by informal controls...(Wilson and Kelling, 1982: 31)

Broken windows policing encourages the police to be concerned with problems of disorder, and moves crime itself to a secondary, or at least second-stage goal of the police. From the perspective of the crisis of policing we have described, broken windows policing again expands the police function. Importantly, it does so at the same time that it suggests that the police can be effective in preventing serious crime even if in the short run police tactics have little impact on crime. Indeed, in the Newark Foot Patrol Experiment, the Police Foundation concluded that foot patrol did not lead to reduced crime rates. However, residents in the foot patrolled neighborhoods felt safer and tended to believe that crime had been reduced. Wilson and Kelling argued that they were not fooled, because in the long run such empowerment of the community would indeed work to prevent community decay and the influx of predatory crime. Both in community policing and broken windows policing the failures of crime fighting became less important, because the police function was seen to lie in good part in other activities.

Hot spots policing is part of another very distinct response to the crisis of legitimacy and effectiveness in policing. Unlike community policing and broken windows policing, which implicitly accepted the idea that the police could not, at least directly, ameliorate crime problems, these innovations began with an assumption that the police could be effective. The problem was in the strategies of policing, not in the underlying possibilities of police affecting crime problems. Importantly, this second group of innovations, like community policing and broken windows policing, also accepted that it was important for the police to broaden its mandate and to become closer to the communities that they served. However, while recognizing the importance of this expansion of the police function, they did not assume that the police should abandon or place less emphasis on its primary task of affecting directly crime and other public safety problems.

The first response of this type was termed "problem-oriented policing," and was introduced by the distinguished police scholar Herman Goldstein in 1979. In his original formulation of problem-oriented policing he argued that the "police job requires that they deal with a wide range of behavioral problems that arise in the community" (1979: 242). However, problem-oriented policing responded to the failures of the standard model of policing primarily by arguing that the organization of policing and policing tactics had failed. Police could impact upon crime and other problems if they took a different approach, in this case the problem-oriented-policing approach. In this sense, a second response to the crisis we have described is not to accept as some academic criminologists had that the police could not do something about crime and thus to search to define other important police functions as central (Bayley, 1994; Gottfredson and Hirschi, 1990) but to suggest that the strategies of the standard policing model were flawed and that new more effective models could be developed.

Problem-oriented policing sought to redefine the way in which the police did their job. Goldstein (1979, 1990) argued that the police had "lost sight" of their primary task, which was to do something about crime and other problems, and instead had become focused on the "means" of allocating police resources. He identified this pathology as a common one in large organizations, and sought through the model of problem solving to develop a more successful method of ameliorating crime and other community problems. Police officers following the problem-oriented approach soon found that many crime problems and community concerns were concentrated in particular places within larger communities (Braga, 2008).

In Newport News, Virginia, an early field test of problem-oriented policing led to the identification of crime-and-disorder-problems that were primarily concentrated at particular places within neighborhoods (Eck and Spelman, 1987). These place-based problems included (Eck and Spelman, 1987: 83–90):

- Residential burglaries in the New Briarfield Apartments
- Thefts from automobiles in the Newport News Shipbuilding parking lots
- Personal robberies in the Central business district
- Commercial burglaries on Jefferson Avenue
- Vacant buildings in the Central business district
- Residential burglaries in the Glenn Gardens Apartments
- Larcenies in Beechmont Gardens
- Drug dealing at 32nd and Chestnut
- Disorderly youths at the Peninsula Skating Rink
- Shot houses (illegal liquor-selling establishments) in the Aqua Vista Apartments
- Disturbances at the 7-Eleven convenience store on Marshall Avenue
- Noise and property damage by dirt bikes in Newmarket Creek
- Hooliganism at the Village Square Shopping Center

Problem-oriented policing in this context became an important component of what was to later be defined as hot spots policing.

Another innovation, which was to have important impacts on hot spots policing, is what has come to be called "third-party policing." Third-party policing follows suggestions made by Herman Goldstein (1979) that the "tool box" of police strategies be expanded. In this case however, the resources of the police are expanded to "third parties" that

Third Party policing

are believed to offer significant new resources for doing something about crime and disorder. The opportunity for a third-party policing approach developed in part from more general trends in the relationship between civil and criminal law (Mazerolle and Ransley, 2006). The expansion of the civil law and its use in other legal contexts as a method of dealing with problems that were once considered to be the exclusive province of criminal statutes created important new tools for the police. Third-party policing asserts that the police cannot successfully deal with many problems on their own, and thus that the failures of traditional policing models may be found in the limits of police powers. Using civil ordinances and civil courts, or the resources of private agencies, third-party policing recognizes that much social control is exercised by institutions other than the police and that crime can be managed through agencies other than the criminal law.

Third-party policing initiatives typically involve police efforts to persuade or coerce organizations or non-offending persons, such as public-housing agencies, property owners, parents, health and building inspectors, and business owners to take some responsibility for preventing crime or reducing crime problems (Buerger and Mazerolle, 1998). The police seek to create or enhance crime prevention nodes in locations or situations where crime-control guardianship was previously absent or not effective. In this sense, third-party policing is often place oriented. Third-party policing initiatives tend to proliferate in efforts to control low-level, street crime such as controlling drug problems at problem addresses (Green, 1996; Mazerolle and Ransley, 2005).

Compstat also responds to the failures of the standard policing model by critiquing the ways in which the police carry out their tasks (Silverman, 2006; Weisburd et al., 2003). However, in the case of Compstat the focus is less on the specific strategies that the police are involved in and more on the nature of police organization itself. If, as Herman Goldstein noted in 1979, the failures of the standard model of policing could be explained by the fact that police organizations were poorly organized to do something about crime, Compstat sought to overcome that pathology. It sought to empower the command structure to do something about crime problems. William Bratton, the New York City police commissioner who coined the term and developed the program, writes:

> We created a system in which the police commissioner, with his executive core, first empowers and then interrogates the precinct commander, forcing him or her to come up with a plan to attack crime. But it should not stop there. At the next level down, it should be the precinct commander, taking the same role as the commissioner, empowering and interrogating the platoon commander. Then, at the third level, the platoon commander should be asking his sergeants...all the way down until everyone in the entire organization is empowered and motivated, active and assessed and successful. It works in all organizations, whether it's 38,000 cops or Mayberry, R.F.D. (Bratton, 1998: 239)

Compstat has also been adopted widely by larger American police agencies over the last decade (Weisburd, Mastrofski, et al., 2001; Weisburd et al., 2003). And though Compstat is an innovation that seeks to concentrate police efforts on specific goals and increase organizational control and accountability, it has encouraged geographic analysis of crime to focus on hot spots as one of its innovations (Silverman, 1999). In the words of then–NYPD Deputy Commissioner Jack Maple, "the main principle of deployment can be expressed in one sentence: 'map the crime and put the cops where the dots are.' Or, more succinctly: 'Put cops on dots'" (1999: 128). Computerized crime mapping has become an integral part of many Compstat programs and, according to a recent Police Foundation survey (Weisburd et al., 2001), Compstat departments are much more likely to utilize crime mapping and try to identify crime hot spots than are agencies that do not have Compstat programs.

Thus far, we have traced the wide diffusion of innovations in the 1990s to a crisis of police practices that developed in previous decades. We have argued that it is not accidental that so much innovation was brought to American policing during this period. Indeed, such innovation was a direct response to a growing sense among police managers and police scholars that the standard model of policing had failed. We have also argued that the paths of police innovation can be understood in the context of the critiques that developed of the standard policing model. Innovation generally developed in two main trends. In some cases, the innovations minimized the importance of crime fighting, which had been the main focus of earlier policing research. Such innovations responded to the crisis of policing by defining a broader or new set of tasks that the police could perform more effectively. Other innovations, however, started with a critique of the methods used in the standard model. They argued that the police could be more effective, even in preventing or controlling crime, if the tactics used were changed. Hot spots policing can be placed among this latter group of innovations. However, unlike many other of the innovations in policing we have reviewed, hot spots policing can be traced directly to theoretical developments in criminology and basic research on crime. In this sense, hot spots policing represents an important innovation not only because of the evidence of its effectiveness that we will review in Chapter 4, but also because of the way in which it has developed.

Crime Theory, Basic Research, and Hot Spots Policing

Looking at the major police innovations of the last decade, what is most striking from a criminologist's perspective is the extent to which new programs and practices have been developed without reference to either criminological theory or research evidence. Some institutional theorists might argue that this is understandable given the limited ability of police agencies to reliably demonstrate their successes, and the political environments within which police agencies must operate (Meyer and Rowan, 1977; Mastrofski and Ritti, 2000; Willis, Mastrofski, and Weisburd, 2004). However, this reality is very much at odds with a model of policing that would seek to draw new policies and practices from a solid research base (Sherman, 1998), and suggests an approach to policing that is based more on intuition and luck than on research and experimentation. Recent studies of the adoption of police innovation reinforce this problematic portrait of American police innovation (Weisburd and Braga, 2006).

In this context, hot spots policing- represents a particularly important innovation on the American police scene. Its origins can be traced to innovations in criminological theory and basic research on the distribution of crime. In this section, we describe the origins of hot spots policing in theory and basic research.

From Theory to Practice: An Evidence-Based Model

The idea of hot spots policing can be traced to recent critiques of traditional criminological theory (Weisburd and Braga, 2003, 2006). For most of the last century, criminologists have focused their understanding of crime on individuals and communities (Nettler, 1978; Sherman, 1995). In the case of individuals, criminologists have sought to understand why certain people as opposed to others become criminals (e.g., see Akers, 1973; Gottfredson and Hirschi, 1990; Hirschi, 1969; Raine, 1993), or to explain why certain offenders become involved in criminal activity at different stages of the life course or cease involvement at other stages (e.g., see Moffitt, 1993; Sampson and Laub, 1993). In the case of communities, criminologists have often tried to explain why certain types of crime or different levels of criminality are found in some communities as contrasted with others (e.g., see Agnew, 1999; Bursik and Grasmick, 1993; Sampson and Groves, 1989; Shaw and McKay, 1972) or how community-level variables, such as relative deprivation, low socioeconomic status, or lack of economic opportunity may affect individual criminality (e.g., see Agnew, 1992; Cloward and Ohlin, 1960; Merton, 1968; Wolfgang and Ferracuti, 1967). In most cases, research on communities has focused on the "macro" level, often studying states (Loftin and Hill, 1974), cities (Baumer et al., 1998), and neighborhoods (Sampson, 1985; Bursik and Grasmick, 1993).

This is not to say that criminologists did not recognize that the opportunities found at more micro levels of place can impact upon the occurrence of crime. Edwin Sutherland (1947), for example, whose main focus was upon the learning processes that bring offenders to participate in criminal behavior, noted in his classic criminology textbook that the immediate situation influences crime in many ways. For example, "a thief may steal from a fruit stand when the owner is not in sight but refrain when the owner is in sight; a bank burglar may attack a bank which is poorly protected but refrain from attacking a bank protected by watchmen and burglar alarms" (Sutherland, 1947: 5). Nonetheless, Sutherland, as other criminologists, did not see micro crime places as a relevant focus of criminological study. This was the case, in part, because crime opportunities provided by such places were assumed to be so numerous as to make concentration on specific places of little utility for theory or policy. In turn, criminologists traditionally assumed that situational factors played a relatively minor role in explaining crime as compared with the "driving force of criminal dispositions" (Clarke and Felson, 1993: 4; Trasler, 1993). Combining an assumption of a wide array of criminal opportunities, and a view of offenders that saw them as highly motivated to commit crime, it is understandable that criminologists paid little attention to the problem of the development of crime at micro levels of place.

While the focus on individuals and communities has continued to play a central role in criminological theory and practice, traditional theories and approaches were subjected to substantial criticism beginning in the 1970s. Starting with Robert Martinson's critique of rehabilitation programs in 1974, a series of studies documented the failures of traditional crime prevention initiatives (e.g. Sechrest, White, and Brown, 1979; Whitehead and Lab, 1989). In policing as well, as discussed earlier in this chapter, there was substantial criticism of traditional approaches.

A number of scholars argued that the failures of traditional crime prevention could be found in the inadequacies in program development and research design in prior studies (e.g., Farrington, Ohlin, and Wilson, 1986; Goldstein, 1990). Other reviews stressed that there are examples of successful offender-focused crime prevention efforts, which can provide guidance for the development of more effective prevention policies (Farrington, 1983; Lipsey, 1992). Nonetheless, even those scholars that looked to improve such policies came to recognize the difficulties inherent in trying to do something about criminality (Visher and Weisburd, 1998). Summarizing the overall standing of what they define as traditional "offender-centered" crime prevention, Patricia and Paul Brantingham (1990: 19) write: "If traditional approaches worked well, of course, there would be little pressure to find new forms of crime prevention. If traditional approaches worked well, few people would possess criminal motivation and fewer still would actually commit crimes."

One influential critique of traditional criminological approaches to understanding crime that had strong influence on the development of hot spots policing was introduced by Cohen and Felson (1979). They argued that the emphasis placed on individual motivation in criminological theory failed to recognize the importance of other elements of the crime equation. They noted that for criminal events to occur there is need not only of a criminal, but also of a suitable target and the absence of a capable guardian. They showed that crime rates could be affected by changing the nature of targets or of guardianship, irrespective of the nature of criminal motivations. Cohen and Felson's suggestion that crime could be affected without reference to the motivations of individual offenders was a truly radical idea in criminological circles in 1979. The routine activities perspective they presented established the context of crime as an important focus of study.

Drawing upon similar themes, British scholars led by Ronald V. Clarke began to explore the theoretical and practical possibilities of situational crime prevention (Clarke, 1983, 1995; Cornish and Clarke, 1986). Their focus was on criminal contexts and the possibilities for reducing the opportunities for crime in very specific situations. Their approach, like that of Cohen and Felson, turned traditional crime prevention theory on its head. At the center of their crime equation was opportunity. And they sought to change opportunity rather than reform offenders. In situational crime prevention, more often than not "opportunity made the thief" (Felson and Clarke, 1998). This was in sharp contrast to the traditional view that the thief simply took advantage of a very large number of potential opportunities. Importantly, in a series of case studies situational crime prevention advocates showed that reducing criminal opportunities in very specific contexts can lead to crime reduction and prevention (Clarke, 1997).

One natural outgrowth of these perspectives was that the specific places where crime occurs would become an important focus for crime prevention researchers (Eck and Weisburd, 1995; Taylor, 1997). While concern with the relationship between crime and place goes back to the founding generations of modern criminology (Guerry, 1833; Quetelet, 1842), the "micro" approach to places emerged only in the last few decades (e.g., see Brantingham and Brantingham, 1975, 1981; Duffala, 1976; LeBeau, 1987; Hunter, 1988; Mayhew et al., 1976; Rengert, 1980, 1981).[1] Places in this "micro" context are specific locations within the larger social environments of communities and neighborhoods (Eck and Weisburd, 1995). They are sometimes defined as buildings or addresses (see Green, 1996; Sherman, Buerger, and Gartin, 1989), sometimes as block faces or street segments (see Sherman and Weisburd, 1995; Taylor, 1997), and sometimes as clusters of addresses, block faces or street segments (see Block, Dabdoub, and Fregly, 1995; Weisburd and Green, 1995; Weisburd, Bernasco and Bruinsma, 2009).

In the mid-to-late 1980s, a group of criminologists began to examine the distribution of crime at micro places. Their findings were to radically alter the way many criminologists understood the crime equation, drawing them into a new area of inquiry that was to have important implications for police practice. Perhaps the most influential of these studies, described in our introduction, was conducted by Lawrence Sherman and his colleagues (Sherman, Gartin, and Buerger, 1989). Looking at crime addresses in the city of Minneapolis, they found a concentration of crime at place that was startling. Only 3 percent of the addresses in Minneapolis accounted for 50 percent of the crime calls to the police. Similar results were reported in a series of other studies in different locations and using different methodologies, each suggesting a very high concentration of crime in micro places (e.g., see Pierce, Spaar, and Briggs, 1988; Eck, Gersh, and Taylor, 2000; Weisburd, Maher, and Sherman, 1992; Weisburd and Green, 1994). As we described in chapter 1,

Weisburd et al. (2004) shows moreover that the concentration of crime in hot spots is fairly stable across time.

Importantly, such concentration of crime at discrete places does not necessarily follow traditional ideas about crime and communities. There were often discrete places free of crime in neighborhoods that were considered troubled, and crime hot spots in neighborhoods that were seen generally as advantaged and not crime prone (Weisburd and Green, 1994). This empirical research thus reinforced theoretical perspectives that emphasized the importance of crime places, and suggested a focus upon small areas, often encompassing only one or a few city blocks that could be defined as hot spots of crime.

The Development of Hot Spots Policing

These emerging theoretical paradigms and empirical findings led Sherman and Weisburd (1995) to explore the practical implications of the hot spots approach for policing. The theoretical innovations and basic research we have described led them to believe that the police could be effective in responding to crime if they focused police interventions on hot spots. As we described in our introduction, with cooperation from the Minneapolis Police Department they developed a large experimental field study of "police patrol in crime hot spots." They sought to challenge the conclusions of the Kansas City Preventive Patrol Experiment noted earlier, then well established, that police patrol has little value in preventing or controlling crime. But they also sought to show that the focus of police efforts on crime hot spots presented a new and promising approach for police practice. The results of the study were impressive and challenged the Kansas City experiment's assertion that varying levels of patrol do not affect crime. Overall reported crime in the treatment areas was reduced by 13 percent and robbery was reduced by 20 percent (statistically significant results; Sherman and Weisburd, 1995). Further, researcher observations of disorder noted a 50 percent reduction in experimental hot spots when compared to control places (Sherman and Weisburd, 1995). A follow-up study by Koper (1995) of the optimal amount of time that patrol cars should spend in hot spots found that patrol stops should last between 11 and 15 minutes; after that, continued police presence during a single patrol stop brings diminishing returns.

The encouraging results of the Minneapolis Hot Spots Patrol Experiment generated considerable academic and practical interest in hot spots policing that led to a series of rigorous evaluations of the effects of focused police attention in street-level drug markets (Weisburd and Green, 1995), gun violence hot spots (Sherman and Rogan, 1995a), violent crime hot spots (Braga et al., 1999), and crime and disorder hot spots (Braga and Bond, 2008). Several reviews of the available scientific evidence have concluded that, when applied properly, hot spots policing programs generate noteworthy crime prevention gains (Braga, 2001, 2005; Sherman, 1997; Skogan and Frydl, 2004). The details of these programs and evaluation results are reviewed in chapter 4. As a result of these well-publicized research findings, and a strong desire by police managers to adopt proven crime prevention practices, hot spots policing has become a very popular way for police departments to address crime problems (Weisburd and Braga, 2006).

Conclusion

The origins of hot spots policing can be found in the crisis of legitimacy and effectiveness of American policing of the 1970s and 1980s, just as other innovations of the last two decades. Its response was to argue that the police could be effective in doing something about crime, and other community problems, if it changed the unit of geographic focus of police interventions. The major police innovations reviewed in this chapter contributed to and complemented the development of hot spots policing as these approaches challenged the police to focus on local crime-and-disorder-problems which often were manifested at very specific places within communities. But, as we have described, a major difference between other innovations in this period and hot spots policing can be found in the use of innovations in criminological theory and basic research in the identification and early development of the approach.

The Theoretical Importance of Place in Crime Prevention

3

Police crime prevention practices have traditionally been focused on identifying and arresting criminal offenders. Police attention has also been directed at dealing with broader community problems, securing communities in emergencies, and, more recently, in responding to homeland security threats. The hot spots policing paradigm reorients police practices to small high-activity crime places as a central concern in dealing with crime problems. As discussed in the previous chapter, academic criminology played a key role in the development of hot spots policing programs. Theoretical and empirical developments pointed to the importance of place in crime causation and suggested that police crime-control strategy should consider the micro-contexts of criminal behavior. Academic interest in the criminology of a place developed from research suggesting that microlevel variation in crime existed within communities and the attributes of specific places were important in understanding the concentration of crime at particular locations.

The observation that the distribution of crime varied within neighborhoods has existed for some time (see Hawley, 1944; Hawley, 1950; Shaw and McKay, 1942; Weisburd, Bernasco and Bruinsma, 2009). However, due to limited analytical capacities, little empirical research examined this variance beyond the community level of analysis. As we have already described, with the advent of powerful computer systems and software packages in the late 1980s researchers have provided a strong body of evidence that crime is very concentrated in crime hot spots. Indeed, the earliest studies in this regard (Pierce, Spaar, and Briggs, 1988; Sherman, Gartin, and Buerger, 1989) which found that fewer than 5 percent of the addresses in a city generated more than 50 percent of emergency-calls-for-service to the police have been replicated in a series of subsequent studies. Even within high-crime neighborhoods, research found that crime clusters at a few discrete locations, leaving blocks of areas relatively crime-free (Sherman, Gartin, and Buerger, 1989; Weisburd and Green, 1994; Groff, Weisburd, and Morris, 2009). Further, research by Taylor and Gottfredson (1986) revealed conclusive evidence that links this spatial variation to the physical and social characteristics of particular blocks and multiple dwellings within a neighborhood. Crime clustering at specific locations within neighborhoods has been reported in studies of a variety of crimes, including burglary (Forrester et al., 1988, 1990; Farrell, 1995), convenience-store robberies (Crow and Bull, 1975; Hunter and Jeffrey, 1992), gun crimes (Sherman and Rogan, 1995a) and drug selling (Weisburd and Green, 1994).

The study of places as a means to explain the variation of crime within communities has developed from an interest in improving crime control policies (Weisburd, Maher, and Sherman, 1992). The attributes of a place are viewed as key factors in explaining clusters of criminal events (Braga, 2008; Eck and Weisburd, 1995). For example, a poorly lit street corner with an abandoned building, located near a major thoroughfare, provides an ideal location for a drug market. The lack of proper lighting, an abundance of "stash" locations around the derelict property, a steady flow of potential customers on the thoroughfare, and a lack of defensive ownership (informal social control) at the place all generate an attractive opportunity for drug sellers. In many such cases, the police spend considerable time and effort arresting sellers without noticeably affecting the drug trade (Weisburd and Green, 1995). The compelling criminal opportunities at the place attract sellers and buyers, and thus sustain the market. If the police want to disrupt the market, they should focus on the features of the place that causes the drug dealing to cluster at that particular location. This approach to focusing on the characteristicsof high-crime locations is considered to be a radical departure from traditional criminological theories, which centered prevention efforts on the individual and ignored the importance of place (Sherman, Gartin, and Buerger, 1989).

This chapter develops the theoretical basis for policing crime hot spots by exploring more closely our understanding of the relationship between place and crime. While the larger worlds of communities and neighborhood have been the primary focus of crime prevention theory and research in the past, there is a growing recognition of the importance of shifting that focus to the small worlds in which the attributes of place and its routine activities combine to develop crime events (Eck and Weisburd, 1995). This chapter presents complementary theoretical perspectives that influence our understanding of the importance of place in criminology. It also presents findings from criminological research that identifies facilities, such as taverns and convenience stores, and site features, such as easy access, the presence of valuable goods, and a lack of guardianship, in influencing the presence of criminal opportunities at particular places.

Defining Places and Crime Hot Spots

Before we turn to a discussion of the theoretical importance of place in crime, it is important to begin by defining what we mean by places and crime hot spots. Hot spots policing is not simply the application of police strategies to units of geography. Traditional policing in this sense can be seen as place-based, since police have routinely defined their units of operation in terms of large areas, such as police precincts and beats. In hot spots policing, place refers to a very different level of geographic aggregation than has traditionally interested police executives and planners. Places in this context are very small micro units of analysis, such as buildings or addresses; block faces or street segments; or clusters of addresses, block faces, or street segments (Eck andWeisburd, 1995). When crime is concentrated at such places, they are commonly called hot spots.

Two illustrations of crime hot spots are useful since they point to the different ways that place may be important in understanding crime and in police interventions. In the Minneapolis Hot Spots Experiment, Sherman and Weisburd (1995) identified street segments or street blocks for increased patrol presence (see figure 3.1). Street blocks were used, in part, because they represented a unit of analysis that was easily identified by police and could provide a natural setting for police interventions. But Sherman and Weisburd (1995) also recognized, as have other scholars, that such factors as the visual closeness of residents of a block; interrelated role obligations; acceptance of certain common norms and behavior; common, regularly recurring rhythms of activity; the physical boundaries of the street; and the historical evolution of the street segment make the street block a particularly useful unit for analysis for policing places (Hunter and Baumer, 1982; Taylor, Gottfredson, and Brower, 1984).

In the Jersey City Displacement and Diffusion Project (Weisburd et al., 2006), the researchers also sought to identify a discrete place for police attention. However, they specifically sought to examine specific types of criminal markets. Such markets often spread across street segments in a larger area of criminal activity. Figure 3.2 illustrates the boundaries of a prostitution market identified for intervention in Jersey City. Included in

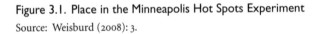

Figure 3.1. Place in the Minneapolis Hot Spots Experiment
Source: Weisburd (2008): 3.

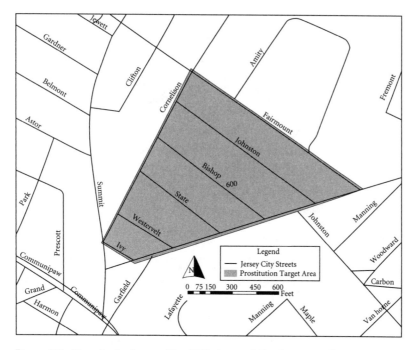

Figure 3.2. Place in the Jersey City Diffusion and Displacement Experiment
Source: Weisburd (2008): 3.

this case is a group of city blocks but, importantly, this is still much smaller than the neighborhoods or police precincts that have often been the focus of police interventions and scientific study of crime. The displacement project and the Minneapolis experiment illustrate more generally the ways in which units of place might differ depending on the interests of the police and the underlying structure of crime problems.

It is important to note that such clustering of crime at small units of geography does not simply mask trends that are occurring at a larger geographic level, such as communities. Research has shown, for example, that in what are generally seen as good parts of town there are often streets with strong crime concentrations, and in what are often defined as bad neighborhoods, many places are relatively free of crime (Weisburd and Green, 1994). The extent to which crime at micro units of place varies from street to street is illustrated in a recent study of hot spots of juvenile crime (Groff, Weisburd, and Morris, 2009). Using geographic statistics that identify spatial independence, Groff and her colleagues (2009) show that street segments right next to each other tend to have very different levels and patterns of crime over time. This issue of defining units of analysis for hot spots policing is one that certainly will demand more attention if police adopt this approach on a large scale (see also Weisburd, Bruinsma, and Bernasco, 2009).

Crime Places and Crime Theory

Theories of crime can be divided into those that seek to explain the development of criminal offenders, and those that seek to explain the development of criminal events (Eck and Weisburd, 1995). Theories of and research on offenders have been dominant in the development of criminology (Clarke, 1980). Most research on crime and crime prevention has been focused on why certain types of people commit crime and what we can do about them. It is only recently that serious attention has begun to be paid to explaining crimes rather than the criminality of people involved in crime. Concern with why certain places become crime hot spots and other places do not is very much central to this approach.

While theories of crime and criminality are often seen as competing explanations of the crime problem, Eck and Weisburd (1995) suggest that it useful to begin with the idea that offender and event explanations are complements to each other rather than competitors. Offenders may be highly motivated, but unless they create a crime event there is nothing to explain. Similarly, given a criminal act, the full etiology of the event must in some manner include an explanation of the offender. Offender theories should eventually tell us how people come to be criminal offenders, and the circumstances under which they desist from offending. Such theories may suggest crime prevention strategies that are focused on those individuals who are likely to become serious violent offenders, or high-rate offenders committing less serious crimes. However, to date theories about the development of criminality do not provide a solid basis for making such predictions, and there is little consensus as to what such a theory in the future would look like. Consequently, a preventive strategy based on offender theories is not near at hand. But even if we were to understand more about the development of criminality than we presently do, it is not clear whether all or even most offenders can be prevented from involvement in crime (see Clarke and Weisburd, 1990).

So even if we had a good explanation for the development of offenders, we would still need a good explanation for criminal events (Eck and Weisburd, 1995). Specifically, we would want a theory that could tell us why certain targets are selected by offenders—why some targets are attractive and others are repellent. What are the impediments to offending that are presented to offenders, and how are they overcome? What types of routine activities of offenders, victims and what have sometimes been termed guardians contribute to the likelihood of crime occurringin particular places? Though a comprehensive crime-event theory that would provide unambiguous answers to such questions is decades away, there is considerable consensus among criminologists who study crime events as to what such a theory should look like. Moreover, there is growing evidence that event-prevention strategies can have a dramatic and immediate impact on specific crime problems (see Braga, 2008; Clarke, 1997).

Theoretical Perspectives Supporting the Importance of Crime Places

The study of crime events at places is influenced and supported by three complementary theoretical perspectives: rational choice, routine activities, and environmental criminology. The importance of focusing police resources on crime hot spots is also informed by the "broken windows" thesis on the relationship between disorder and more serious crimes.

Rational Choice Perspective

The rational choice perspective assumes that "crime is purposive behavior designed to meet the offender's commonplace needs for such things as money, status, sex, and excitement, and that meeting these needs involves the making of (sometimes quite rudimentary) decisions and choices, constrained as these are by limits of time and ability and the availability of relevant information" (Clarke, 1995: 98; see also Cornish and Clarke, 1986). Rational choice makes distinctions between the decisions to initially become involved in crime, to continue criminal involvement, and to desist from criminal offending, as well as the decisions made to complete a particular criminal act. This separation of the decision-making processes in the criminal event from the stages of criminal involvement allows the modeling of the commission of crime events in a way that yields potentially valuable insights for crime prevention. Of particular importance to effective crime prevention practice, the decision processes and information utilized in committing criminal acts can vary greatly across offenses; ignoring these differences and the situational contingencies associated with making choices may reduce the ability to effectively intervene (Clarke, 1995). In the case of places, modeling an offender's choice of committing crimes at one place over another may provide avenues for intervention. For example, a robber may choose a "favorite" spot because of certain desirable attributes that facilitate an ambush, such as poor lighting and untrimmed bushes. One obvious response to this situation would be to improve the lighting and trim the bushes.

The emphasis of the rational choice perspective on concepts of risk, reward, and effort in criminal decision making has been used to inform the development of situational crime prevention strategies that seek to change offender appraisals of criminal opportunities (Clarke, 1997). As suggested above, improving formal and natural surveillance in public spaces can be helpful in changing offender perceptions of risk. Welsh and Farrington (2004) find that closed-circuit televisions and improved street lighting are equally effective in reducing crime. More detailed analyses found that improved street lighting was more effective in reducing crime in city centers and both were more effective in reducing property crimes than violent crimes (Welsh and Farrington, 2004). Table 3.1 details a variety of situational crime prevention approaches that seek to change the decision-making processes of offenders in their appraisal of

Table 3.1. Twenty-Five Techniques of Situational Prevention

Increase the Effort	Increase the Risks	Reduce the Rewards	Reduce Provocations	Remove Excuses
1. Target harden * Steering column locks and immobilizers * Anti-robbery screens * Tamper-proof packaging	**6. Extend guardianship** * Take routine precautions: go out in group at night, leave signs of occupancy, carry phone * "Cocoon" neighborhood watch	**11. Conceal targets** * Off-street parking * Gender-neutral phone directories * Unmarked bullion trucks	**16. Reduce frustrations and stress** * Efficient queues and polite service * Expanding seating * Soothing music / muted lights	**21. Set rules** * Rental agreements * Harassment codes * Hotel registration
2. Control access to facilities * Entry phones * Electronic card access * Baggage screening	**7. Assist natural surveillance** * Improved street lighting * Defensible space design * Support whistleblowers	**12. Remove targets** * Removable car radio * Women's refuges * Pre-paid cash cards for pay phones	**17. Avoid disputes** * Separate enclosures for rival soccer fans * Reduce crowding in pubs * Fixed cab fares	**22. Post instructions** * "No Parking" * "Private Property" * "Extinguish camp fires"

(continued)

Table 3.1. Continued

Increase the Effort	Increase the Risks	Reduce the Rewards	Reduce Provocations	Remove Excuses
3. Screen exits	**8. Reduce anonymity**	**13. Identify property**	**18. Reduce emotional arousal**	**23. Alert conscience**
* Ticket needed for exit	* Taxi driver IDs	* Property marking	* Controls on violent pornography	* Roadside speed display boards
* Export documents	* "How's my driving?" decals	* Vehicle licensing and parts marking	* Enforce good behavior on soccer field	* Signatures for customs declarations
* Electronic merchandise tags	* School uniforms	* Cattle branding	* Prohibit racial slurs	* "Shoplifting is stealing"
4. Deflect offenders	**9. Utilize Place Managers**	**14. Disrupt markets**	**19. Neutralize peer pressure**	**24. Assist compliance**
* Street closures	* CCTV for double-deck buses	* Monitor pawn shops	* "Idiots drink and drive"	* Easy library checkout
* Separate bathrooms for women	* Two clerks for convenience stores	* Controls on classified ads	* "Its OK to say No"	* Public lavatories
* Disperse pubs	* Reward vigilance	* License street vendors	* Disperse troublemakers at school	* Litter bins

5. Control tools/weapons	10. Strengthen formal surveillance	15. Deny benefits	20. Discourage imitation	25. Control drugs and alcohol
* "Smart" guns	Red light cameras Burglar alarms Security guards	* Ink merchandise tags	* Rapid repair of vandalism	* Breathalyzers in pubs
* Disabling stolen cell phones		* Graffiti cleaning	* V-chips in TVs	* Server intervention
* Restrict spray paint sales to juveniles		* Speed humps	* Censor details of modus operandi	* Alcohol-free events

Source: Cornish and Clarke (2003): 90.

criminal opportunities. Indeed, many of these strategies seek to change the attributes and dynamics of specific places.

The rational choice perspective has also provided a theoretical grounding for the development of a "script analytic approach" through its emphasis on the person-situation interaction in explanations of criminal events (Cornish, 1994). Interviews with offenders can be very informative in unraveling the nature of crime problems and the identification of preventive responses. Many crime prevention scholars argue that "opportunity makes the thief" and, as such, it is important to "always think thief" (Clarke and Eck, 2003: 11). The underlying idea is that any particular category of crime requires a set of standard actions to be performed in a particular order like a script in a play (Clarke and Eck, 2003).

The use of crime scripts can assist crime prevention designers in focusing their prevention efforts at different points in the series of actions that make up a crime. For example, a script analysis of the motivations of young vandals in the Greater London area found that the presence of graffiti, as well as the width of the fence surface and the materials out of which the fence was made, structured their choices in rating the attractiveness of fences to vandalize (Smith, 2003). The implications for prevention included the "rapid repair" of vandalized fences that send cues that encourage additional graffiti writing (i.e., prompt removal reduces the rewards offenders receive from having their work displayed), the use of fences with narrow bars to decrease the surface area for graffiti writing, and the construction of fences from "hard" materials that were difficult to for vandals to damage (Smith, 2003). When the New York City subway system understood the motivation of "taggers" (to "get up" or see their handiwork displayed as the trains repeatedly traveled around the city), they succeeded in eliminating graffiti by implementing an immediate cleaning program (Sloan-Howitt and Kelling, 1990).

Routine Activity Theory

Rational choice is often combined with routine activity theory to explain criminal behavior during the crime event (Clarke and Felson, 1993). Rational offenders come across criminal opportunities as they go about their daily routine activities and make decisions whether to take action. The source of the offender's motivation to commit a crime is not addressed (it is assumed that offenders commit crimes for any number of reasons); rather, the basic ingredients for a criminal act to be completed are closely examined. Routine activity posits that a criminal act occurs when a likely offender converges in space and time with a suitable target (e.g., victim or property) in the absence of a capable guardian (e.g., property owner or security guard; Cohen and Felson, 1979). The routine activity approach was used to demonstrate that increases in residential burglary in the United States between 1960 and 1970 could be largely explained by changes in the routine activities of households. During this time period, the number of empty homes during the day increased as the number of single-person households and female participation in the workforce grew. At the same time, households increasingly contained attractive items to steal, such as more portable televisions and other electronic goods. Burglary increased, as fewer capable guardians were present in the home to protect the new suitable targets from burglars.

Routine activities theory provides the theoretical underpinnings for the well-known problem analysis crime triangle that breaks crime down into the features of places, features of offenders, and features of victims (see, e.g., Hough and Tilley, 1998; Leigh, Read, and Tilley, 1996). This analytic device was intended to help crime analysts and police officers visualize crime problems and understand relationships between the three elements. Moreover, research suggests that crime tends to cluster among a few places, offenders, and victims. Spelman and Eck (1989) examined several studies and estimated that 10 percent of the victims in the United States are involved in 40 percent of victimizations, 10 percent of offenders are involved in over 50 percent of crimes, and 10 percent of places are the sites of about 60 percent of crimes. These broad categories of crime problems are useful ways to think about focusing limited police resources.

The crime triangle has been reformulated to help police think about the response as well as the analysis (figure 3.3). The latest formulation of the crime triangle adds an outer level of "controller" for each of the

Figure 3.3. Revised Crime Problem Analysis Triangle
Source: Clarke and Eck (2007), section 8.

original three elements; problems are created when offenders and targets come together and controllers fail to act (Eck, 2003):

- For the target/victim, the *guardian* is usually someone who protects their own belongings or those of family members, friends, neighbors, and co-workers.
- For the offender, this is the *handler,* someone who knows the offender well and who is in a position to exert some control over his or her actions. Handlers include parents, siblings, teachers, friends, and spouses.
- For the place, the controller is the *place manager,* a person who has some responsibility for controlling behavior in the specific location such as a bus conductor or teacher in school [adapted from Clarke and Eck, 2003: 9].

When searching for appropriate responses, the revised crime triangle can help police think about what might be done to prevent offenders from re-offending by making better use of handlers, what victims can do to reduce the probability of being targets, and what changes could be made to the places where crimes occur (Clarke and Eck, 2003). Place management is discussed further in chapter 5.

Many crime problems are a mixture of repeat offenders, repeat victims, and repeat locations (Braga, 2008). However, routine activity theory can assist in figuring out which dimension of a crime problem is the most dominant (Clarke and Eck, 2003; Eck, 2003). A poorly managed tavern with repeated fights involving different participants is an example of a crime problem that may be most powerfully addressed through a place-based response. In this case, the setting continues to facilitate the problem events, even though handlers suppress offending, and guardians suppress victimization (Clarke and Eck, 2003). These insights would suggest that police should pay close attention to the characteristics and features of the place when devising appropriate prevention strategies.

Environmental Criminology

Environmental criminology, also known as crime pattern theory, explores the distribution and interaction of targets, offenders, and opportunities across time and space (Brantingham and Brantingham, 1991). According to Eck and Weisburd (1995), this occurs because offenders engage in routine activities. Environmental criminology is important in understanding the nature of crime at places because it combines rational choice and routine activity theory to explain the distribution of crime across places. Understanding the characteristics of places, such as facilities, is important as these attributes give rise to the opportunities that rational offenders will encounter during their routine activities. Environmental criminologists unravel crime problems through studying offender decision-making processes and small (e.g., shopping mall or housing project) and intermediate-level (e.g., neighborhood or city) analyses of very specific types of crimes occurring at very particular locations in these areas (Brantingham and Brantingham, 1991).

Studies of environmental factors of crime have shown that commercial properties located near main roads have an increased risk of robbery, and affluent homes located adjacent to poorer areas are more likely to be burglarized. In both cases, the offenders' "journey to work" was greatly reduced by the proximity of the targeted places to the offenders' homes or to a major thoroughfare. A key insight from these studies was that the offender's target search time, the amount of effort expended by the offender to locate a suitable target, was related to risk of victimization at that place (as described by Clarke, 1995). According to Marcus Felson (2006), offenders find suitable targets through *personal knowledge* of the victim (your neighbor's son might know when you are away from your house), *work* (a burglar working as a telephone engineer might overhear that you will be taking vacation next week), and overlapping *activity spaces* (where people live, work, shop, or seek entertainment).

The concept of place is essential to crime pattern theory (Eck and Weisburd, 1995). Not only are places logically required (an offender must be in a place when an offense is committed), their characteristics influence the likelihood of a crime and the likelihood that particular places become crime hot spots. Place characteristics highlighted by routine activity theory include the presence and effectiveness of managers and the presence of capable guardians. Crime pattern theory links places with desirable targets and the context within which they are found by focusing on how places come to the attention of potential offenders.

It is worth noting that although crime pattern theory and routine activity theory are mutually supportive in many respects, they can give rise to differing explanations of crime at specific locations (Eck and Weisburd, 1995). Given a set of crime hot spot locations, a crime pattern theorist would focus on how offenders discover and gain access to the place. A routine activity theorist would focus instead on the behaviors of the targets and the possible absence of controllers whose presence could have prevented the offenses from taking place—guardians, handlers, and place managers. In other words, for the crime pattern theorist, particular places are problematic because of their location and relationship to the environment. For the routine activity theorist, certain places are problematic because of the types of people present and absent from the location. Clearly, both explanations can be valid in different contexts and situations. It is possible that crime-specific explanations may show that for some events crime pattern theory is a particularly useful explanation, for other events routine activity theory offers greater insights, and for still a third group of events some combination of the two theories is needed.

"Broken Windows" Thesis

In their seminal "broken windows" article, Wilson and Kelling (1982) argue that social incivilities (e.g., loitering, public drinking, and prostitution) and physical incivilities (e.g., vacant lots, trash, and abandoned buildings) cause residents and workers in a neighborhood to be fearful. Fear causes many stable families to move out of the neighborhood and the remaining residents isolate themselves and avoid others. Anonymity increases and the level of informal social control decreases. The lack of control and escalating disorder attracts more potential offenders to the area and this increases serious criminal behavior (see also Kelling and Coles, 1996). Wilson and Kelling (1982) suggest that serious crime developed because the police and citizens did not work together to prevent urban decay and social disorder.

Research on crime hot spots suggests that disorder clusters in space and time with more serious crimes. In their closer look at crime in Minneapolis hot spots, Weisburd and his colleagues (1992) found that assault calls for service and robbery of person calls for service were significantly correlated with "drunken person" calls for service. In Jersey City, New Jersey, Braga and his colleagues (1999) found that violent crime hot spots also suffered from serious disorder problems.

At the neighborhood level, however, the available research evidence on the connections between disorder and more serious crime is mixed. Skogan's (1990) survey research found disorder to be significantly correlated with perceived crime problems in a neighborhood even after controlling for the population's poverty, stability, and racial composition. Further, Skogan's (1990) analysis of robbery victimization data from thirty neighborhoods found that economic and social factors' links to crime were indirect and mediated through disorder. In his reanalysis of the Skogan data, Harcourt (1998, 2001) removed several neighborhoods with very strong disorder-crime connections from Newark, New Jersey, and reported no significant relationship between disorder and more serious crime in the remaining neighborhoods. Eck and Maguire (2000) suggest that Harcourt's analyses do not disprove Skogan's results; rather, his analyses simply document that the data are sensitive to outliers. The removal of different neighborhoods from Harcourt's analysis may have strengthened the disorder-crime connection (Eck and Maguire, 2000).

In his longitudinal analysis of Baltimore neighborhoods, Taylor (2001) finds some support that disorderly conditions lead to more serious crime. However, these results varied according to types of disorder and types of crime. Taylor (2001) suggests that other indicators, such as initial neighborhood status, are more consistent predictors of later serious crimes. Using systematic social-observation data to capture social and physical incivilities on the streets of Chicago, Sampson and Raudenbush (1999) found that, with the exception of robbery, public disorder was not significantly related to most forms of serious crime when neighborhood characteristics such as poverty, stability, race, and collective efficacy were considered.[1]

Sampson and Raudenbush's findings have been criticized because their social observation data on disorder were collected during the day rather than at night (Sousa and Kelling, 2006) and based on their decision to test a model in which disorder mediates the effects of neighborhoods' characteristics on crime rather than neighborhood characteristics mediating the effects of disorder on crime (Jang and Johnson, 2001). A recent study of crime hot spot areas in Chicago found some support for both broken windows and collective efficacy theories in explaining the concentration of specific crime types at places (St. Jean, 2007). However, this research also found that different kinds of crime occur most often in locations that offer perpetrators specific "ecological advantages." For instance, drug dealers and robbers were primarily attracted to locations with businesses like liquor stores, fast-food restaurants, and check-cashing outlets (St. Jean, 2007). In St. Jean's research, interviews with offenders revealed that criminals found certain facilities and site features at specific places provided compelling opportunities to commit crimes.

Eck and Weisburd's (1995) Review of Crime Place Research

Recent perspectives in criminological theory provide a basis for constructing a theory of crime hot spots. However, such a theory must be developed in reference to a growing literature about the relationship between crime and place. Eck and Weisburd (1995) review five different types of research that shed light on the role of place in crime events (see figure 3.4; see also Eck, 1994). The research evidence on crime clustering was reviewed in chapter 1. In this section, we present the four remaining types of research on crime and place from the Eck and Weisburd review.

As Eck and Weisburd (1995) report, three of the research enterprises use the place as a unit of analysis, making crime events problematic at the outset. In these studies researchers have tried to understand how the facilities associated with place influence crime, why crime clusters at places, and finally how the social and physical characteristics of places alter opportunities for crime. Two of the research categories focus on people but nonetheless lead to an understanding of the role of place in crime. Mobility and target-selection studies provide insight into how offenders choose crime places and the social factors that inhibit their reach.

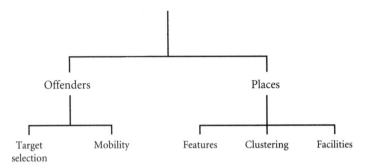

Figure 3.4. Studies of Crime and Place
Source: Eck and Weisburd (1995): 8.

Facilities and Crime

Facilities are special-purpose structures operated for specific functions. Examples of place facilities include high schools, taverns, convenience stores, churches, apartment buildings, and public housing projects. Different types of facilities increase or decrease crime in their immediate environment and can be important determinants of whether particular places become crime hot spots or not. As suggested by offender-search theory, this could occur because it draws people, some of whom are offenders, to the area. Or, as routine activity theory suggests, this occurs because of the way the facility is managed, the desirability and accessibility of targets found in the facility, the likelihood of handlers being at the location, and the level of guardianship found at the site. Evidence supporting either theory can be found in studies of crime around facilities (see, for example, Roncek, 1981). Unfortunately, these studies cannot comparethe relative evidence supporting the two explanations because the studies do not differentiate between offenses at the facility and those in the surrounding block.

Another problem with some of these studies is that they often do not differentiate between crime density (crimes per land area) and victimization risk (crimes per target) (Wikstrom, 1995). More than thirty years ago Boggs (1965) pointed out that most calculations of crime rates are not estimates of crime risk because inappropriate measures of the crime opportunities (targets) are used for the denominator in the calculations. Burglary rates are normally calculated by dividing the number of burglary events by the population of the area being studied. The appropriate denominator for calculating risk is the number of buildings in the area. Burglaries may be concentrated in one area relative to another because there are more places to break into in the first area, or because they differ in some other factor (e.g., the first neighborhood may be populated by childless couples in which both partners work, whereas the second area is populated by retired couples who spend a great deal of time around their homes).

Measures of opportunities have been used in some of these studies, but they are often indirect measures of the number of targets at risk.

Engstad (1975), for example, used the number of bar seats as an indirect measure of the opportunity for assaults in and around bars. If bar seats are used to capacity, or if the vacancy rate for these spots is constant across bars, then they may be reasonable approximations of the number of targets at risk. If, however, some bars have a greater proportion of their seating empty than other bars, and vacancy rates are related to crime (e.g., bars with many crimes scare off potential customers), the opportunity measures may introduce a confounding influence to the estimated relationship being examined.

Roncek and his colleagues have conducted a series of facilities studies in Cleveland and San Diego, and they follow a standard methodology. The numbers of facilities of interest are counted in each of the city's census blocks using phone directories or other locally available rosters. The crime count by census block is derived from police data, and census files provide demographic information for control variables. These studies have found that bars and high schools are associated with ele-vated crime counts in the blocks in which they are located, but have little impact beyond the immediate block (Roncek, 1981; Roncek and Bell, 1981; Roncek and Faggiani, 1985; Roncek and Lobosco, 1983; Roncek and Meier, 1991; Roncek and Pravatiner, 1989).

The research has also found that public housing projects in Cleveland are associated with small but significant increases in crime on their blocks (Roncek and Faggiani, 1985; Roncek and Lobosco, 1983). Because compositional variables have been controlled for, the facility effects are assumed due to the place and not to the people who reside on the block. A number of other studies report similar findings. Frisbie and colleagues (1977) reported clustering of crimes within .15 of a mile around bars in Minneapolis. These counts were not standardized by controlling for the number of criminal opportunities available at different distances from the bars, so it is unclear whether this is due to an opportunity gradient around bars or whether bars enhance the criminal propensity of people who are attracted to bars.

While much research points to the relationship between bars and crime in proximate areas (Block and Block, 1995; Roncek and Meier,

1991), most bars experience little crime while a few may be hot spots of crime (Homel and Clark, 1994; Sherman, Schmidt, and Velke, 1992). According to Eck (1997: 7–10), "the behavior of bartenders and bouncers may contribute to violence in these places and changes in bar management practices (from server training and changes in legal liability of bartenders) may reduce assaults, drunk driving, and traffic accidents." As Clarke and Eck (2007) observe, only a small proportion of any type of facility will account for the majority of crime and disorder problems experienced or produced by the group of facilities as a whole.

Engstad (1975) compared the number of auto crimes and bar crimes (assault, disorderly conduct, and violations of the liquor act) in small areas with hotels to the same crime counts in adjacent areas without hotels. He standardized the crime counts by the number of residents living in the areas and found an association between the presence of hotels and higher rates of crime per thousand people. When Engstad (1975) compared hotel areas and standardized the crime counts by calculating opportunity-based rates for each crime (i.e., dividing auto crimes in each hotel area by the number of parking places in each area, and dividing the bar crimes in the area by the number of seats in bars), he found that one particular hotel area had higher auto and bar crime rates than the other hotel areas.

Engstad (1975) conducted the same types of analysis for shopping centers using auto crimes, thefts, and other property crimes and found that areas with shopping centers had higher rates of crime per thousand population than areas without shopping centers. When he compared the shopping center areas for these crimes standardized by opportunity-based measures (i.e., parking places for auto crime, retail space per 1,000 square feet for thefts, and acres of shopping center for mischief), Engstad (1975) again found variation among the shopping-center areas. Because Engstad did not compare crime events in target areas to crime events in their surrounding areas controlling for opportunities, we cannot determine if the associations he found are due to different opportunities available or to the people who use the areas. Even when controls for opportunity were introduced, controls for other structural and compositional variables were not used. Consequently, we have no idea why such variation might exist.

Spelman (1993) examined the association between abandoned unsecured residential homes and crime on the blocks on which these homes were located. He found a positive association, though he did not control for the criminal opportunities on the blocks. He does provide evidence that the only significant difference between the blocks with abandoned homes and those without such homes was that the former had more owner-occupied buildings. More recently, Felson (2006) identified eleven ways that abandoned sites, such as shells of factories, closed businesses, abandoned residences, and empty lots, can feed crime problems.

Brantingham and Brantingham (1982) studied the association between commercial burglaries per store on blocks and the presence of five types of "commercial landmarks": fast-food restaurants, traditional restaurants, supermarkets, department stores, and pubs. Though supermarket and department-store blocks had commercial burglary rates comparable to blocks without these landmarks, the other three landmarks had commercial burglary rates 2 to 2.5 times higher than the non-landmark average (Brantingham and Brantingham, 1982).

Rengert and Wasilchick (1990) provide evidence from interviews with burglars that drug dealing locations might draw predatory offenders to an area to purchase drugs. These offenders then may commit predatory crimes in the area surrounding the drug places. Providing partial support for the view that places attract offenders for one purpose who then participate in other crimes, Weisburd and colleagues (1994) found an overrepresentation of crime calls for a series of crime categories in places that were identified primarily as drug markets. These studies suggest three possible hypotheses: there is something about the place that fosters deviance in the block; the facilities draw people into the block; or both. Unfortunately, these studies cannot test these hypotheses separately.

Several studies suggest that the more access people have to an area or place, the more crime in the area or place. Friedman, Hakim, and Weinblatt (1989) examined the effects of casino gambling in Atlantic

City on crime in the small towns along the main routes to this resort. They found that crime counts increased in these towns relative to towns not located on routes to Atlantic City, controlling for town population, unemployment, value of commercial and residential real estate per square mile, and population density. If we could assume that the small towns on the route did not change in social composition or structure at the same time casino gambling was introduced, the increase in crime would be most plausibly explained by the increases in outsiders passing through the towns. Unfortunately, the authors provide no evidence that the social composition and structure were not changed by the growth of Atlantic City.

Duffala (1976) and Nasar (1981) examined stores with varying crime counts (convenience-store robberies and commercial burglaries, respectively) and found that those with the most crime were located on major thoroughfares. Comparisons of high- and low-crime neighborhoods (Greenberg and Rohe, 1984; White, 1990) and street segments (Frisbie et al., 1977) show that area accessibility is associated with higher crime rates. The more people who pass a place, the greater the chances that the place will be the scene of a crime. This conclusion is consistent with the hypothesis that places that attract large numbers of people will suffer more victimizations (these studies do not rule out the alternative hypothesis, however). This suggests that facilities attract people into the block, some of whom are motivated to commit crimes (Brantingham and Brantingham, 1981).

Though facilities may attract offenders onto a block, the variation in crime among blocks with the same facilities suggests that there may be important differences in the social structure of the places that account for differences in crime counts, even when controlling for crime opportunities (see Engstad, 1975). Further, all of the studies to date have been of facilities that may have low guardianship (because they attract large numbers of people with little in common) and/or low levels of place management (because of inadequate staffing or training). A study of the effects of facilities with high guardianship and place management (e.g., churches) on block crime would be revealing in this respect.

Site Features

Studies of crime hot spots show offenses occurring at places but provide scant information as to why some places are more criminogenic than others. Are these hot spots the hangouts of deviants? Is there a failure of social control at these hot spots? Or are there features present at these hot spot locations that attract offenders from the surrounding areas? Some insight as to possible answers can be gained by examining studies of place features and crime.

The strategy of defensible space entails organizing the physical environment to enhance peoples' sense of territoriality, make it possible for them to observe their environment, and communicate to would-be offenders that they are being watched (Newman, 1972). Newman (1972) purported to find that public housing projects with defensible space features had less crime than projects that did not have these features.

Critics have attacked Newman's research and theory. Mawby (1977) suggested that Newman misrepresented his findings, purposely selecting the two principal study sites to bolster his premise and failing to describe the characteristics of the resident populations and offender rates of the two sites. Merry (1981) found that people do not automatically scrutinize their environment even when the physical arrangements make surveillance feasible, and that offenders know this. She criticized defensible space theory for neglecting the social dimensions of crime prevention. Mayhew (1981) concluded that consistent surveillance is unlikely except by employees of organizations who control places; a number of studies sponsored by the U.K. Home Office support this assertion (Poyner, 1988; Webb and Laycock, 1992). Other reviews of research on defensible space consistently reported that the theory is vague and omits critical mediating variables (Mawby, 1977; Mayhew, 1979; Taylor, Gottfredson, and Brower, 1984).

Research on convenience stores also supports Mayhew's (1981) hypothesis that employees can prevent crimes through improved surveillance. Reviews of studies comparing stores with few and many robberies point to such physical features as unobstructed windows, placement of the cash register so that the entrance can be monitored, and lighted parking areas fully visible from inside the store (Hunter and Jeffrey, 1992; LaVigne, 1991).

It is unclear whether the number of employees conducting surveillance makes a difference. Evaluating the impact of a Gainesville, Florida, city ordinance that required two clerks to be present in the evening, Clifton (1987) contends that robberies were reduced. This contention has been challenged by Wilson (1990) and by Sherman (1991), both of whom claim that Clifton failed to rule out several important rival hypotheses. Nevertheless, Hunter and Jeffrey (1992) contend that this crime prevention measure had the strongest empirical support of all measures tested. LaVigne (1991), however, could find no such evidence in her study of Austin, Texas, convenience-store crime.

Finally, from studies of the deterrent effects of guards, there is additional evidence that offenders avoid places with people trained to watch their environment and to intervene if criminal behavior is suspected. Hannan (1982) used multivariate cross-sectional analysis to investigate the deterrent value of bank guards in Philadelphia. He found that the presence of guards was associated with fewer robberies, even when the volume of banking business and the demographics of the surrounding areas were held constant. Landes (1978) demonstrated that the decline in aircraft hijacking in the United States was due principally to the installation of metal detectors in airports and secondarily to increased use of armed air marshals on flights. Additional police security in New York City's subway system apparently reduced robberies there for a time, even when problems with police falsification of crime statistics were accounted for (Chaiken, 1978; Chaiken, Lawless, and Stevenson, 1974). Book theft from libraries was deterred through the introduction of electronic security systems (Scherdin, 1992), while placing attendants in some parking facilities (Laycock and Austin, 1992) or installing closed circuit television (Poyner, 1988) reduced auto thefts. In summary, offenders avoid targets with evidence of high guardianship.

But note that effective guardianship is linked to place management. In each of the studies just cited, the additional security was put in place by the owner or manager of the place, not by the users of the place. Site features are not only useful for enhancing surveillance, they can also control access to places. Studies in the security literature highlight the effectiveness of physical barriers that prevent access to targets. Grandjean (1990) reported that Swiss banks with security screens have fewer robberies than those without such barriers. The installation of security screens in British post offices resulted in fewer robberies of these places (Ekblom, 1987). The value of access-control features for controlling crime depends on the crime. Eck (1994) found evidence that crack and powder cocaine dealers may prefer apartment buildings with physical features that control access. Thus the features that may prevent burglary may attract drug dealing.

A third way in which site features may influence offender decisions about places involves making the targets at the place less desirable or hard to attack. Protecting targets at places can be accomplished by such tactics as securing targets, removing targets from places, or making them appear to be less attractive. Property marking can sometimes reduce burglaries by reducing the value of the stolen goods (Laycock, 1985). Exact fares on buses were found to reduce robberies by securing the target to the floor of the bus (Chaiken, Lawless, and Stevenson, 1974). Cash-control methods (introducing timelock cash boxes, setting cash limits on draws at each teller, installing safes with adjustable time locks) have been reported to reduce robberies in betting shops (Clarke and McGrath, 1990). The removal of pre-payment gas meters from residences in a housing complex in Britain was partially responsible for reducing burglaries there (Forrester et al., 1990).

Finally, how places are managed may have an effect on the risks of crime at a location. The ways in which bartenders and bouncers regulate drinking, for example, seems to have an effect on violence in drinking establishments (Homel and Clark, 1994). Offenders may select sites for criminal activity based on the level of control owners (or their hired surrogates) exercise over behavior at the location. Evidence for offender site selection based on place management can be gleaned from systematic comparison of crime and noncrime places. By examining the characteristics of drug-dealing places and nondrug-dealing places in the same area of San Diego, Eck (1994) found that crack and powder cocaine dealers seem to prefer small apartment buildings. Smaller apartment buildings appear to be owned by people who are not professional landlords and who do not have great financial assets. The majority of the apartment buildings that contain drug dealing are encumbered with debt, have lost value, and are either just breaking even or losing money for the owner. Thus, place management may be weaker at these locations; the landlords either do not know how to control the behavior of their residents or they cannot afford to do much about drug dealing. Drug dealers may select places with weak management, either because they are kept out of strong management places or they prefer weak management places, or both (see Eck, 1994).

In summary, there are a variety of physical and social features of places that enhance their attractiveness to offenders and can be important determinants whether particular places become crime hot spots. These features include an obvious lack of guardianship, easy access to the site, and the presence of readily attainable valuables. Sites without these features have been shown to have fewer crimes committed than similar sites with them. Additionally, evaluations of crime prevention programs demonstrate that removal of these attractive features reduces crime. Finally, how places are managed may influence the crime at sites. These studies demonstrate that offenders make choices about places based on site-level social and physical features.

Offender Mobility

The fact that criminals are mobile reinforces the importance of places for criminologists. Since offenders move about and crimes occur in a variety of settings, place and movement matter. Studies of offender mobility are based on official arrest and incident data from police and prosecutors' files. Reliance on crimes resulting in an arrest creates a potential source of bias in the results of these studies, given the low clearance rates of the crimes studied. Mobility studies may underestimate the distances offenders travel, if people who offend near their homes are more likely to be caught than people who commit their crimes further away.

Two aspects of mobility—distance and direction—have been examined in this literature. Distance and direction have been measured in a variety of ways, but for the most part they are calculated by connecting the address of a crime to the address of the offender's home. Distances traveled by offenders from homes to crime sites usually appear to be short, with the number of offenses declining rapidly as one moves further from the offender's home (Capone and Nichols, 1976; Phillips, 1980; Rhodes and Conley, 1981). At the same time, Brantingham and Brantingham (1981) hypothesize that offenders may avoid targets immediately adjacent to their homes to avoid being recognized (see also Weisburd et al., 2006).

Mobility may also be constrained between crime sites. Weisburd and Green (1994) argue that drug markets within close proximity to each other have clear and defined boundaries, often circumscribed by the nature of drug activities found in a specific place. Examining offenders who were arrested more than once for narcotics sales in Jersey City, they found it was very unlikely for an offender to be arrested in drug markets adjacent to each other. Indeed, suggesting a high degree of territoriality among offenders, it was more likely for a repeat arrestee to be arrested in a different district in the city than in a drug market a block or two away.

Evidence suggests that there may also be substantial variation by age, race, sex, and crime type in offender mobility. Young offenders appear not to travel as far from home as older offenders (Phillips, 1980; Nichols, 1980). African American offenders may not travel as far to commit crimes as whites (Phillips, 1980; Nichols, 1980). Women may travel further than men to commit crimes (Phillips, 1980), but may not travel as far from home to engage in robberies (Nichols, 1980). Expressive crimes—for example, rapes and assaults—are usually committed closer to home than instrumental crimes—burglary and robbery (Phillips, 1980; Rhodes and Conley, 1981). For robberies, offenders attacking commercial targets seem to travel further than offenders attacking individuals (Capone and Nichols, 1976). Drug dealers may have the shortest travel distances of offenders studied, since a large proportion is arrested at their home address (Eck, 1992).

Offender mobility studies investigating direction consistently demonstrate that offenders move from residential areas with fewer targets to areas with more targets (Boggs, 1965; Phillips, 1980; Costanzo, Halperin, and Gale, 1986). If the residential areas of offenders are target-rich, then travel distances are shorter than when the offenders' residential areas are target-poor (Rhodes and Conley, 1981). Property offenders avoid targets close to home where they might be recognized (Suttles, 1968). Rand (1986) compared offense place addresses to offender and victim home addresses and found that the most common pattern was that of each address located in a different census tract. Further, as the distribution of targets in a metropolitan area changes over time, offenders' direction and travel distance follow the targets (Lenz, 1986).

Though the search area of offenders may be limited, it does not seem to be random. Offenders appear to search for targets, though age, race and possibly gender may affect search strategy. Carter and Hill (1976) suggest that black and white offenders have different cognitive maps (i.e., mental images of their environments), and these may influence target-search patterns.

The preceding studies have often been interpreted as evidence of rational and deliberative target-searching behavior, and the influence of personal characteristics and the distribution of crime targets on this behavior. These studies, however, are consistent with two different target-search hypotheses: that offenders actively seek out attractive targets with low guardianship, and that they chance upon such opportunities while engaged in routine noncriminal activities. For example, Rhodes and Conley (1981) puzzle over an anomalous finding: that offenders seem to skip over areas of small businesses close to their home neighborhoods but prey on small businesses further away. Presumably, if offenders were aggressively seeking targets, then closer opportunities would be victimized more frequently than those further away. However, if offenders are finding opportunities while going to and from work, school, stores, recreation facilities and other sites for common activities, and these places are located at some distance from offenders' places of residence, then this skip pattern may be more explicable.

Offenders' cognitive maps may not include much information about areas they pass through, but may be rich in detail about places where they go for legitimate purposes (Brantingham and Brantingham, 1981). An example of this can be found in a study of crime in Stockholm. Wikstrom (1995) describes how youths living outside the center city use public transportation to go to the center city for entertainment and shopping. The concentration of legitimate activities that are attractive to youths also creates an environment rich in targets. As a consequence, center-city Stockholm has more crimes per land area than other parts of the city (Wikstrom, 1995).

Offender Target Selection

Offenders themselves should be able to describe their decision-making processes, and a number of studies have examined crime-site selection from their point of view. Most of these studies involve interviewing either a sample of subjects in custody or several offenders freely plying their craft. Most of the studies are of persistent adult offenders, so the conclusions one draws from them are unlikely to match the conclusions one would draw from a representative sample of offenders. Further compromising the conclusions we can draw from this approach is the fact that offenders do not always provide accurate accounts of their own decision making (Carroll and Weaver, 1986; Cromwell, Olson, and Avary, 1991).

These studies consistently conclude that offenders are rational, even though their rationality is bounded (Rengert and Wasilchick, 1990; Feeney, 1986; Kube, 1988; Maguire, 1988; Biron and Ladouceur, 1991; Cromwell, Olson, and Avary, 1991). Burglars report looking for cues that suggest a place is likely to yield acceptable gains with manageable risks, though among burglars there is variation in the salience of specific cues (Rengert and Wasilchick, 1990; Cromwell, Olson, and Avary, 1991). Planning is limited, and the more experienced the offender, the less planning that takes place (Feeney, 1986; Cromwell, Olson, and Avary, 1991). Offenders find targets by chancing upon them during routine, noncriminal activities, and through intentional searches (Rengert and Wasilchick, 1990; Cromwell, Olson, and Avary, 1991).

Thus, interviews of offenders confirm many of the studies that rely on official data: offenders make choices about places based on cues at the sites; and their discovery of places is in large part reliant on routine activities that are unrelated to crimes. This suggests that crime hot spots are likely to be easily accessible (i.e., on major thoroughfares), have things of value that can be taken, and emit cues that risks are low for committing crimes.

Repeat Victimization and its Relevance to Hot Spots Policing

Crime hot spots are often populated by specific targets that repeatedly attract offenders. For instance, an apartment building could have a particular unit that is burglarized over and over again. The same apartment building could have another unit that generates a large number of calls to the police as a result of violent husband who repeatedly abuses his wife and children. The growing body of research that seeks to understand and prevent repeat victimization has much to offer in developing our understanding of the underlying conditions and situations that cause particular places to be crime hot spots.

Criminological research has demonstrated that small proportions of the population, and of victims, suffer large proportions of all criminal victimizations. As mentioned earlier, in the United States, 10 percent of the victims are involved in 40 percent of the victimizations (Spelman and Eck, 1989). Using data from the 1992 British Crime Survey, Farrell and Pease (1993) reported that 4 percent of people experience 44 percent of all victimizations. In his review of the international research evidence on repeat victimization, Farrell (1995) found that the 2 or 3 percent of victim-survey respondents who are most commonly victimized report between a quarter and a third of all incidents. As such, preventing repeat victimization may prevent a large percentage of all crimes. Focusing on repeat victims also provides the police with an opportunity to detect more serious offenders, as well as addressing specific problems within crime hot spots.

Repeat targets can include an individual, a group of persons, a property (residential, commercial, or other), a motor vehicle, or some other single target (Farrell, 1995). Repeat victimization can involve either the same or different types of crime. As such, there is possible ambiguity in defining the target of repeat crimes. As Farrell and Sousa (2001) describe, in the case of auto theft, it could be unclear whether it is the car or the person that is repeatedly victimized. In practice, the former definition of the target is likely to provide greater utility as the preventive response is developed. In this chapter therefore, except where noted the focus will be primarily on the repeat victimization of individuals and groups of individuals.

Repeat victimization is not a random occurrence, and vulnerable individuals are prone to repeat victimization by the same type of crime (Reiss, 1980). Repeat victims can include individuals who are repeatedly victimized by the same offender (e.g., spouse assault cases) and individuals who are repeatedly victimized by a variety of offenders (e.g., a local merchant who is repeatedly visited by shoplifters, robbers, and vandals). The "lifestyle" theory of victimization suggests that differential risks of victimization are related to differential exposure to offenders (Hindelang, Gottfredson, and Garofalo, 1978). Exposure to potential offenders varies with the characteristics of the victim (age, race, place of residence, etc.) as well as the victim's lifestyle (Clarke, 1992). Work and leisure activities, such as drinking alcohol in public or using public transportation late at night, can increase an individual's risk of victimization.

For individuals with particularly risky lifestyles, the probability of victimization can be quite high. For example, during Boston's youth-homicide epidemic in the early to mid-1990s, youth gang members stood a roughly one in seven chance of being killed at some point during an average nine-year gang membership (Kennedy, Piehl, and Braga, 1996). Youth gunshot-wound victims treated in Boston emergency rooms often had scars from past gun and knife wounds (Rich and Stone, 1996). Routine activity theory also suggests that repeat victimization can be influenced by the activities and vulnerabilities of the victim (Cohen and

Felson, 1979). As Clarke (1992) observes, the implication is that modifying patterns of activity may reduce the risks of victimization.

Farrell, Sousa, and Lamm Weisel (2002) suggest that repeat crimes can be understood in terms of "risk heterogeneity" and "event dependency." Risk heterogeneity refers to the persisting attributes of repeat victims that make them more attractive to offenders relative to other potential victims. For example, a violent father may be more likely to repeatedly assault his 120-pound wife relative to his 250-pound college-age son who plays football. Event dependency is simply when one crime leads to another for the same victim. In the case of burglary, the same dwelling could suffer repeat burglaries because the successful offender decided to make a return visit to exploit a suitable target, informed his criminal associates of the easy opportunity, or the initial break-in caused the dwelling to become somehow more attractive to other burglars (e.g., the broken lock on the door had not yet been replaced). Unfortunately, many burglary victims do not heed crime prevention advice from police (Scott, 2004a). Weak doors, door-frames, window-frames,and window locks contribute to forced-entry burglaries and many low-income victims lack the resources to improve these house features (Scott, 2004a).

Pease (1998) explains repeat victimization by distinguishing between "boost" accounts and "flag" accounts. Like event dependency, boost accounts explain repetitions in terms of positive experiences at the initial offense; the likelihood of subsequent victimization for the same target is increased (or "boosted"). Flag accounts explain repeated victimization in terms of the unusual attractiveness or vulnerability of specific targets to a variety of offenders (sending a signal or "flag" to them). Some professions, such as taxi drivers, have much higher victimization rates than others, and some "hot" products, such as sports cars attractive to joy riders, also increase the likelihood of repeat victimization (Clarke and Eck, 2003).

An important dimension of revictimization is the length of time between one victimization and the next. Research demonstrates that the risk of revictimization is greatest in the period immediately after the preceding victimization and that this risk declines over time (Farrell, 1995). Thus, a study of residential burglary in Saskatoon, Canada, revealed that the likelihood of a repeat burglary at a residence within a month was over twelve times the expected rate of burglary, but that rate declined to less than twice the expected rate when burglaries six months apart were considered. An analysis of the repeat burglaries within a single month revealed that half of the second burglaries occurred within seven days of the first (Polvi et al., 1990, 1991). Similarly, in a study of families suffering violent racial attacks on an estate in the East End of London, Sampson and Phillips (1992) found that 67 percent of the thirty families in the study had been repeatedly victimized and that subsequent attacks were most frequent within the first week of the first attack. The most heavily victimized family was harassed, on average, once every six days. Further, it is well established that domestic violence is frequently a repeated crime (Crowell and Burgess, 1996).

An analysis of domestic-dispute calls to the police revealed a "heightened risk period" for repeat domestic-violence victimizations; when a woman calls the police, she is more likely to call them repeatedly within a short period of time (Farrell, Buck, and Pease, 1993). This body of research suggests that crime prevention measures need to be implemented as soon as possible following victimization and that temporary measures to provide security during the high-risk period after victimization may be an efficient and effective way to prevent crime (Farrell, 1995).

Pease and Laycock (1996) argue that repeat victimization provides two types of opportunities for crime prevention: (1) crime deflection and (2) the detection of offenders. Crime deflection involves turning offenders away from crime targets. For example, to reduce fighting at soccer matches in Britain, rival groups of fans have been segregated in the stadium, and their arrivals and departures have been scheduled to avoid waiting periods that promote trouble (Clarke, 1983). Second, repeat victimization gives law enforcement an opportunity to predict where and when crimes will occur and, as such, facilitates the detection of offenders. As much as 80 percent of repeat burglary victims are likely to have been revictimized by the same offender (Pease, 1998). From interviews with offenders, Anderson and Pease (1997) learned the degree to which burglary and theft repeats are rational and market-driven. Repeats involved less risk, since the place was known, including escape routes; offered the prospect of capturing new, insurance-replaced goods, which will attract a better price; and permitted offenders to learn the value of goods known to remain available during the period between offenses. Anderson and Pease (1997) also found that substantial change (or perceived substantial change) at places previously targeted decreased the likelihood that the same offenders would target these places again. Gill and Pease (1998) revealed that bank robbers who targeted the same branch more than once were more serious offenders than those who did not repeat offenses against the same target. The prospects of apprehending chronic offenders by protecting repeat victims underscore the potential crime prevention value of this approach.

Examining repeat victimization patterns can also assist in making predictions about those who are not yet victims. "Virtual repeat victimization" refers to instances where offenders select targets because they have already offended against similar or identical targets (Pease, 1998). As Farrell (2005: 147) describes,

> For example, the same make and model of car offers similar prospects to offenders. If the car is parked in a similar location or situation, the virtual-repeat is all the more identical. Nearby households with the same layout are prone to virtual repeats because, for the offender, there is a good chance that the same types of efforts and skills are needed, and the risks and rewards are similar to those of the previous target. These virtual repeats provide a useful angle for thinking about crime prevention: whether virtual-repeat victimization occurs due to a target's design (easy to break into), its location (in an unlit area) or its high resale value and low traceability (for example, a laptop, a portable MP3 player), can influence the choice of tactics for a preventive response.

The victimization of targets located next to one that was victimized is referred to as "near-repeat victimization." A series of studies have shown that the risk of burglary is communicable—properties next to a burgled home are temporarily victimized at a rate that is much higher than what would be expected on the basis of chance alone (Townsley, Homel, and Chaseling, 2003; Johnson and Bowers, 2004). The increased burglary risk is communicated to neighboring households and, for any given distance, there is a greater risk for homes on the same side of the street as the burgled home (Johnson and Bowers, 2004). The elevation in risk is temporary, however, and diminishes as the distance from the burgled property increases. According to Johnson and Bowers (2007), more detailed analyses revealed that the increased risk was communicated to houses up to 400 meters away and for a period of one month after the original burglary event. Obviously, these insights suggest that police officers should give priority to protecting homes close to the initial burgled home over the next several weeks.

The Convergence of High-Crime Areas, Crime Hot Spots, and Repeat Victimization

While focusing on repeat victims may be a particularly valuable way to detect and apprehend highly active offenders, it also provides a way to better focus police efforts at crime hot spots. Indeed, since both hot spots policing and protecting repeat victims involve the prevention of repeated crimes, it is conceptually diffiscult to draw a distinct line between the two approaches. Common themes include the use of empirical data to identify crime patterns, a policy interest in predicting the next crime or victimization, and an interest in identifying the causal mechanisms of crime (Farrell, 1995).

Pease and Laycock (1996) suggest that repeat targets could be thought of as "hot dots" of crime on a crime map. This conception of repeat targets facilitates the description of different types of problems within a troubled neighborhood, ranging from hot dots to hot spots to high-crime areas. In the search for appropriate responses to crime problems, it could be very important to distinguish between high-crime areas, crime hot spots, and repeat victimization. In this discussion, a high-crime area is simply a larger hot spot area, such as a high-crime public-housing site, rather than a specific location, such as a common playground area within the public housing site.

As Farrell and Sousa (2001) describe, repeat victimization may occur either inside or outside buildings, and it can cluster into both hot spots and high-crime areas. It is also important to note that not all hot spots or high-crime areas will involve repeat victimization, not all high-crime areas will be made up of hot spots, and not all hot spots are located in high-crime areas (Farrell and Sousa, 2001). However, it does seem likely that there will be more repeat victimization in hot spots because repeat crimes may be committed by more prolific offenders who return sooner and more often to the same target while generally operating in the same area (Farrell and Sousa, 2001). More likely offenders may also pass by a suitable target in a hot spot sooner and notice that something has changed to make it even more attractive.

Conclusion

The theoretical and empirical criminological evidence reviewed here suggests that criminogenic dynamics, situations, and attributes of particular places cause them to become crime hot spot locations. The obvious policy implication is that the police need to address the underlying conditions that cause a place to be attractive to criminals. Robust hot spots policing efforts would then require the expansion of the toolbox of policing far beyond traditional law enforcement responses to crime such as heightened presence and increased arrests. Alternative prevention strategies, such as razing abandoned buildings, controlling access to venues, target hardening, and protecting repeat victims, requires activities that are very different from traditional law enforcement actions and the development of partnerships with a wider range of individuals and organizations. In this context, hot spots policing requires that police be concerned not only about places, offenders, and victims but also about potential nonpolice guardians. If the goal of the police is to improve safety at places, then it is natural in hot spots policing to be concerned with place managers, guardians, and handlers of offenders who frequent the area. More generally, dealing with crime hot spots brings the attention of the police to the full range of people and contexts that are part of the crime problem.

The Empirical Evidence for Hot Spots Policing **4**

Although tradition and experience often provide the only guidance for criminal justice practitioners, there is a growing consensus among scholars, practitioners, and policymakers that crime prevention practices and policies should be rooted as much as possible in scientific evidence about "what works" (Cullen and Gendreau, 2000; MacKenzie, 2000; Sherman, 1998; Sherman et al., 2002). "Evidence-based crime prevention" is a part of a larger and increasingly expanding movement in social policy to use scientific research evidence to guide program development and implementation. In general terms, this movement is dedicated to the improvement of society through the utilization of the highest quality scientific evidence on what works best (see, e.g., Sherman et al., 1997).

In an evidence-based model, the source of scientific evidence is empirical research in the form of evaluations of programs, practices, and policies. Not all evaluation designs are considered equal, however. Some evaluation designs, such as randomized controlled experiments, are considered more scientifically valid than others (Campbell and Stanley, 1966; Cook and Campbell, 1979; Weisburd, 2003). The findings of stronger evaluation designs are privileged over the findings of weaker research designs in determining "what works" in crime and justice interventions. For instance, in their report to the United States Congress on what works in preventing crime, University of Maryland researchers developed the

Maryland Scientific Methods Scale to indicate to scholars, practitioners, and policymakers that studies evaluating criminological interventions may differ in terms of methodological quality of evaluation techniques (Sherman et al., 1997).

Common evaluation designs include randomized experiments, quasi-experiments, and observational research designs. In this chapter, we briefly describe the strengths and weaknesses of these three common research designs in order to place our discussion of prioritization of research findings in context. We then present results of three rigorous research reviews that assess the crime prevention value of hot spots policing. In this chapter, the important issue of whether focused police efforts in hot spot areas lead to displacement of crime to other locations (Repetto, 1976) or a "diffusion" of crime-control benefits to nearby locations (Clarke and Weisburd, 1994) is also considered. Using scientific-evaluation evidence as a criterion, we find substantial support for the crime prevention effectiveness of hot spots policing.

Experimental, Quasi-Experimental, and Non-Experimental Research Designs

There is no hard rule for determining when studies provide more reliable or valid results, or any clear line to indicate when there is enough evidence to come to an unambiguous conclusion. Nonetheless, social scientists generally agree on some basic guidelines for assessing the strength of the evidence available. Perhaps the most widely agreed on criterion relates to what is often referred to as internal validity (Sherman et al., 2002; Weisburd, Lum, and Petrosino, 2001). Research designs that allow the researcher to make a stronger link between the interventions or programs examined and the outcomes observed are generally considered to provide more valid evidence than designs that provide for a more ambiguous connection between cause and effect. In formal terms, the former designs are considered to have higher internal validity. In reviewing studies, internal validity is often used as a primary criterion for assessing the strength of the evidence provided.

Randomized Experimental Designs

Randomized experimental designs allow researchers to assume that the only systematic difference between the control and treatment groups is the presence of the intervention; this permits a clear assessment of causes and effects (Cook and Campbell, 1979; Campbell and Stanley, 1966; Sechrest and Rosenblatt, 1987). The classical experimental design involves three major pairs of components: (1) independent and dependent variables, (2) treatment and control groups, (3) pretesting and posttesting.[1]

Experiments essentially examine the effect of an independent variable on a dependent variable. The independent variable usually takes the form of a treatment stimulus which is either present or not. For instance, an experiment could examine the effect of an in-prison education program (the independent variable) on recidivism (the dependent variable) when offenders are released from prison. The key element of an experiment is the random allocation of subjects or units of analysis to treatment and control groups. This randomization approach allows the researcher to determine with confidence what would have happened if the treatment stimulus or intervention were not applied to the treatment group (often referred to as the "counterfactual"). The treatment group (sometimes called the "experimental" group) receives the stimulus or intervention to be tested and the control group does not. During the pretest period, treatment and control groups are both measured in terms of the dependent variable. After the stimulus or intervention is administered to the control group, the dependent variable is measured again in the posttest period. Differences noted between the pretest and posttest period on the dependent variable are then attributed to the influence of the treatment.

Randomization provides a simple and convincing method for achieving comparability in the treatment and control groups. After subjects are recruited by whatever means, the researchers randomly assign those subjects to either the treatment or control group. If randomization is done correctly, the only systematic difference between the two groups should be the presence or absence of the treatment. Experiments that use randomization to create equivalent groups are often called "randomized controlled trials."

Quasi-Experimental Designs

A quasi-experimental design seeks to approximate characteristics of a true experiment without the benefit of random allocation of units to treatment and control conditions (Cook and Campbell, 1979). As such, quasi-experiments do not have the same high degree of internal validity as randomized controlled trials. While there are many types of quasi-experimental research designs, researchers often use matching instead of randomization to create equivalence between the groups studied. Importantly, a randomized experiment makes the differences between groups unsystematic, meaning that there is no reason to believe that the people or places allocated to one group are different from another.

In a quasi-experiment, the researcher tries to create "equivalence" by using knowledge about a phenomenon to develop groups that are similar except for the fact that one received an intervention and the other did not. For example, a researcher interested in investigating the effects of a new juvenile curfew on crime in a particular city would try to find a city with similar crime rates and citizen demographics in the same geographic region. This matching strategy is sometimes called a nonequivalent-group-comparison design as the treatment and "control" cities will not be exactly the same. In the statistical analysis of quasi-experimental data, researchers will often attempt to isolate treatment effects by including covariates to account for any measurable factors that could also influence observed differences in the dependent variable (such as poverty levels, youth population size, and the like). Quasi-experimental designs result in less confidence in study findings than true experimental approaches because it is usually not possible to create groups that are alike on all possible characteristics. In the example above we might expect specific differences between cities. In turn, we recognize at the outset that we may not be aware of all those differences, and if aware we may not have the data available to fully take them into account.

Quasi-experimental interrupted time series analysis, involving before and after measurements for a particular dependent variable, represents a common type of evaluation research found in criminology and criminal justice. One of the intended purposes for doing this type of quasi-experimental research is to capture longer time periods and a sufficient number of different events to control for various threats to validity and reliability (Cook and Campbell, 1979). Long series of observations are made before and after the treatment. The established before-treatment trend allows researchers to predict what may have happened without the intervention. The difference between what actually happened after the intervention and the predicted outcome based on the before-treatment trend determines the actual treatment effect.

These approaches are often criticized for not accounting for other confounding factors that may have caused the observed differences.[2] It can also be difficult to model the trend in the time series so the treatment effect can be properly estimated. For instance, in their evaluation of the 1975 Massachusetts Bartley-Fox gun control law that mandated a year in prison for illegal carrying of firearms, Deutsch and Alt (1977) used an interrupted time series quasi-experimental design and found the passage of the law was associated with a statistically significant reduction in armed robbery in Boston. However, Hay and McCleary (1979) reanalyzed these data using a different quasi-experimental time series modeling approach and found no statistically significant reduction in Boston armed robberies associated with the passage of the law. In contrast, Pierce and Bowers (1981) found statistically significant violence reductions associated with the passage of the law using quasi-experimental interrupted time series analysis with multiple control-group comparisons.

While these designs are still likely to have lower internal validity than randomized experimental evaluations, quasi-experiments that combine the use of a control group with time series data can sometimes produce results that are of similar quality to randomized controlled trials (Lipsey and Wilson, 1993). Others, however, found that even strongly designed quasi-experiments produce less valid outcomes when compared to well-executed randomized controlled trials (see Weisburd, Lum, and Petrosino, 2001). In general, the persuasiveness of quasi-experiments should be judged on a case-by-case basis (Weisburd, Lum, and Petrosino,

2001). For evidence-based crime prevention, the implication is that randomized controlled trials are necessary to produce the most valid and unbiased estimates of the effects of criminal justice interventions.

Another type of quasi-experimental design is known as a natural experiment, where nature, or some event, has created treatment and control groups. In contrast to laboratory experiments, these events are not created by scientists, but yield scientific data nonetheless. The classic example is the comparison of crime rates in areas after the passage of a new law or implementation of a crime prevention initiative that affects one area and not another. For instance, the 1994 Brady Handgun Violence Prevention Act established a nationwide requirement that licensed firearms dealers observe a waiting period and initiate a background check for handgun sales. To assess the impact of the Brady Law on violence, Ludwig and Cook (2000) examined trends in homicide and suicide rates, controlling for population age, race, poverty, and other covariates, in the thirty-two "treatment" states directly affected by the Brady Act requirements were compared with the eighteen "control" states and the District of Columbia, which had equivalent legislation already in place. They found that the Brady Act appeared to be associated with reductions in the firearm suicide rate for persons aged fifty-five years or older but not with reductions in homicide rates or overall suicide rates.

Non-Experimental Designs

Studies that rely only on statistical controls are often seen to represent the weakest level of confidence in research findings (Cook and Campbell, 1979; Sherman et al., 1997). These studies are typically called non-experimental or observational research designs. In these studies, researchers do not vary treatments to observe their effects on outcomes. Rather, researchers will examine natural variation in a dependent variable of interest, such as crime, and estimate the effect of an independent variable, such as police staffing levels, based on its covariation with the dependent variable. Additional covariates, such as employment and demographic data, related to variation in the dependent variable will be included in the model as statistical controls to isolate the effect of the key independent variable of interest. The difficulty of this approach is that there could easily be excluded factors related to both the key independent variable and dependent variable that bias the estimated relationship between these variables. Unfortunately, for some sensitive areas in crime and justice, non-experimental research designs are the only method of investigation possible. While some scholars argue that it is possible to develop statistical models that provide highly valid results (e.g., Heckman and Smith, 1995), it is generally agreed that causes unknown or unmeasured by the researcher are likely to be a serious threat to the internal validity of non-experimental research designs (Cook and Campbell, 1979).

External Validity

Our discussion of methodological quality so far has focused on the internal validity of different types of research designs. However, another important indicator of the quality of a study is its external validity. External validity gauges the extent to which the findings of a study can be generalized to the population of interest. Accordingly, external validity measures whether the results of a study have meaning for the "real" world of crime and justice with which we are concerned (Cook and Campbell, 1979). A study can have very high internal validity but be relevant only to a very limited number of contexts or problems. Clearly, strongly designed studies should be capable of being generalized widely. Inferences about cause-effect relationships based on a specific scientific study are said to possess external validity if they may be generalized from the unique and idiosyncratic experimental settings, procedures, and participants to other populations and conditions.

Randomized experiments are sometimes seen as having lower external validity than other types of studies (Clarke and Cornish, 1972; Eck, 2002; Pawson and Tilley, 1997). This is especially seen to be the case in comparing observational non-experimental studies with randomized field trials. Randomized experiments are still not widely accepted by practitioners in criminal justice, and often require significant interventions in the daily routines of police agencies to be implemented successfully. This often means that only the most progressive police agencies are willing to be involved in randomized experiments. One consequence of this is that experiments are conducted in relatively special environments, ones which are willing and able to participate in a randomized study. We know of no study to date that has actually shown a relationship between study design and external validity, and we suspect that differences are not substantial. Nonetheless, the problem of external validity should be kept in mind in reviewing study findings.

The well-known Minneapolis Domestic Violence Experiment and its subsequent replications offer a cautionary tale on the external validity of study findings when interventions are applied to other subjects and in other settings (Sherman, 1992a). The Minneapolis experiment was undertaken to determine the best way to prevent the risk of repeated violence by the suspect against the same victim in the future. Three approaches were tested. The traditional approach was to do very little as it was believed that the offenders would not be punished harshly by the courts and the arrest might provoke further violence against the victim. A second approach was for the police to undergo special training enabling them to mediate ongoing domestic disputes. The third approach was to treat misdemeanor violence as a criminal offense and arrest offenders in order to teach them that their conduct was serious and to deter them from repeating it. The experiment revealed that, in Minneapolis, arrest worked best: it significantly reduced repeat offenses relative to the other two approaches (Sherman and Berk, 1984). The results of the experiment were very influential as many police departments adopted mandatory misdemeanor arrest policies and a number of states adopted mandatory misdemeanor arrest and prosecution laws. However, replications of the Minneapolis domestic violence experiment in five other cities did not produce the same findings. In his review of those differing findings, Sherman (1992a: 19) identified four policy dilemmas for policing domestic violence:

1. Arrest reduces domestic violence in some cities but increases it in others.
2. Arrest reduces domestic violence among employed people but increases it among unemployed people.
3. Arrest reduces domestic violence in the short run but can increase it in the long run.
4. Police can predict which couples are most likely to suffer future violence, but our society values privacy too highly to encourage preventive action.

This experience suggests that even experimental findings need to be replicated before enacting mandatory interventions that could, in fact, have varied effects across different settings and subjects.

Statistical Power

In designing evaluations, researchers need to ensure that the research design is powerful enough to detect a treatment effect if one exists. The power of a statistical test is the probability that the test will reject a false null hypothesis (Lipsey, 1990; Weisburd and Britt, 2007) that there is no statistically significant difference in the outcomes of the treatment and control groups. Statistical power is a very complex problem, especially in experimental research. Power estimates are often based simply on the number of cases in the study, with the general observation that larger numbers of subjects increases the power of statistical tests to detect treatment effects (Lipsey, 1990). However, as Weisburd (1993) points out, the number of cases may be a misleading measure because there is often a relationship between the number of cases studied and other elements of a research design, for example the intensity of interventions. He finds that the smaller the experiment, the better the control of variability in treatment and design. In the reviews below, scholars considered statistical power in evaluating the impact of studies included.

University of Maryland Report to the United States Congress (Sherman et al. 1997, 2002)

In 1996, the United States Congress commissioned the Department of Criminology and Criminal Justice at the University of Maryland to provide an independent, scientifically rigorous assessment of more than $4 billion worth of federally sponsored crime prevention programs. Lawrence Sherman and his colleagues (1997) reviewed scientific evaluations of programs intended to prevent crime in seven settings in which crime prevention takes place: families, schools, communities, labor markets, places (e.g., urban centers, homes), police, courts, and corrections. Programs were evaluated on the Scientific Methods Scale, mentioned earlier, which ranked scientific studies from one (weakest) to five (strongest) on overall internal validity. Properly implemented randomized experiments were rated highest on the scale and non-experimental correlational studies lowest. The scale was one of the first attempts in crime and justice studies to rank studies scientifically and to communicate quality in science more effectively to policymakers, practitioners, media, and general public. The findings of the original 1997 report were updated in a 2002 book (Sherman et al., 2002).

In the policing section of the updated Maryland report, Lawrence Sherman and John Eck (2002) examined eight major hypotheses about policing and crime. These hypotheses examined a variety of police crime prevention strategies, including increasing numbers of police, rapid response to 911, random patrols, directed patrols, reactive arrests, proactive arrests, community policing, and problem-oriented policing. Their examination of directed patrol strategies closely resembled a careful review of patrol-based hot spots policing programs. Sherman and Eck distinguished directed patrols from traditional random patrols by observing that the advent of computerized crime analysis allowed greater precision in the identification of crime patterns. In turn, the police used this precision to focus police resources on the times and places at greatest risk of serious crime. Sherman and Eck suggested that the police were operating under the hypothesis that the more precisely patrol presence is concentrated at the "hot spots" and "hot times" of criminal activity, the less crime there will be in those places and times.

To be included in the directed-patrol program category, the studies had to indicate that they were somehow focused on high-crime places, times or areas. Sherman and Eck (2002) identified nine studies in his review (table 4.1). All nine studies reported crime reductions in response to the directed patrol strategy. Using a standard of at least two consistent findings from level three methods score (well-measured, before-after studies with a comparison group) studies and a preponderance of the other evidence in support of the same conclusion, the review concluded that increased directed patrols in street-corner hot spots "works" in preventing crime. The review also noted that most of these studies had not examined the issue of crime displacement and, as such, the results could be questioned on the grounds that offenders simply may have focused on other areas. The Fritsch, Caeti, and Taylor (1999) study, however, measured displacement effects and found evidence of slight spatial displacement.

In another section of the updated Maryland report, John Eck (2002) examined the prospects of preventing crime at high-activity crime places, in other words, crime hot spots. Eck identified 109 place-oriented interventions reported in 89 studies. While the methodological quality, interventions, and settings varied in these studies, Eck's review found that 90 percent of the evaluated place-oriented crime prevention interventions displayed evidence of crime-reductioneffects. Often the reported reductions were large. The review also concluded that, when measured, crime displacement was often limited or often nonexistent. Several studies reported a diffusion of prevention benefits to targets and areas not protected by the place-based intervention.

About half of the reviewed interventions were considered to be problem-oriented policing or situational crime prevention efforts. Eck (2002) suggested that, rather than looking for generic solutions to problems at crime places, it was preferable to undertake a thorough examination of the problem and then craft a unique set of interventions to address this problem. Situational crime prevention and problem-oriented

Table 4.1. Studies Examining the Crime Prevention Effects of Directed Patrol

Studies	Scientific Methods Score	Findings
Press, 1971	3	40% more police, reductions of outdoors crime
Chaiken et al., 1975; Chaiken, 1978	3	Police on subways at night reduced crime
Dahman, 1975	2	More police, reductions of outdoors crime
Schnelle et al., 1977	2	400% more patrol, less Part I crime
Sherman and Weisburd, 1995	5	100% more patrol, less observed hot spot crime
Koper, 1995	4	Longer patrol visits, longer post-visit crime-free time
Reiss, 1995 Review:		
Barker et al., 1993	2	Squad focused on hot spots, where street crime dropped
Burney, 1990	2	Saturation patrols, reduced street crime
Fritsch, Caeti, and Taylor, 1999	3	Undirected saturation patrolling was less effective than truancy and curfew patrolling in curbing gang violence

Source: Sherman and Eck (2002): 308.

policing were recommended as promising avenues to prevent crime in high-activity crime places. Similarly, in the police review, Sherman and Eck (2002) identified five problem-oriented policing projects that specifically focused on crime hot spots. Four of the five studies reported substantial and significant reductions in target offenses at treatment places when compared to control places. The Maryland directed patrol and place-oriented interventions reviews strongly suggested that police, when appropriately focused on specific problems at a place, can prevent crime at hot spot locations.

National Research Council's Committee to Review Research on Police Policy and Practices (2004)

The Violent Crime Control and Law Enforcement Act of 1994 encouraged the adoption of community policing, increased use of modern information technology, and the hiring of many new police officers. The 1994 Act also mandated that policing programs already underway or to be sponsored by funds from the legislation needed to be evaluated. As part of their considerable investment in law enforcement practice and research, the U.S. Department of Justice requested the National Research Council to establish the Committee to Review Research on Police Policy and Practices (Skogan and Frydl, 2004). The committee assessed police research and its influence on policing and the influence and operation of the community-policing philosophy (Skogan and Frydl, 2004).

The committee was charged with a number of specific tasks including evaluating the effectiveness of police activities in reducing crime, disorder, and fear (see also Weisburd and Eck, 2004). In reviewing the existing evaluation literature on police crime prevention programs, the Committee used internal validity as a primary criterion for assessing the strength of the evidence provided. As such, the findings of more rigorous research designs, such as randomized experiments, were privileged over the findings of weaker research designs such as quasi-experimental or correlational studies (Skogan, and Frydl, 2004; Weisburd and Eck, 2004).

Since randomized field experiments can be compromised by implementation difficulties, the committee also considered the integrity of the implementation design in their assessment of research evidence.

As part of their review of focused policing efforts to reduce crime, the committee closely examined the research evidence on the crime prevention effectiveness of hot spots policing. The committee's assessment drew strongly on preliminary results from a systematic review of hot spots policing conducted for the Campbell Collaboration (Braga, 2001). Findings of the completed Campbell systematic review are presented in the next section of this chapter. The committee reported that a series of randomized field trials showed that policing focused on crime hot spots can result in meaningful reductions in crime and disorder (Skogan and Frydl, 2004; Weisburd and Eck, 2004).

An early evaluation of problem-oriented policing tactics that were focused on high rate crime addresses, the Repeat Call Policing (RECAP) experiment (Sherman, Buerger, and Gartin, 1989; Buerger, 1993) did not report encouraging findings. The randomized experiment included five hundred commercial and residential addresses with the highest frequency of citizen calls for service in Minneapolis that were randomly allocated to treatment and control conditions. The treatment involved the application of problem-oriented policing by a specialized unit. The evaluation reported no significant differences between the treatment and control locations. However, the investigators reported a number of threats to the integrity of research design. In particular, the large caseload of high-activity addresses assigned to the RECAP unit made it impossible to apply problem-oriented policing with sufficient depth (Buerger, 1993). Moreover, the simple randomization procedure led to the placing of some of the highest event addresses into the treatment group; this led to high variability between the treatment and control groups and low statistical power.

While the RECAP experiment did not provide promising findings, six subsequent studies with strong experimental designs suggested that hot spots policing was effective in responding to crime and disorder problems (Skogan and Frydl, 2004; Weisburd and Eck, 2004). The first of these studies was the Minneapolis Hot Spots Patrol Experiment (Sherman and Weisburd,

1995), described in chapters 1 and 2. This study found the treatment as compared to the control hot spots experienced statistically significant reductions in crime calls. In another randomized experiment, the Kansas City Crack House Raids Experiment (Sherman and Rogan, 1995b), crackdowns on drug locations were also found to lead to significant relative improvement in citizen calls and crime reports in the treatment sites, although the effects were modest and decayed in a short period. However, in another randomized field experiment, Eck and Wartell (1996) found that if the raids were immediately followed by police contacts, crime prevention gains could be reinforced and sustained for longer periods of time.

Two other randomized controlled experiments tested a more tailored problem-oriented policing approach to dealing with crime hot spots and reported more general crime and disorder effects. In the Jersey City Problem-Oriented Policing in Violent Places experiment (Braga et al., 1999), strong statistically significant reductions in total crime incidents and total crime calls were found in the treatment hot spots relative to the control hot spots. Importantly, all crime categories experienced reductions and observational data revealed statistically significant declines in social and physical disorder as well. In the Jersey City Drug Market Analysis Program experiment (Weisburd and Green, 1995), hot spots policing tactics were found to be more effective at reducing disorder at drug hot spots than generalized enforcement. Violent crime was not significantly reduced as a result of the tailored approaches to local drug hot spots. In both Jersey City experiments, problem-solving interventions were implemented at the treatment hot spots. However, in practice, aggressive disorder-enforcement tactics were often the central strategy. In the Oakland Beat Health study, Green Mazerolle and Roehl (1998) also reported strong reductions in crime and disorder in an experimental evaluation of civil-remedy interventions at specific drug-involved locations.

The Committee also found that these experimental findings were supported by a series of quasi-experimental research studies (Skogan and Frydl, 2004). For instance, the Kansas City Gun Project evaluation (Sherman and Rogan, 1995a) found strong crime-control gains for hot spots policing approaches. Using intensive enforcement in an eight by ten block area, including traffic stops and searches, Sherman and Rogan (1995a) reported a 65 percent increase in guns seized by the police and a 49 percent increase in gun crimes in the treatment area relative to a matched control area. Hope (1994) examined the effects of a problem-oriented policing strategy, which relied primarily on traditional law enforcement tactics, on total calls for service in three drug hot spot locations in St. Louis, Missouri. The evaluation compared total calls in the targeted drug hot spots to addresses proximate to the treatment locations and blocks in the surrounding areas. Hope (1994) reported significant crime reductions in the treatment locations when compared to the control locations.

The Committee also considered the issue of crime displacement in their assessment of the crime prevention value of hot spots policing and concluded these approaches did not simply cause crime to move else-where (Skogan and Frydl, 2004; Weisburd and Eck, 2004). Several of the reviewed studies examined the issue of immediate spatial displacement in their evaluation of the approach. In the Jersey City Drug Market Analysis Program experiment, two block-displacement areas surround-ing each treatment hot spots were compared to two block-displacement areas around control hot spots (Weisburd and Green 1995). The investi-gators did not report significant displacement of crime and disorder calls. They did note, however, that drug-related and public-morals calls actually decreased significantly in the treatment displacement areas relative to the control displacement areas. This "diffusion of crime con-trol benefits" (Clarke and Weisburd, 1994) was also reported in the Jersey City Problem-Oriented Policing in Violent Places experiment (Braga et al., 1999), the Oakland Beat Health study (Green Mazerolle and Roehl, 1998), and Kansas City Gun Project (Sherman and Rogan, 1995a). Only the St. Louis Problem-Oriented Policing in Three Drug Market Locations study reported direct spatial displacement of crime in areas immediately surrounding only one targeted area and this displacement effect was much smaller than the overall crime prevention effect (Hope, 1994). The primary cause of the observed displacement was a shift in drug sales from a targeted apartment building to a similar nontargeted apartment building on the same block.

The National Research Council report was not ambiguous in its conclusions regarding the effectiveness and importance of hot spots policing. The committee concluded:

> There has been increasing interest over the past two decades in police practices that target very specific types of criminals, and crime places. In particular, policing crime hot spots has become a common police strategy for addressing public safety problems. While there is only weak evidence suggesting the effectiveness of targeting specific types of offenders, a strong body of evidence suggests that taking a focused geographic approach to crime problems can increase policing effectiveness in reducing crime and disorder. (Skogan and Frydl, 2004: 246–47)

Campbell Collaboration Systematic Review and Meta-Analysis of Hot Spots Policing Programs

There is consensus among those who advocate for evidence-based crime policy that systematic reviews are an important tool in this process. In systematic reviews, researchers attempt to gather relevant evaluative studies in a specific area (e.g., the impact of correctional boot camps on offending), critically appraise them, and come to judgments about what works "using explicit, transparent, state-of-the-art methods" (Petrosino et al., 2001: 21). Rigorous methods are used to summarize, analyze, and combine study findings. Formed in 2000, the Campbell Collaboration Crime and Justice Group aims to prepare and maintain systematic reviews of criminological interventions and to make them electronically accessible to scholars, practitioners, policymakers and the general public (Farrington and Petrosino, 2001; see also www.campbellcollaboration. org). The Crime and Justice Group requires reviewers of criminological interventions to select studies with high internal validity (Farrington and Petrosino, 2001).

Meta-analysis is a method of systematic reviewing and was designed to synthesize empirical relationships across studies, such as the effects of a specific crime prevention intervention on criminal offending behavior (Wilson, 2001). Meta-analysis uses specialized statistical methods to analyze the relationships between findings and study features (Lipsey and Wilson, 1993; Wilson, 2001). The "effect size statistic" is the index used to represent the findings of each study in the overall meta-analysis of study findings and represents the strength and direction (positive or negative) of the relationship observed in a particular study (e.g., the size of the treatment effect found; Lipsey and Wilson, 1993). The "mean effect size" represents the average effect of treatment on the outcome of interest across all eligible studies in a particular area, and is estimated by calculating a mean that is weighted by the precision of the effect size for each individual study.

Although the methods are technical, meta-analysis provides a defensible strategy for summarizing the effects of crime prevention and intervention efforts for informing public policy (Wilson, 2001). For instance, Farrington and Welsh (2005) carried out a series of meta-analyses of criminological experiments in the last twenty years and concluded that prevention methods in general, and multisystemic therapy in particular, were effective in reducing offending. They also reported that correctional therapy, batterer treatment programs, hot spots policing programs, drug courts, and juvenile restitution were effective crime prevention approaches. However, "Scared Straight" programs and boot camps for offenders were not reported to be effective at preventing crime.

As part of the Campbell Collaboration Crime and Justice Group's efforts to build a scientific knowledge base on effective crime prevention practices, a systematic review has been conducted on an ongoing basis on the crime prevention effects of hot spots policing programs (Braga, 2001, 2005). This section presents the methodology and findings of the Campbell review.

Systematic-Review Selection Criteria

In keeping with the conventions established by the systematic-reviews-methods literature, the stages of the Campbell hot spots policing review and the criteria used to select eligible studies are described below. In many hot spots policing experiments (e.g., Braga et al., 1999; Weisburd and Green, 1995) and quasi-experiments (e.g., Sherman and Rogan, 1995a), the control group experiences routine police interventions (e.g., regular levels of random patrol, ad-hoc investigations, etc.). In eligible studies, crime places that received the hot spots policing intervention were compared to places that experienced routine levels of traditional police service. The comparison-group study had to be either experimental or quasi-experimental (nonrandomized control group).

The units of analysis were crime hot spots or high-activity crime "places." As Eck (1997, 7–s1) suggests, "a place is a very small area reserved for a narrow range of functions, often controlled by a single owner, and separated from the surrounding area … examples of places include stores, homes, apartment buildings, street corners, subway stations, and airports." All studies using units of analysis smaller than a neighborhood or community were considered. This constraint was placed on the review process to ensure that identified studies were evaluating police strategies focused on the small number of locations that generate a disproportionate amount of crime in urban areas. As described in chapters 2 and 3, hot spots policing was a natural outgrowth of theoretical perspectives that suggested specific places where crime concentrates were an important focus for strategic crime prevention efforts. Police interventions implemented at the community or neighborhood level would not be specifically focused on small places, often encompassing only one or a few city blocks, that would be considered hot spots of crime.

The methodological approaches used to identify hot spots in the eligible studies were also reviewed. Diverse types of hot spots may respond to treatment in different ways. As such, the review needed to be sensitive to varying hot spots identification methods that could influence whether or not the treatment generated crime prevention gains.

To be eligible for the Campbell hot spots policing review, interventions used to control crime hot spots were limited to police enforcement efforts. Suitable police enforcement efforts included traditional tactics such as directed patrol and heightened levels of traffic enforcement as well as alternative strategies such as aggressive disorder-enforcement and problem-oriented policing with limited situational responses and limited engagement of the public. Eligible problem-oriented policing initiatives must engage primarily traditional policing tactics such as law enforcement actions, informal counseling and cautioning, and referrals to other agencies (known as "enforcement" problem-oriented policing; see Eck, 1993a). Problem-oriented policing programs that involved multiple interventions implemented by other stakeholders such as community members, business owners, or resident managers (e.g., Green Mazerolle and Roehl, 1998), were not considered by the Campbell review (see Weisburd et al., 2010 for a Campbell review focused on problem-oriented policing).

Studies of police crackdown programs were also considered (see, e.g., Sherman, 1990). However, to be included in the review, crackdown programs had to be focused on very specific places and not limited to a one-time-only swamping of police resources. Some ongoing attention to crime hot spots must be a characteristic of the program whether it was a series of subsequent crackdowns or simple maintenance of the targeted area through other means (e.g., additional follow-up directed patrol). This inclusion criterion ensured that only crackdown programs that were similar to more formal hot spots policing programs were considered.

Eligible studies also had to measure the effects of police intervention on officially recorded levels of crime at places. Appropriate measures of crime included crime incident reports, citizen emergency calls for service, or arrest data. Other outcomes measures such as survey, interview, systematic observations of social disorder (such as loitering, public drinking, and the solicitation of prostitution), systematic observations of physical disorder (such as trash, broken windows, graffiti, abandoned homes, and vacant lots), and victimization measures used by eligible studies to measure program effectiveness were also coded and analyzed. Particular attention was paid to studies that measured crime displacement effects and diffusion of crime-control benefit effects. The quality of the methodologies used to measure displacement and diffusion effects, as well as the types of displacement (spatial, temporal, target, modus operandi) examined, was assessed.

Search Strategy Results

To identify studies meeting the selection criteria, the Campbell review used four search strategies: searches of eleven online social science databases for study abstracts, searches of narrative and empirical reviews of literature that examine the effectiveness of police interventions on crime hot spots, searches of bibliographies of police crime prevention efforts and place-oriented crime prevention programs, and contacts with leading researchers. These search strategies complemented each other in the identification of eligible hot spots policing studies. For example, if an eligible study existed that did not appear in one of the online databases, contacts with leading researchers and searches of existing bibliographies were likely to discover the study in question. All published and unpublished studies were considered for the Campbell review. Each online database was searched as far back as possible. However, since hot spots policing is a very recent development in crime prevention, the search strategies described above were considered by the Campbell review to be sufficient to identify all relevant studies.

Search strategies in the systematic review process generate a large number of citations and abstracts for potentially relevant studies that must be closely screened to determine whether the studies meet the eligibility criteria (Farrington and Petrosino, 2001). The screening process yields a much smaller pool of eligible studies for inclusion in the review. In May 2003, the four search strategies produced 697 distinct abstracts.[3] The contents of the 697 abstracts were reviewed for any suggestion of an experimental or quasi-experimental evaluation of hot spots policing interventions. Fifty-seven distinct abstracts were selected for closer review and the full-text reports, journal articles, and books for these abstracts were acquired and carefully assessed to determine whether the interventions involved focused police-enforcement efforts at crime hot spots and whether the studies used randomized controlled trial designs or nonrandomized quasi-experimental designs. Nine eligible studies were identified and included in the Campbell review:

1. Minneapolis Repeat Call Address Policing (RECAP) Program (Sherman, Buerger, and Gartin, 1989)*
2. Minneapolis Hot Spots Patrol Program (Sherman and Weisburd, 1995)*
3. Jersey City Drug Markets Analysis Program (DMAP; Weisburd and Green, 1995)*
4. Jersey City Problem-Oriented Policing at Violent Places Project (Braga et al., 1999)*
5. St. Louis Problem-Oriented Policing in Three Drug Market Locations Study (Hope, 1994)
6. Kansas City Gun Project (Sherman and Rogan, 1995a)
7. Kansas City Crack House Police Raids Program (Sherman and Rogan, 1995b)*
8. Houston Targeted Beat Program (Caeti, 1999)
9. Beenleigh, Australia, Calls for Service Project (Criminal Justice Commission, 1998)

Characteristics of Selected Studies

The nine evaluations were conducted in five large cities in the United States and one suburb in Australia. Five of the selected studies used randomized experimental designs (indicated with an asterisk in the list above) and four used non-equivalent control group quasi-experimental designs. The treatments used to prevent crime at hot spots fell into three broad categories: enforcement problem-oriented policing interventions, directed and aggressive patrol programs, and police crackdowns and raids (see table 4.2). The effects of problem-oriented policing initiatives comprised of mostly traditional tactics with limited situational responses were evaluated in the Minneapolis RECAP Program, the Jersey City Drug Market Analysis Project, the Jersey City Problem-Oriented Policing at Violent Places Study, the St. Louis Problem-Oriented Policing at Drug Market Locations Study, and the Beenleigh, Australia, Calls for Service Project. The evaluation of the Houston Targeted Beat Program examined the effects of three types of treatments applied in different target

Table 4.2. Hot Spots Policing Experiments and Quasi-Experiments

Study	Treatment	Hot Spot Definition	Research Design*
Minneapolis (MN) RECAP Sherman, Buerger, and Gartin (1989) Buerger (1993)	Problem-oriented policing interventions comprised of mostly traditional enforcement tactics with some situational responses 1 year intervention period Integrity of treatment threatened by large caseloads that outstripped the resources the RECAP unit could bring to bear	Addresses ranked by frequency of citizen calls for service divided into commercial and residential lists; the top 250 commercial and top 250 residential addresses were included in experiment	Randomized experiment; control and treatment groups were each randomly allocated 125 commercial and 125 residential addresses Differences in the number of calls to each address from a baseline year to the experimental year were compared between RECAP and control groups
Minneapolis (MN) Hot Spots Sherman and Weisburd (1995)	Uniformed police patrol; experimental group, on average, experienced twice as much patrol presence 1 year intervention period Breakdown in the treatment noted during the summer months	110 hot spots comprised of address clusters that experienced high volumes of citizen calls for service, had stable numbers of calls for over two years, and were visually proximate	Randomized experiment; control and treatment groups were each randomly allocated 55 hot spots within statistical blocks Differences of differences between citizen calls in baseline and experimental years, comparing control and experimental groups

(continued)

Table 4.2. Continued

Study	Treatment	Hot Spot Definition	Research Design*
Jersey City (NJ) DMAP Weisburd and Green (1995)	Well-planned crackdowns followed by preventive patrol to maintain crime control gains 15 month intervention period Slow progress at treatment places caused intervention time period to be extended by 3 months	56 drug hot spot areas identified based on ranking intersection areas with high levels of drug-related calls and narcotics arrests, types of drugs sold, police perceptions of drug areas, and offender movement patterns	Randomized experiment; control and treatment groups were each randomly allocated 28 drug hot spots within statistical blocks Differences of differences between citizen calls during 7 month pre-test and post-test periods, comparing control and experimental groups
Jersey City (NJ) POP at Violent Places Braga et al. (1999)	Problem-oriented policing interventions comprised of mostly aggressive disorder enforcement tactics w/some situational responses 16 month intervention period Initial slow progress at places caused by resistance of officers to implement intervention	24 violent crime places identified based on ranking intersection areas with high levels of assault and robbery calls and incidents, and police and researcher perceptions of violent areas	Randomized experiment; 24 places were matched into like pairs based on simple quantitative and qualitative analyses; control and treatment groups were each randomly allocated 12 places within matched pairs Differences of differences between a number of indicators during 6 month pre-test and post-test periods, comparing control and experimental groups

St. Louis (MO) POP in 3 Drug Areas Hope (1994)	Problem-oriented policing interventions comprised of mostly traditional enforcement tactics with some situational responses 9 month intervention period No threats to the integrity of the treatment reported	Subjective selection of POP efforts made at 3 hot spot locations comprised of specific addresses associated with street-level drug sales	Quasi-experiment with non-equivalent control group; changes in citizen calls at hot spot addresses location were compared to changes in calls at other addresses on the block as well as other blocks in surrounding areas Simple trend analyses including 12 month pre- and 6 month post-intervention periods
Kansas City (MO) Crack House Raids Sherman and Rogan (1995b)	Court-authorized raids on crack houses conducted by uniformed police officers Intervention period was the day of the raid All but 7 cases received randomly assigned treatment as assigned No threats to the integrity of the treatment reported	207 blocks with at least 5 calls for service in the 30 days preceding an undercover drug buy; sample was restricted to raids on the inside of residences where a drug buy was made that was eligible for a search warrant	Randomized experiment; raids were randomly allocated to 104 blocks and were conducted at 98 of those sites; the other 103 blocks did not receive raids Differences of differences analytic design; pre-post time periods were 30 days before and after raid for experimental blocks, and 30 days before and after controlled buy at treatment block for control blocks

(continued)

Table 4.2. Continued

Study	Treatment	Hot Spot Definition	Research Design*
Kansas City (MO) Gun Project Sherman and Rogan (1995a)	Intensive enforcement of laws against illegally carrying concealed firearms via safety frisks during traffic stops, plain view, and searches incident to arrest on other charges 29 week intervention period No threats to the integrity of the treatment reported; Two phases of patrols reported due to shifts in grant funding	8 by 10 block target beat selected by federal officials for Weed and Seed grant Enforcement actions targeted at hot spots in beat identified by computer analyses	Quasi-experiment with non-equivalent control group; target beat matched to a control beat with nearly identical levels of drive-by shootings Difference of means comparing weekly gun crimes between intervention period and 29 week pre-test period Time series analyses of weekly gun crimes for 52 week before-after period (ARIMA—effect of abrupt intervention in time series) Analysis of variance models with one extra pre year and post year to examine changes in homicides and drive-by shootings for both patrol phases

Houston (TX) Targeted Beat Program Caeti (1999)	Patrol initiative designed to reduce Index crimes in 7 beats. 3 beats used "high visibility patrol" at hot spots 3 beats used "zero tolerance" policing at hot spots 1 beat used a problem-oriented policing approach comprised of mostly traditional tactics to control hot spots 2 year intervention period 3 "high visibility" patrol beats managed by one substation experienced police resistance to the program	7 highest crime beats were selected for this program Enforcement actions targeted at hot spots in beats identified by computer analyses	Quasi-experiment with non-equivalent control groups; target beats were matched to non-contiguous comparison beats through cluster analysis and correlations of Census data Difference of means in reported crime were used to evaluate program effects for 3 year pre-intervention and 2 year intervention period

(continued)

Table 4.2. Continued

Study	Treatment	Hot Spot Definition	Research Design*
Beenleigh (AUS) Calls for Service Project	Problem-oriented policing interventions comprised of mostly traditional enforcement tactics with some situational responses	Two groups of 10 addresses that experienced the highest volume of calls during separate 6 month periods	Quasi-experiment with non-equivalent control group. Beenleigh, a lower income suburb with a population of 40,000, was matched to similar Brown Plains suburb
Criminal Justice Commission (1998)	6 month intervention period		Simple time series analyses of total monthly calls for service in 5 month pre-test, 6 month intervention, and 3 month post-test periods
	No threats to the integrity of the treatment reported		19 pre/post no control case studies

Adapted from Braga (2001): 110–13.

areas; these interventions included high-visibility patrol, "zero toler-ance" disorder policing,[4] and enforcement problem-oriented policing. The Kansas City Gun Project examined the gun violence prevention effects of proactive patrol and intensive enforcement of firearms laws via safety frisks during traffic stops, plain-view searches and seizures, and searches incident to arrests on other charges. The Minneapolis Hot Spots Patrol program evaluated the effects of increased levels of preventive patrol on crime. The Kansas City Crack House Raids Programs evalu-ated the effects of court-authorized raids on crack houses.

Effects of Hot Spots Policing Programs on Crime and Disorder

The Campbell review reported noteworthy crime and disorder reductions in seven of the nine selected studies (Braga, 2001; see table 4.3). The stron-gest crime-control gains were reported in the Jersey City Problem-Oriented Policing at Violent Places experiment and the Kansas City Gun Project quasi-experiment. The Beenleigh, Australia, Calls for Service quasi-exper-iment found no noteworthy differences in the total number of calls in the town of Beenleigh relative to the matched town of Brown Plains (Criminal Justice Commission, 1998). However, simple nonexperimental pre/post comparisons found noteworthy reductions in total citizen calls for service in sixteen of nineteen case studies included in the report. The research team concluded that the problem-oriented policing strategy enjoyed some success in reducing calls for service at the targeted locations, but due to the small scale of the project and limitations of the research design, these crime prevention gains were not large enough to be detected at the aggregate town level (Criminal Justice Commission, 1998).

As described earlier, the Minneapolis RECAP experiment showed no statistically significant differences in the prevalence of citizen calls for service at addresses that received the problem-oriented policing treatment as compared to control addresses (Sherman, Buerger, and Gartin, 1989). Despite the methodological and statistical concerns iden-tified by the research team, a case study analysis of the RECAP experiment revealed that several addresses experienced dramatic reductions in total

Table 4.3. Results of Hot Spots Policing Experiments and Quasi-Experiments

Study	Crime Outcomes	Other Outcomes	Displacement/Diffusion
Minneapolis (MN) RECAP Sherman, Buerger, and Gartin (1989)	No statistically significant differences in the prevalence of citizen calls for service	None	Not measured
Minneapolis (MN) Hot Spots Sherman and Weisburd (1995)	Modest, but statistically significant reductions in total crime calls for service ranging from 6% to 13%	Systematic observations of crime and disorder were half as prevalent in experimental as in control hot spots	Not measured
Jersey City (NJ) DMAP Weisburd and Green (1995)	Statistically significant reductions in disorder calls for service in treatment drug markets relative to control drug markets No change in violent and property crime calls	None	Examined displacement and diffusion effects in two-block catchment areas surrounding the treatment and control drug places and replicated the drug market identification process Little evidence of displacement; analyses suggest modest diffusion of benefits

Jersey City (NJ) POP at Violent Places Braga et al. (1999) Braga (1997)	Statistically significant reductions in total calls for service and total crime incidents All crime categories experienced varying reductions; statistically significant reductions in street fight calls, property calls, narcotics calls, robbery incidents, and property crime incidents	Observation data revealed that social disorder was alleviated at 10 of 11 treatment places relative to control places Non-experimental observation data revealed that physical disorder was alleviated at 10 of 11 treatment places Non-experimental interviews with key community members in target locations suggest no noteworthy improvements in citizen perceptions of places	Examined displacement and diffusion effects in two-block catchment areas surrounding the treatment and control drug places Little evidence of immediate spatial displacement or diffusion

(*continued*)

Table 4.3. Continued

Study	Crime Outcomes	Other Outcomes	Displacement/Diffusion
St. Louis (MO) POP in 3 Drug Areas Hope (1994)	All 3 drug locations experienced varying reductions in total calls Regression analysis suggests that reductions on blocks where drug locations were located were greater than other blocks and intersections in surrounding areas	None	Compared trends in calls at targeted addresses to trends in calls at other addresses on same block Location 1- significant displacement into surrounding addresses; Location 2- no displacement or diffusion; Location 3- no displacement or diffusion
Kansas City (MO) Crack House Raids Sherman and Rogan (1995b)	Modest decreases in citizen calls and offense reports that decayed in two weeks	None	Not measured

Kansas City (MO) Gun Project Sherman and Rogan (1995a)	65% increase in guns seized by the police; 49% decrease in gun crimes in treatment area 15% reduction in guns seized by the police; 4% increase in gun crimes in control area	Separate pre/post quasi-experiment surveying citizens opinions of KC gun project suggests citizens were aware of the project, generally supported the intensive approach, and perceived an improvement in the quality of life in treatment neighborhood compared to residents in comparison beat	Displacement tests using pre/post difference in means and ARIMA time series analyses were conducted in 7 contiguous beats No significant displacement into specific beats; 2 beats showed significant reductions in gun crimes

(*continued*)

Table 4.3. Continued

Study	Crime Outcomes	Other Outcomes	Displacement/Diffusion
Houston (TX) Targeted Beat Program Caeti (1999)	Aggregated experimental beats experienced significant reductions in auto theft, total Part I Index crimes, and total Part I suppressible (robbery, burglary, auto theft) index crimes relative to aggregate control beats 3 "zero tolerance" beats experienced mixed results; certain reported crimes decreased in particular beats 3 "high visibility" beats experienced reductions in a wide variety of Index crimes Problem solving beat experienced no significant decrease relative to control beat	None	Simple pre/post analyses of reported crimes in beats contiguous to treatment beats No evidence of significant displacement; contiguous beats surrounding 3 target areas (problem-solving beat, 2 zero-tolerance beats) experienced possible diffusion of benefits in particular reported crimes

Beenleigh (AUS) Calls for Service Project	No noteworthy differences in total number of calls between Beenleigh and Brown Plains areas	None	Not measured
Criminal Justice Commission (1998)	Noteworthy reductions in calls reported by non-experimental pre/post impact assessments in 16 of the 19 case studies		

Adapted from Braga (2001): 115–18.

calls for service as a direct result of the implemented problem-solving interventions (Buerger, 1992).

Displacement and Diffusion Effects

Five studies in the Campbell review examined whether focused police efforts were associated with crime displacement or diffusion of crime-control benefits (Braga, 2001; see table 4.3). Prior to a discussion of the research findings, it must be noted that it is very difficult to detect displacement effects, because the potential manifestations of displacement are quite diverse (Barr and Pease, 1990). Diffusion effects are likely to be as difficult to assess. All five studies were limited to examining immediate spatial-displacement and diffusion effects; that is, whether focused police efforts in targeted areas resulted in crime "moving around the corner" or whether these proximate areas experienced unintended crime control benefits.

The Campbell review found that none of the five studies reported substantial immediate spatial-displacement of crime into areas surrounding the targeted locations (Braga, 2001). Four studies suggested possible diffusion of crime control benefits effects associated with the focused police interventions. The two Jersey City experiments used the most sophisticated methodologies to measure immediate spatial-displacement and diffusion effects. The Jersey City Problem-Oriented Policing at Violent Places experiment found little evidence of displacement in the catchment areas and reported significant decreases in total calls for service and disorder calls for service in the catchment areas.[5] As reported earlier, the Jersey City DMAP experiment found significant decreases in public morals calls for service and narcotics calls for service in treatment catchment areas relative to controls; the Kansas City Gun Project reported evidence of diffusion rather than displacement of crime while the St. Louis study reported limited displacement. The Houston Targeted Beat quasi-experiment examined displacement and diffusion effects by conducting simple pre/post comparisons of reported Part I index crimes in beats contiguous to the treatment beats. The analyses revealed no overall evidence of displacement and contiguous beats surrounding three targeted beats experienced possible diffusion of crime control benefits effects as several types of reported Index crimes decreased notably.

Meta-Analysis of the Effects of Hot Spots Policing on Crime and Disorder

Due to inconsistent reporting of program effects in the quasi-experimental studies, only randomized trials were included in the Campbell review meta-analysis (Braga, 2005).[6] Since all hot spots policing experiments used citizen calls for service as an outcome measure, the main effect size for each study was calculated based on the statistics reported for key calls for service findings.[7] In the Jersey City Problem-Oriented Policing at Violent Places, Kansas City Crack House Raids, and Minneapolis Hot Spots Patrol experiments, the effects of the treatment on total calls for service were used to calculate the effect-size measures. In the Jersey City Drug Market Analysis Program experiment, the authors examined the effects of the treatment on varying call subcategories and reported the effects of the treatment on disorder calls for service as the key finding of the study. As such, the Campbell review included effect size for disorder calls as the main outcome measure. The Minneapolis RECAP experiment reported the effect of the treatment on total calls for service separately for the residential addresses and the commercial addresses. Since the residential and commercial addresses represented distinct locations, two independent effect sizes for total calls for service were calculated for the RECAP experiment in the Campbell review.

Table 4.4 presents the standardized mean difference effect sizes and inverse variance weights for the hot spots experiments from the Campbell review (Braga, 2005).[8] For those readers not familiar with meta-analytic techniques and terminology, these concepts are quickly defined here. The standardized mean difference effect size statistic applies to research findings that contrast two groups on their respective mean scores on some dependent variable that is not operationalized the same across

Table 4.4. Meta-Analysis of Hot Spots Experiment Effect Sizes for Main Outcomes

Experiment	Effect Size	Standard Error	Inv. Var. Weight (% Total Weight)	95% C.I.
Jersey City POP	2.05*	.504	3.93 (1.8%)	Upper 3.04 Lower 1.06
Jersey City DMAP	.689*	.275	13.21 (6.0%)	Upper 1.23 Lower .15
Minneapolis Patrol	.322*	.142	27.15 (12.3%)	Upper .60 Lower .044
Kansas City Crack	.219	.139	51.32 (23.3%)	Upper .492 Lower −.054
Minneapolis RECAP Commercial	.089	.127	62.49 (28.3%)	Upper .337 Lower −.159
Minneapolis RECAP Residential	−.009	.127	62.49 (28.3%)	Upper .238 Lower −.256
Meta-Analysis All Studies	.345*	.150	Total Weight = 220.59	Upper .640 Lower .058
Meta-Analysis w/o RECAP	.632*	.253	Total Weight w/o RECAP = 95.61	Upper 1.13 Lower .138

$p < .05$
Adapted from Braga (2005): 333.

study samples (Lipsey and Wilson, 1993). In lay terms, this metric provides a standard score for the differences in calls for service between treatment and control groups of places that can be used to compare crime control effects across studies using call data collected from different police departments that may use varying collection and reporting procedures. The inverse variance weight is a metric that weighs each effect size in a meta-analysis by its precision (Lipsey and Wilson, 1993). Studies with more precise effect sizes, determined in part by the number of places in a particular study, will be more influential in the meta-analytic calculation of the overall mean effect size for the impact of hot spots policing programs on citizen calls for service.

The effect size of the hot spots policing intervention on the treatment places relative to control places was very large (2.05) and statistically significant in the Jersey City Problem-Oriented Policing at Violent Places experiment. While the Jersey City Problem-Oriented Policing experiment reported a very large effect size, the influence of the study on the overall meta-analysis was moderated by its small sample size and correspondingly small inverse variance weight (only 1.8% of the total weight). The Jersey City DMAP experiment intervention also had a large statistically significant effect size (.689) and the Minneapolis Hot Spots Patrol experiment intervention had a moderate statistically significant effect size (.322). The Kansas City Crack House Raid experiment and the Minneapolis RECAP experiment's commercial-addresses interventions had smaller nonstatistically significant effect sizes that favored the treatment places relative to the controls (.219 and .089, respectively). The Minneapolis RECAP experiment's residential-addresses intervention had a very small, nonstatistically significant effect size that slightly favored the control places relative to the treatment places.

Overall, the Campbell review found that hot spots policing interventions reduced citizen calls for service in the treatment places relative to the control places (Braga, 2005).[9] The mean effect size for the hot spots policing intervention for the six studies was medium (.345) and statistically significant.[10] When the RECAP study was not included in the meta-analysis due to methodological concerns, the mean effect size was large (.632) and statistically significant.[11]

The Campbell review examined the sensitivity of these findings to the selection of one effect size per study by conducting a meta-analysis of all reported crime and disorder calls for service outcome measures across the studies (Braga, 2005). Table 4.5 presents the standardized mean

Table 4.5. Meta-Analysis of Hot Spots Experiment Effect Sizes for All Reported Crime and Disorder Calls for Service Outcomes

Experiment and Measures	Effect Size	Standard Error	Inv. Var. Weight	95% C.I.
Jersey City POP				
Robbery calls	.077	.41	5.99	−.723 to .878
Street fight calls	.946*	.43	5.39	.102 to 1.79
Property calls	1.145*	.44	5.16	.282 to 2.01
Disorder/Nuisance calls	.1979	.41	5.97	−.60 to 1.00
Narcotics calls	1.302*	.45	4.95	.421 to 2.18
Total calls	2.05*	.504	3.93	1.06 to 3.04
Jersey City DMAP				
Disorder calls	.689*	.275	13.21	.15 to 1.23
Violence calls	−.19	.268	13.93	−.71 to .335
Property calls	−.059	.267	13.99	−.583 to .465
Kansas City Crack				
Disorder calls	.164	.139	51.43	−.109 to .437
Violence calls	.061	.139	51.57	−.211 to .334
Property calls	.171	.139	51.54	−.102 to .444
Total calls	.219	.139	51.32	−.054 to .492
Minneapolis Patrol				
"Hard" crime calls	.159	.191	27.41	−.215 to .5337
"Soft" crime calls	.382*	.192	27.0	.005 to .759
Total calls	.322*	.142	27.15	.044 to .60
Minn. RECAP Commercial				
Disorder calls	.086	.127	62.44	−.162 to .334
Property calls	.162	.127	62.30	−.086 to .410
Personal crime calls	−.132	.127	62.36	−.38 to .116
Total calls	.089	.127	62.49	−.159 to .337

Minn. RECAP

Residential

Disorder calls	.024	.126	62.49	−.224 to .272
Property calls	−.076	.127	62.45	−.323 to .172
Personal crime calls	.174	.127	62.26	−.075 to .423
Total calls	−.009	.127	62.49	−.256 to .238
Meta-Analysis – All Outcomes	**.129**	**.067**	**Total weight = 222.42**	**−.002 to .261**
Disorder calls	.161*	.067	Total weight = 222.54	.021 to .292
Property calls	.098	.071	Total weight = 195.44	−.041 to .239
Property calls w/hard crime	.106	.067	Total weight = 222.85	−.025 to .237
Violence calls	.043	.070	Total weight = 195.81	−.095 to .181
Violence calls w/hard crime	.057	.066	Total weight = 223.22	−.072 to .186
Meta-Analysis – All Outcomes w/o RECAP	**.231***	**.101**	**Total weight = 97.49**	**.033 to .429**
Disorder calls	.297*	.101	Total weight = 97.61	.099 to .496
Property calls	.197	.119	Total weight = 70.69	−.037 to .429
Property calls w/hard crime	.186	.101	Total weight = 98.1	−.012 to .384
Violence calls	.048	.119	Total weight = 71.19	−.184 to .280
Violence calls w/hard crime	.079	.101	Total weight = 98.6	−.119 to .276

* $p < .05$

Note: The p-level for the "all outcomes" meta-analysis with RECAP included was $p = .0537$.

Adapted from Braga (2005): 334–35.

difference effect sizes and inverse variance weights for twenty-four reported outcomemeasures from the eligible randomized controlled experiments. Nineteen of the twenty-four reported outcome measures in the hot spots experiments favored a treatment effect. The mean effect size for all reported calls for service outcome measures favored a treatment effect.[12] However, when RECAP was included in the Campbell meta-analysis, the mean effect size for all reported outcomes was smaller (.129) and not quite statistically significant at the conventional .05 level. When RECAP was not included, the meta-analysis yielded a mean effect size for all reported outcomes that favored treatment (.231) and was statistically significant.[13]

The Campbell review also aggregated the reported outcomes into three categories of calls for service: disorder calls, property calls, and violence calls (Braga, 2005). Since the reported effects were not independent, a mean violence effect size was calculated for robbery and street fight call categories in the Jersey City Problem-Oriented Policing experiment for inclusion in the overall violence calls meta-analysis. The Minneapolis Hot Spots Patrol experiment reported the effects of the intervention on "hard" crime and "soft" crime calls for service (Sherman and Weisburd, 1995). The hard-crime category included both property and violent crimes while the soft-crime category included mostly disorder offenses. As such, the mean effect sizes for the aggregate property calls and violence calls categories were calculated with and without the hard-crime call outcomes from the Minneapolis Hot Spots Patrol experiment. All estimated mean effect sizes favored a treatment effect for the hot spots policing programs across the specific call categories.[14] With and without hard-crime calls considered in the calculation of mean effect sizes, the treatment effects of hot spots policing on property and violence call categories were small and not statistically significant. However, hot spots policing interventions had a statistically significant treatment effect on disorder calls for service. When RECAP was included in the meta-analysis, the mean effect size was small (.161). When RECAP was not included, the mean effect size was moderate (.297).

More Recent Scientific Evidence on the Crime Prevention Value of Hot Spots Policing

Since the publication of the most recent iteration of the Campbell review, two additional randomized controlled experiments evaluating the crime prevention benefits of hot spots policing have been completed. In Lowell, Massachusetts, a randomized controlled experiment evaluated the effects of policing disorder, within a problem-oriented policing framework, at crime and disorder hot spots (Braga and Bond, 2008). Thirty-four hot spots were matched into seventeen pairs and one member of each pair was allocated to treatment conditions in a randomized block field experiment. The impact evaluation revealed a statistically significant 20 percent reduction in crime and disorder calls for service at the treatment places relative to the control places with no evidence of significant immediate spatial crime displacement. Analyses of systematic-observation data also revealed significant reductions in social and physical disorder at the treatment places relative to the control places.

Drawing upon the literature from developmental criminology (Hawkins, Arthur, and Catalano, 1995; Loeber and Farrington, 1998) and hot spots policing, the Redlands, California, police department developed the Risk-Focused Policing at Places (RFPP) approach to preventing and reducing juvenile delinquency (Weisburd, Morris, and Ready, 2008). The RFPP program was a community-oriented policing and problem-solving strategy that targets risk factors relatedto delinquency and problem behaviors of youths living in census-block group areas. A matched block randomized experimental design was used to evaluate the effects of the program on youths living in twenty-six census-block groups in Redlands. The evaluation found that RFPP did not significantly reduce self-reported delinquency, or perceptions of risk-protective factors and police legitimacy. Weisburd, Morris, and Ready (2008) suggest that the primary explanation for the absence of a program effect centered on the unit of analysis used for the program. They argue that the census-block group was too large a geographic unit of analysis to achieve the kind of targeted and focused interventions that generate crime prevention benefits.

Rethinking the Purported Inevitability of Crime Displacement

Crime displacement is the notion that efforts to eliminate specific crimes at a place will simply cause criminal activity to move elsewhere, be committed in another way, or even be manifested as another type of crime, thus negating any crime control gains (Repetto, 1976). This perspective on the crime prevention effectiveness of police efforts to control problem places developed from dispositional theories of criminal motivations, and the views of these skeptics were supported by early studies of opportunity-reducing measures (Gabor, 1990; Clarke, 1980). For instance, although exact-fare systems reduced the number of robberies on New York City buses, a corresponding increase in robberies occurred in the subways (Chaiken, Lawless, and Stevenson, 1974). And Mayhew, Clarke, and Hough (1980) found that reductions in the theft of newer cars after the implementation of a new law in England—which required all new domestic and imported cars to be fitted with steering column locks—were offset by displacement to older, unprotected autos. After a successful police crackdown on street crimes in one New York City precinct, Press (1971) found that street crimes increased in surrounding precincts. Finally,traditional police efforts to control street-level drug markets have been found to be quite susceptible to spatial, temporal, and tactical displacement. Offenders have been found to change the time and place they sell drugs and use different tactics to sell drugs, such as hiring lookouts to detect police surveillance, wearing disguises, and inventing complex transaction schemes (see Eck, 1993b; Sherman, 1990; Caulkins, 1992).

Recent studies, however, have indicated that the purported inevitability of displacement was very much overestimated. Indeed, the review of hot spots policing initiatives presented here revealed that, when displacement was measured it was quite limited and often-unintended crime prevention benefits were associated with the hot spots policing programs. Several reviews of situational crime prevention measures have concluded that crime displacement was absent or never complete (Gabor, 1990; Clarke, 1992; Hesseling, 1994). For example, Matthews (1990) reported that prostitutes were not displaced to other locations in London after the "red-light" district was cleaned up by police officers. After the progressive detoxification of domestic gas, Clarke and Mayhew (1988) found that the resulting decline in the number of suicides in England and Wales was not displaced to other suicide methods. Neither the Jersey City Problem-Oriented Policing in Violent Places experiment (Braga et al., 1999), Lowell Policing Crime and Disorder Hot Spots experiment (Braga and Bond, 2008), nor the Kansas City Gun project (Sherman and Rogan, 1995a) discussed in this chapter resulted in the significant displacement of crime to surrounding areas. Even when displacement is present, it is rarely complete. For example, in New York City's crackdown on street crimes, the estimate of displaced crime was less than the reduction of crime in the targeted precinct (Press, 1971).

Offenders are most likely to displace when other crime targets share the same "choice-structuring properties" as the original crime-opportunity structure (Cornish and Clarke, 1987), but as Clarke (1995) suggests, the easy and/or profitable criminal opportunities of the targeted offenses may not be available elsewhere. Moreover, the level of displacement may be dependent on the offender's familiarity with alternative tactics, places, times, and targets. As Bennett and Wright's (1984) interview research on residential burglars revealed, only 40 percent of their respondents would seek targets elsewhere if their original opportunities were blocked. Similarly, in a recent study of armed robberies, a lack of displacement from newly protected banks to alternative targets such as convenience stores and gas stations was attributed to smaller cash bounties that were not as attractive to organized robbery gangs (Clarke, Field, and McGrath, 1991). Likewise, the reductions in suicides from the detoxification of domestic gas in England and Wales were not followed by substantial increases in other suicide techniques (Clarke and Mayhew, 1988) because the alternative methods were not as readily available, painless, or lethal. Hesseling's (1994) review of ethnographic studies of serious offenders (imprisoned robbers, burglars, and drug addicts) and blocked criminal opportunities suggests that between one-half and two-thirds of these offenders are likely to displace. However, he also argues that these committed offenders are not representative of general criminal populations; it is very probable that less committed offenders are less likely to displace.

Beyond the absence of complete displacement, Barr and Pease (1990) argue that the severity of displacement could be "benign" if it were to lesser crimes, such as from burglary to shoplifting, or if victimization were more evenly distributed so that a few victims would not suffer disproportionate amounts of crime. In support of these assertions, Gabor and colleagues' (1987) study of imprisoned inmates found that criminals who desisted from armed robbery had shifted their focus to lesser forms of criminality such as fraud and drug selling.

Hesseling (1994) reviewed fifty-five studies on crime prevention measures that had examined evidence of displacement. Thirty-three studies reported some form of displacement. No study reported complete crime displacement; in fact, most studies observed that the displacement was very limited in scope. The forms of displacement that were most likely to occur were temporal, target, and spatial—the types that required the least amount of effort on the part of the offender. Hesseling (1994) suggests that the costs associated with these types of displacement are lower than the costs associated with changes in offense or tactics. Twenty-two of the studies did not report any evidence of displacement, and six of the studies reported unexpected beneficial effects of reducing crime in adjacent areas.

Several scholars have suggested that crime prevention efforts may result in the complete opposite of displacement—that anticipated crime control benefits may be greater than expected and "spill over" into places beyond the target areas. Generally referred to as "diffusion of benefits" (Clarke and Weisburd, 1994), these unexpected benefits have been reported by a number of studies on crime prevention measures. For example, Chaiken, Lawless, and Stevenson (1974) found that sharp increases in police patrol in the New York City subway between the hours of 8:00 PM and 4:00 AM decreased robbery rates during both the day and night hours. Poyner's (1988) evaluation of the use of closed-circuit television to combat vandalism and graffiti on a fleet of eighty double-deck buses in northern England reported that vandalism and graffiti declined for the entire fleet even though only two buses were protected by live cameras and three buses had dummy cameras installed. The Jersey City Drug Market Analysis Experiment revealed that drug-related calls for service declined in two-block buffer zones constructed around experimental hot spots as compared to catchment zones surrounding the control locations (Weisburd and Green, 1995a). Similarly, Green (1996) found improvements in the physical appearance and reductions in the number of police contacts in housing units surrounding "nuisance" addresses targeted by the Oakland Beat Health Program.

Clarke and Weisburd (1994) classified diffusion effects using a rational choice framework into two processes—deterrence and discouragement. In the deterrent-diffusion process, offenders may overestimate the reach of the crime control measure and believe that they face a greater risk of arrest than is the case. Sherman (1990) described this effect as the "free bonus" of deterrence beyond the period that a police crackdown is actually in force. Poyner's (1988) evaluation of the use of CCTV on buses to prevent graffiti and vandalism exemplifies the deterrent-diffusion process: "the children have learned…that the cameras will enable misbehaving individuals to be picked out and that action will be taken. However, what they do not know is how extensive the risk is. They appear to believe that most buses have cameras, or at least they are uncertain about which buses have cameras" (Poyner, 1988: 50).

Alternatively, discouragement may cause crime control benefits to diffuse to other places, targets, and times by discouragement. According to the rational choice perspective, offenders consider effort and reward, in addition to the risk of apprehension. Offenders may become discouraged from crime if the amount of effort is not commensurate with the reward. Thus, the replacement of coin-fed gas and electricity meters with ordinary billed meters in residences that suffered repeat victimization caused a reduction in burglary in the protected homes as well as other homes across the Kirkholt estate (Pease, 1991). The burglars were uncertain which homes in the estate still had the profitable coin-fed meters; the increased amount of effort necessary to locate a residence that still had the coin-fed version outweighed the rewards of finding the device. Similarly, Decker's (1972) evaluation of slug-rejecter devices on parking meters found a decline in slug use in control areas where the devices had not been installed on the meters. This effect was presumably explained by the inability of prospective offenders to distinguish easily between parking meters that had the device and those which did not.

A recent controlled study of displacement and diffusion effects generated by intensive police interventions in two hot spots areas in Jersey City found that the most likely outcome of focused crime prevention efforts was a diffusion of crime control benefits to the surrounding areas (Weisburd et al., 2006). As described in chapter 1, qualitative data collected by Weisburd and his colleagues (2006) suggested that spatial movement from the targeted crime sites involves substantial effort and risk by offenders.

These empirical studies also pointed to the difficulty of detecting displacement effects because the potential manifestations of displacement are quite diverse. Weisburd and his colleagues (2006) for example find little evidence of spatial displacement, but describe examples of method displacement such as the use of telephones and beepers to arrange meetings as opposed to ordinary market behavior on the street. As Barr and Pease (1990: 293) suggest,

> If, in truth, displacement is complete, some displaced crime will probably fall outside the areas and types of crime being studied or be so dispersed as to be masked by background variation. In such an event, the optimist would speculate about why the unmeasured areas or types of crime probably escaped displaced crime, while the pessimist would speculate why they probably did not. No research study,

however massive, is likely to resolve the issue. The wider the scope of the study in terms of types of crimes and places, the thinner the patina of displaced crime could be spread across them; thus disappearing into the realm of measurement error.

Different forms of displacement can also occur in combination; as Hesseling (1994: 198) observes, "a burglar may move to a different neighborhood, employ new tactics, *and* offend at a different time of day…it may be impossible to confirm empirically the existence or magnitude of displacement." Hesseling further argues that researchers must be aware of factors independent of the crime control intervention that could produce what appears to be a displacement effect, such as changes in offender populations, opportunity structures, and overall crime-rate trends. While diffusion effects are likely to be as difficult to assess, a failure to examine diffusion effects may mean that program evaluators are underestimating the crime control benefits of interventions (Clarke and Weisburd, 1994). Although measurement of displacement and diffusion effects is very complex, evaluations of place-oriented crime-control strategies must assess the possibility of displacement and diffusion before any conclusions can be made about the overall effectiveness of the intervention. The evidence so far suggests that hot spots policing is much more likely to result in diffusion of crime prevention benefits than displacement of crime.

Conclusion

The scientific evidence reviewed here strongly suggests that police can prevent crime and disorder at specific places without simply displacing problems to another location. While the available evidence supports the assertion that hot spots policing is an effective crime prevention strategy, there are important gaps in our knowledge about the approach. For example, we know little of which specific hot spots strategies work best in which specific types of situations. The Committee to Review Research on Police Policy and Practice suggests that the most generalized strategies, for example preventive patrol and drug raids, are likely to have less impact than engaging a diverse set of approaches that include more problem-solving elements, such as working with landlords to deal with disorderly conditions and problem tenants (Skogan and Frydl, 2004; Weisburd and Eck, 2004). The commitee's findings suggest that problem-oriented policing, with its attention to the development of local responses that are tailored to the conditions that give rise to ongoing crime and disorder problems, may be used to good effect in dealing with crime hot spots. Moreover, the Campbell Collaboration meta-analysis revealed that the largest crime prevention effect sizes were generated by more tailored responses, such as the interventions in the Jersey City DMAP and Problem-Oriented Policing in Violent Crime Places experiments, rather than more one-dimensional traditional enforcement strategies in the Minneapolis Hot Spots Patrol and Kansas City Crack House Raids experiments. As will be discussed further in chapter 5, the recent Lowell experimental evaluation further suggests that the strongest crime prevention gains at the crime and disorder hot spots were driven by situational problem-oriented policing strategies that attempted to modify the criminal opportunity structure in the treatment places (Braga and Bond, 2008).

We also know very little about community reactions to focused police action in crime hot spot areas. While research suggests that residents of crime and disorder hot spots welcome increased police attention (McGarrell et al., 2001; Shaw, 1995), there have been well-documented increases in community complaints against the police for engaging overly aggressive "zero tolerance" policing strategies (Greene, 1999). Is it possible for the police to deal with problem places in a manner that improves their relationships with the communities they seek to protect and serve? The potential impacts of different approaches to address crime hots spots on community relations and police legitimacy are discussed in chapter 6.

Clearly, our understanding of the effects of hot spots policing remains very general. If we are to maximize the crime prevention effects of hot spots approaches we need to examine carefully the interaction of different strategies with different hot spots settings. This effort would demand a large group of studies. But given the promise of hot spots policing, such an investment in research in this area seems appropriate. The next chapter considers the prospects of different forms of problem-oriented policing in controlling crime hot spots by reviewing the available research evidence on its application at specific crime places.

Dealing with Problem Places

Criminal opportunities attract offenders to crime hot spot locations. The underlying conditions, situations, and dynamics generate an opportunity structure at specific places that produces and sustains an elevated rate of criminal and disorderly behavior. There are numerous ways police can address the problems at crime hot spots. As the Minneapolis Hot Spots Patrol experiment suggests, simply increasing patrol presence in hot spot areas can generate modest crime prevention gains (Sherman and Weisburd, 1995). Unfortunately, such one-dimensional strategies do little to change the attributes of a place that cause it to be a hot spot for crime. The presence of a patrol car may deter criminals and disorderly persons in the short run, but the problems of the place still remain when the car moves out of the area. To reduce and better manage problems at crime hot spots, the police need to change the underlying conditions, situations, and dynamics that make them attractive to criminals and disorderly persons.

Problem-oriented policing holds great promise in addressing the criminogenic attributes of places that cause them to be crime hot spots. Problem-oriented policing works to identify *why* things are going wrong and to frame responses using a wide variety of often-untraditional approaches (Goldstein, 1979). Using a basic iterative approach of problem identification, analysis, response, assessment, and adjustment of the response, problem-oriented policing has been effective against a wide variety of crime, fear, and order concerns (Braga, 2008; Eck and Spelman, 1987; Goldstein, 1990). As chapter 3 suggests, the attributes of a place should be viewed as key in understanding and developing appropriate strategies to deal with clusters of criminal events at specific locations. This adaptable and dynamic analytic approach in the problem-oriented policing model provides an appropriate framework to uncover the complex mechanisms at play in crime hot spots and to develop tailor-made interventions to control recurring problems at these deviant locations.

Unfortunately, research suggests that it is difficult for the police to implement problem-oriented policing. Police officers often conduct only a superficial analysis of problems and then rush to implement responses. Shallow problem analysis results in a tendency for police officers to rely upon traditional or faddish responses rather than conducting a wider search for creative responses. In this chapter, we present the problem-oriented policing model and the deficiencies in its practical application, discuss the range of strategies used to prevent crime at places, and conclude that police departments should strive to implement problem-oriented policing properly but recognize that even weak problem solving can be beneficial at crime hot spots.

Problem-Oriented Policing

The reactive methods of the standard model of policing (see chapter 2) are often described as "incident-driven policing." Under this model, departments are aimed at resolving individual incidents instead of solving recurring crime problems (Eck and Spelman, 1987). Officers respond to repeated calls and never look for the underlying conditions that may be causing like groups of incidents. Officers become frustrated because they answer similar calls and seemingly make no real progress. Citizens become dissatisfied because the problems that generate their repeated calls still exist (Eck and Spelman, 1987). In 1979, Herman Goldstein proposed an alternative; he felt that police should go further than answering call after call, that they should search for solutions to recurring problems that generate the repeated calls. Goldstein (1979, 1990) described this strategy as the "problem-oriented approach" and envisioned it as a department-wide activity.

Goldstein's proposition was simple and straightforward. Behind every recurring problem there are underlying conditions that create it. Incident-driven policing never addresses these conditions; therefore incidents are likely to recur. Answering calls for service is an important task and still must be done, but police officers should respond systematically to recurring calls arising from the same problem. In order for the police to be more efficient and effective, they must gather information about incidents and design an appropriate response based on the nature of the underlying conditions that cause the problem(s).

The developing field of situational crime prevention has also supported the problem-oriented policing movement since its genesis in the British Government's Home Office Research Unit in the early 1980s (Clarke, 1992). Instead of preventing crime by altering broad social conditions such as poverty and inequality, situational crime prevention advocates changes in local environments to decrease opportunities for crimes to be committed. Situational crime prevention techniques comprise "opportunity-reducing measures that are, (1) directed at highly specific forms of crime (2) that involve the management, design, or manipulation of the immediate environment in as systematic and permanent way as possible (3) so as to increase the effort and risks of crime and reduce the rewards as perceived by a wide range of offenders" (Clarke, 1992: 4).

The situational analysis of crime problems follows an action-research model that systematically identifies and examines problems, develops solutions, and evaluates results (Clarke, 1992; Lewin, 1947). The applications of situational crime prevention have shown convincing crime prevention results to a variety problems ranging from obscene phone callers (Clarke, 1990) to burglary (Pease, 1991) to car-radio theft (Braga and Clarke, 1994). This simple but powerful perspective is applicable to crime problems facing the police, security personnel, business owners, local government officials, and private citizens. Indeed, Goldstein's (1990) formulation of problem-oriented policing shares many similarities to the action-research underpinnings of situational prevention (Clarke, 1992).

The problem-oriented policing approach was given an operational structure in Newport News, Virginia. Researchers from the Police Executive Research Forum (PERF) and a group of officers selected from the various ranks of the Newport News Police Department crystallized the philosophy into a set of steps known as the SARA model (Eck and Spelman, 1987). The SARA model consists of these stages: *Scanning*—the identification of an issue and determining whether it is a problem; *Analysis*—data collection on the problem to determine its scope, nature, and causes; *Response*—the use of the information from the analysis to design an appropriate response, which can involve other agencies outside the normal police arena; and *Assessment*—the response, whose results can be used to reexamine the problem and change responses or maintain positive conditions (Eck and Spelman, 1987).

In practice, it is important to recognize that the development and implementation of problem-oriented responses do not always follow the linear, distinct steps of the SARA model (Braga and Weisburd, 2006; Capowich and Roehl, 1994). Rather, depending on the complexity of the problems to be addressed, the process can be characterized as a series of disjointed and often simultaneous activities. A wide variety of issues can cause deviations from the SARA model, including identified problems needing to be reanalyzed because initial responses were ineffective, and implemented responses that sometimes reveal new problems (Braga and Weisburd, 2006). It is also important to remember that the SARA model is only one way of operationalizing problem-oriented policing; as Read and Tilley (2000) remind us, it is not the only way and perhaps may not be the best way for police to address problems. Problem-oriented policing is an analytic approach, not a specific set of technologies (Kennedy and Moore, 1995). Interventions implemented as part of the problem-oriented process can be multiple and may evolve over time if field conditions change or offenders adapt to the original response.

There is a growing body of research evidence demonstrating the crime prevention value of the problem-oriented policing approach. Researchers have found problem-oriented policing to be effective in controlling a wide range of specific crime and disorder problems (Braga, 2008; Clarke, 1997). The updated University of Maryland review of existing problem-oriented policing evaluation findings and methods suggested that this strategy "works" in preventing crime (Sherman and Eck, 2002). The National Research Council's Committee to Review Research on Police Policy and Practices concluded that problem-oriented policing was promising in preventing crime as it uses a diversity of approaches tailored to very specific crime problems (Skogan and Frydl, 2004; Weisburd and Eck, 2004). More recently, a systematic review and meta-analysis by Weisburd and colleagues (2010) found that problem-oriented policing programs generated small to moderate-sized statistically significant crime prevention effects on the crime and disorder outcomes.

Deficiencies in the Problem-Oriented Policing Process

Several volumes on problem-oriented case studies provide a good sense of the work being done as well as the strengths and weaknesses of some of the better problem-oriented efforts (see, e.g., O'Connor Shelly and Grant, 1998; Scott, 2000; Sole Brito and Allan, 1999; Sole Brito and Gratto, 2000). The concept seems to have survived what Gary Cordner (1998: 305) has identified as "first-generation" issues:

- the view that problem-oriented policing was not "real" police work;
- the view that problem-oriented policing was a fine idea but not practical because of limited resources (e.g., time and personnel);
- the question of whether ordinary police officers had the analytic ability to conduct sophisticated problem-solving projects;
- the question of whether other government agencies had the capacity to meet police halfway in solving chronic community problems; and
- the danger of falsely raising the community's expectations.

While these issues have not been completely resolved, the implementation of the concept has gone forward as more police managers grew more and more intrigued by the approach (Cordner, 1998).

Although the problem-oriented approach has demonstrated value in preventing crime and improving police practices, research has also documented that it is very difficult for police officers to implement problem-oriented policing strategies (Eck and Spelman, 1987; Clarke, 1998; Braga and Weisburd, 2006). Cordner and Biebel (2005) found that, despite fifteen years of national promotion and a concerted effort at implementation within the San Diego Police Department, problem-oriented policing, as practiced by ordinary police officers fell far short of the ideal model. Cordner and Biebel (2005) suggest that it may be unreasonable to expect every police officer to continuously engage full-fledged problem-oriented policing.

Deficiencies in current problem-oriented policing practices exist in all phases of the process. During the scanning phase, police officers risk undertaking a project that is too small (e.g., the lonely old man who repeatedly calls for companionship) or too broad (e.g., gangdelinquency), which destroys the discrete problem focus of the project and leads to a lack of direction at the beginning of analysis (Clarke, 1998). In San Diego, most problem-oriented policing projects arose out of specific observations or complaints rather than from analysis of data or any other elaborate scanning methodology (Cordner and Biebel, 2005). Some officers skip the analysis phase or conduct an overly simple analysis that does not adequately dissect the problem or does not use relevant information from other agencies, such as hospitals, schools, and private businesses (Clarke, 1998).

Based on his extensive experience with police departments implementing problem-oriented policing, Eck (2000) suggests that most problem analyses consists of a simple examination of police data coupled with the officer's working experience with the problem. Similarly, in their analysis of problem-oriented initiatives in forty-three police departments in England and Wales, Read and Tilley (2000) found that problem analysis was generally weak, with many initiatives accepting the definition of a problem at face value, using only short-term data to unravel the nature of the problem, and failing to adequately examine the genesis of the crime problems. Cordner and Biebel (2005) also found that problem analyses conducted by San Diego police officers tended to be informal and limited. Officers rarely engaged in a discrete analysis phase during their projects; they gathered some information as they proceeded, integrating their analysis with the development of responses.

Analyzing problems at crime hot spots presents a particularly vexing challenge to problem-oriented police officers. High-activity crime places tend to have multiple problems and the problems at crime places can be quite complex and involved. In their close analysis of hot spots in Minneapolis, Weisburd, Maher, and Sherman (1992) suggest that a heterogeneous mix of crime types occur at high-activity crime places rather than a concentration of one type of crime occurring at a place. In their examination of problem-oriented policing in San Diego, Capowich and Roehl (1994: 144) observed that multiple problems tend to coincide at places and report, "at the beat level, there are no pure cases in which the problem can be captured under a single classification. The range of problems is wide, with each presenting unique circumstances." In Oakland's Beat Health program to deal with drug-nuisance locations, officers encountered difficulties unraveling what was happening at a place and deciding how it should be addressed (Green, 1996). The complexity of problems at crime hot spots may discourage police officers from developing innovative responses. For example, frustrated narcotics officers may choose to chase drug dealers at a place rather than implementing a plan to change the multiple underlying characteristics of a place that make it an attractive spot for illicit drug sales (Eck and Wartell, 1998; Green, 1996; Taylor, 1999).

In the response phase, many problem-oriented policing projects rely too much on traditional police tactics (such as arrests, surveillance, and crackdowns) and neglect the wider range of available alternative responses. Read and Tilley (2000) found that officers selected certain responses prior to, or in spite of, analysis; failed to think through the need for a sustained crime reduction; failed to think through the mechanisms by which the response could have a measurable impact; failed to fully involve partners; and narrowly focused responses, usually on offenders, among a number of other weakness in the response-development process. Cordner and Biebel (2005) found that the most common method used by San Diego police officers to develop responses was "personal experience" (62%), followed by "brainstorming" (26%) and "informal discussions with other officers" (slightly more than 10%). Responses generally included enforcement, usually targeted enforcement by uniform patrol, directed or saturation patrol, and targeted investigations, plus one or two more collaborative or nontraditional strategies.

Finally, in the assessment or evaluation phase, Scott and Clarke (2000) observe that assessment of responses is rare and, when undertaken, it is usually cursory and limited to anecdotal or impressionistic data. In San Diego, Cordner and Biebel (2005) report that the most common assessment measure, by far, was "personal observation" (51% of projects), followed distantly by analysis of radio calls (14%) and speaking to residents and businesses (13%).

Strategies to Prevent Crime at Hot Spots

Figure 5.1 presents a continuum of strategies, ranging from traditional to innovative, that police can use to control crime at hot spot locations (see Braga and Weisburd, 2006). At one extreme, police departments use traditional, incident-driven strategies to control crime in the community. Although these activities coincidentally cluster in space and time, these opportunistic enforcement strategies are not specifically targeted at crime hot spots and the limitations of this approach are, as discussed in chapter 2, well known. Drawing on classifications developed in Eck's (1993a) examination of alternative futures for problem-oriented policing, Braga and Weisburd (2006) divided hot spots policing efforts into "enforcement" and "situational" problem-oriented policing programs.

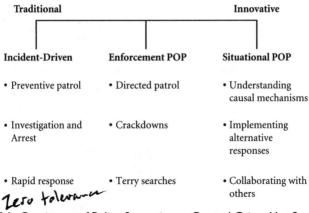

Traditional		Innovative
Incident-Driven	Enforcement POP	Situational POP
• Preventive patrol	• Directed patrol	• Understanding causal mechanisms
• Investigation and Arrest	• Crackdowns	• Implementing alternative responses
• Rapid response	• Terry searches	• Collaborating with others

Zero tolerance

Figure 5.1. Continuum of Police Strategies to Control Crime Hot Spots
Source: Braga and Weisburd (2006): 146.

Problem-oriented enforcement policing interventions move the police response forward by focusing mostly traditional tactics at high-risk times and locations. These focused police-enforcement efforts include directed patrol and heightened levels of traffic enforcement, as well as alternative strategies such as the aggressive enforcement of laws and ordinances regulating disorderly behavior in public places.

In essence, these enforcement-oriented approaches seek to modify the criminogenic routine activities of places by increasing actual and perceived risks of detection and apprehension in a very small area. Offenders seeking to commit crimes at particular places maybe deterred by increased police presence and action. Increasing patrol-car presence in high-crime locations may be the simplest way to generate crime prevention gains. Increasing police contact with serious offenders, through disorder enforcement, conducting *Terry* stops,[1] and implementing crackdowns—a massive short-term swamping of law enforcement resources in a specific area—may extend these crime prevention gains. These enforcement approaches have been found to be effective in controlling crime in the Minneapolis Hot Spots Patrol experiment, Kansas City Gun project, and Kansas City Crack House Raid study.

Although these programs are "problem-oriented" in a global way, their tactics do not employ the individualized treatments for crime problems advocated by Herman Goldstein (1990). Problem-oriented enforcement policing interventions tend to concentrate mainly on the time and location of crime events, rather than focusing on the characteristics and dynamics of a place that make it a hot spot for criminal activity. At the innovative end of the continuum is Goldstein's (1990) vision of situational problem-oriented policing, in which police agencies undertake thorough analysis of crime problems at places, collaborate with community members and other city agencies, and conduct a broad search for situational responses to problems. The following section examines a range of problem-oriented approaches to control crime hot spots and sheds some light on the difficulties experienced by police officers when dealing with crime hot spots.

Implementing Problem-Oriented Policing in Crime Hot Spots

Similar to the findings of other examinations of problem-oriented policing described earlier, the Jersey City Problem-Oriented Policing at Violent Places experiment found that translating problem-solving theory into practice was difficult for the officers (Braga et al., 1999). The complex and varied problems at the violent crime hot spots presented a substantive challenge to the officers charged with preventing crime at the places (Braga and Weisburd, 2006). The number of identified problems per place ranged from three to seven, with a mean of nearly five problems per place (Braga, 1997; Braga, et al., 1999). Figure 5.2 presents the diverse problems encountered by the Jersey City problem-oriented policing officers at one violent-crime hot spot location.

From their training and the reading materials made available to them, the Jersey City problem-oriented officers expected that they would be preventing violence at each hot spot by focusing on very specific underlying characteristics or situational factors. After examining their violent-crime hot spots closely, the officers observed that they would be controlling a multitude of crime and disorder problems at these places

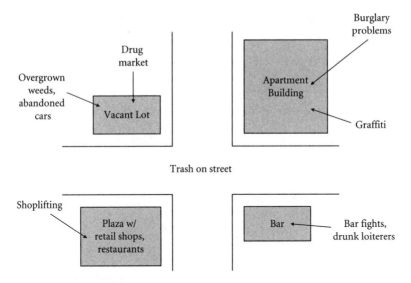

Figure 5.2. Characteristics of a Jersey City Violent Crime Hot Spot Location
Source: Braga (2008): 59.

(Braga, 1997; Braga and Weisburd, 2006). All twelve treatment places were perceived to suffer from social-disorder problems such as loitering, public drinking, and panhandling; eleven places suffered from physical disorder such as trash-filled streets, vacant lots, and abandoned buildings. Seven places had problems with illicit drug selling and three places had problems with property crimes.

Across and within violent hot spots in the Jersey City problem-oriented policing experiment, few problems were analyzed thoroughly. Eck and Spelman (1987) suggest twoclassifications for the depth of problem analysis: limited analysis and extended analysis. Eck and Spelman (1987) grouped problem-solving efforts by the Newport News (VA) Police Department by determining whether there were obvious information sources that were not used, given the nature of the problem; if there were not any obvious unused sources, the effort was classified as extended. Using these definitions, slightly less than one third of the identified problems in the Jersey City study received what could be described as an extended analysis (Braga, 1997; Braga and Weisburd, 2006).

It must be noted that, for certain problems at the Jersey City violent-crime hot spots, a superficial analysis was all that was necessary (e.g., alleviating a trash problem by recognizing that there were not any trash receptacles at the place). Weak problem analyses occurred for two reasons (Braga, 1997; Braga and Weisburd, 2006). First, at ten of twelve places, the officers believed that they "knew what was going on" based on their working knowledge and "on the spot" appraisals of problems. Second, the officers believed that most of the street crime at the place could be linked directly or indirectly to the physical and social disorder of a place. From their problem-oriented policing training, the officers were familiar with the "broken windows" thesis and much preferred the simplicity of a general plan to restore order and reduce crime at places over the specifics of the SARA model to control the multiple and interrelated problems of the violent-crime hot spots (Braga, 1997; Braga and Weisburd, 2006).

Although specific tactics and priorities varied from place to place, the Jersey City officers certainly did not limit themselves to addressing violent crime; the officers generally attempted to control their hot spots by cleaning up the environment via aggressive order maintenance and making physical improvements such as securing vacant lots or removing trash from the street. Therefore, the treatment was a collection of specific problem-oriented tactics that could be broadly categorized as a "policing disorder" strategy. The Jersey City Police Department's program to control violent places went beyond the tactics of most problem-oriented enforcement interventions, but still fell short of Goldstein's vision of the problem-oriented policing process. Nonetheless, the Jersey City approach generated significant reductions in citizen calls for service and crime incidents at the treatment hot spots relative to the control hot spots.

A similar study evaluated the effects of problem-oriented policing interventions on crime and disorder hot spots in Lowell, Massachusetts (Braga and Bond, 2008). Responsibility for the implementation of the problem-oriented policing intervention at the treatment places to the captains that managed Lowell's three police sectors. Within each sector, lieutenants and sergeants spent time analyzing official data sources and discussing problems with community members. Like the Jersey City experience, the problem analysis and community engagement in the Lowell Policing Crime and Disorder Hot Spots project was limited and the implemented problem-oriented policing strategy more closely resembled a general policing-disorder strategy. The strategy was comprised of three key components: situational prevention strategies to modify disorderly conditions, short-term social service strategies such as finding housing for local homeless populations, and increased numbers of misdemeanor arrests for disorderly behavior.

The Lowell impact evaluation revealed significant reductions in crime and disorder calls for service at the treatment hot spots relative to the control hot spots. An analysis of the three key components found that the strongest crime prevention benefits were driven by situational prevention strategies that modified the criminal-opportunity structure at the crime and disorder hot spots (Braga and Bond, 2008). Misdemeanor arrests for disorderly behavior generated much smaller crime prevention gains in the treatment places. Short-term police-led social service strategies did not have a significant impact on citizen calls for service at the hot spots. The Lowell findings suggest that, when developing strategies to deal with crime hot spots, police departments should use an approach that seeks to change the situations, dynamics, and underlying conditions that give rise to crime problems rather than a simplistic "zero-tolerance" policing model that focuses on a subset of social incivilities, such as drunken people, rowdy teens, and street vagrants, and seeks to remove them from the street via arrest. Misdemeanor arrests obviously play a noteworthy role in dealing with disorder; however, these kinds of arrest strategies do not directly deal with criminogenic situations and physical conditions that may facilitate or encourage these problems to exist at specific locations.

On the continuum of police strategies to control high-activity crime places (figure 5.1), the Jersey City and Lowell programs would fit between enforcement and situational problem-oriented interventions. Despite the gap between the desired application of the approach and its actual implementation, the problem-oriented policing approach was found to be effective in reducing crime and disorder in Jersey City and Lowell. This suggests that problem-oriented policing interventions may not need to be implemented in the ways envisioned by Herman Goldstein in order to produce a crime prevention effect. Perhaps, simply focusing police resources on identifiable risks that come to the attention of problem-oriented policing projects, such as crime hot spots, may be enough to produce crime-control gains (Braga and Weisburd, 2006). This is a striking result considering the large body of research that shows the ineffectiveness of many police crime prevention efforts (Visher and Weisburd, 1998).

Of course, this does not mean that had the police more fully implemented the problem-oriented approach and took a more specific, more focused approach to crime and disorder problems, crime-control benefits at places could have been greater. Of course, this requires the development of such skills from both "trial and error" experience of problem solving on thestreet and additional training in the action-research model, particularly in the area of problem analysis. The investment in the acquisition of these skills could be well worth the effort. Indeed, the Campbell Collaboration meta-analysis of randomized experiments suggests that the more customized interventions of the Jersey City DMAP and Problem-Oriented Policing at Violent Places experiments generated larger crime prevention effects when compared to the enforcement-oriented Minneapolis Hot Spots Patrol and Kansas City Crack House Raids interventions (Braga, 2005; see table 4.4 in chapter 4). Moreover, a series of case studies in both problem-oriented policing and situational crime prevention suggest strong crime-control gains in a variety of specific crime and disorder problems ranging from graffiti on the New York City subway (Sloan-Howitt and Kelling, 1990), to prostitution (Matthews, 1990), to the robbery of convenience stores (Hunter and Jeffrey, 1992).

The Prospects of Situational Problem-Oriented Policing in Crime Hot Spots

Although more generalized interventions have produced crime-control gains and have added to law enforcement's array of crime prevention tools, it is commonly assumed that police could be more effective if they focused their efforts on the criminogenic attributes that cause criminally active places to be "hot." In other words, adding an increased level of guardianship at a place by optimizing patrol is a step in controlling crime, but reducing criminal opportunities by changing site features, facilities, and the management at a place (e.g., adding streetlights, razing abandoned buildings, and mobilizing residents) may have a more profound, and longer lasting, effect on crime. However, as described above, research has found that it is difficult for police officers to develop problem-oriented interventions to control the complex problems that cause a place to be hot (Braga and Weisburd, 2006; Braga et al., 1999).

In successful place-oriented problem-solving ventures, the situational interventions designed to control places have been as varied and multi-dimensional as the problems they sought to address at the place. These successful problem-oriented efforts have also been characterized by effective partnerships with outside agencies. Three noteworthy projects that illuminate the varied nature of the responses applied to problem places as well as the crime prevention benefits of developing situational responses that are directly linked to the nature of crime problems at places are described below.

Jersey City was also the site for a problem-oriented policing project designed to address serious crime problems in six public housing projects (Mazerolle, Price, and Roehl, 2000; Mazerolle and Terrill, 1997). At each of the participating housing projects, a problem-oriented site team was created comprising community members, police officers, tenant representatives, a civilian site manager, and a social service liaison. These teams held monthly meetings to identify the places that were associated with serious crime and drug-market problems, unravel the circumstances contributing to these problems, coordinate the implementation of place-specific interventions, and report the progress made on the problem-oriented initiatives.

During the scanning phase, two distinct types of problem places were identified: outdoor common areas (such as parking lots, playgrounds, and walkways) and individual apartments (Mazerolle and Terrill, 1997).

The targeted common areas received situational responses to alter criminal opportunities, such as changing the public phones to allow outgoing calls only and installing floodlights in poorly lit areas (Mazerolle, Price, and Roehl, 2000). The police supplemented these alternative responses with heightened levels of traditional policing tactics such as surveillance and serving warrants. At problem individual apartments, counseling and treatment was provided to leaseholders with drug and alcohol problems and to families withhistories of lease violations (Ready, Green Mazerolle, and Revere, 1998). If the tenants of these "nuisance" apartments did not take advantage of the services, they were advised that noncompliance would lead to eviction. If social services were deemed to be inadequate to deal with these problems, the problem-solving teams used more aggressive tactics such as eviction or having tenants arrested. An evaluation of this program revealed that the problem-oriented strategies, as compared to traditional strategies used prior to the program, led to fewer serious crime calls for service over time and, at two sites, to reductions in violent, property, and vehicle-related crimes (Mazerolle, Price, and Roehl, 2000).

The New York Port Authority Bus Terminal had fallen into such an advanced state of disrepair that Felson and his colleagues (1996) entitled their study of a comprehensive plan to clean up the facility, "Redesigning Hell." Noteworthy problems included phone hustlers placing illegal international phone calls for free from inside the terminal, a bustling community of homeless persons taking over whole sections of the terminal (with accompanying public urination and defecation, drug use, blocking access routes, and aggressive panhandling), male prostitutes, prostitution in the parking structure, and criminal interdependence with the surrounding Times Square area.

Sixty-two interventions were instituted at the terminal including: closing off spaces, improved shopping, cleaning, increased enforcement, and other measures to remove situations that facilitated offending or increased the number of patrons and their ability to watch each other. Beyond addressing physical conditions that facilitated the development of a large homeless population in the terminal, the Port

Authority addressed the homeless problem through a "refer or arrest" process. In partnership with social service agencies, this process allowed the police to offer loitering homeless persons alternative places and programs. If that offer was refused, the officer could ask the person to leave the terminal. If that request was ignored, the officer could make an arrest. The phone-hustling problem was addressed by various measures, including reducing the number of pay phones, removing phones' international dialing capacity, and disabling the keypads to prevent the routing of fraudulent calls through the exchange systems of private businesses (Bichler and Clarke, 1997). Analyses of official crime data revealed that robberies and assaults were significantly reduced in the station (Felson et al., 1996). Noting that robberies and assaults also declined in the surrounding area, Felson and his colleagues (1996) suggest that either outside crime prevention efforts or a diffusion of crime prevention benefits may account for the decreases in crime outside the terminal. An annual survey of terminal patrons that commenced with the 1991 cleanup revealed noteworthy declines in incivilities and disorder in the terminal.

Stronger problem analysis at crime hot spot locations can lead to clearer avenues for place-oriented crime prevention interventions For instance, a situational problem-oriented policing project was implemented to reduce thefts from cars parked in the center city of Charlotte, North Carolina (Clarke and Goldstein, 2003). A detailed analysis of the theft problem revealed that the risks of thefts were much greater in parking lots than in parking decks; these higher risks were associated with inadequate fencing, poor lighting, and the absence of lot attendants. Based on these analyses, the recommended responses included (adapted from Clarke and Goldstein, 2003: 276–77):

1. The Charlotte-Mecklenburg Police Department and the District Attorney's Office would continue to develop aggressive policies of arresting offenders, seeking convictions, and seeking severe sentences for repeat offenders.

2. Parking lot operators would be asked to post the addresses of their lot at the entrance(s) of each lot. This would assist victims in reporting thefts, help police in responding to calls for assistance, and assist future analysis of larcenies from automobiles by allowing these to be assigned to the specific lot in which the larceny occurred.

3. Changes would be sought in the city's zoning ordinance that requires, for aesthetic purposes, that all new lots be surrounded by screening (which in practice is usually a fence) that is no less than four feet in height and can have no more than 25 percent of its surface left open. These fences, most often solid, have reduced surveillance of lots by passing motorists, pedestrians, and police officers on patrol. Furthermore, lots established before the ordinance came into effect in 1993 (and its amendment in 1995), which constitute a majority of all lots, were not required to have screening. The proposed new ordinance would require "see through" fences to be erected for all new lots and, within a period of two or three years, for all existing lots.

4. With the cooperation and agreement of lot operators, the police would seek to implement a rating scheme that would result in every lot being graded for its security on a number of variables. Grades would be determined by either the police or the building inspector and would be posted at the lot entrances, in the same way health inspection results are posted for Charlotte's restaurants. This proposal was intended to provide a strong incentive for parking facility operators to improve security.

5. Funds would be sought for a security bike patrol for the lots. The patrol would be trained in what to look for, how to

focus patrols for greatest effect, how to deal with suspicious persons, and when and how to call the police (their radios would be compatible with police radios). The patrols would give the customers and employees of area businesses the same type of security that private patrols give to customers and employees at large shopping malls.

A new closed-circuit television (CCTV) surveillance system was also installed by private security companies charged with monitoring particular lots. Before the plan was fully implemented and the CCTVs were operational, the targeted lots experienced an unexpected 38 percent decrease in larcenies from motor vehicles (Clarke and Goldstein, 2003). The evaluators credited increased police and security-patrol attention given to the high-risk lots after the problem-oriented policing process commenced. The decline in larcenies continued as the newly devised situational strategies were implemented, and the authors anticipated that these strategies would contribute to a long-term, permanent reduction in larcenies from automobiles.

The Importance of Engaging Place Managers

Properties and facilities are owned by people and entities other than the police. These individuals play a key role in the internal dynamics and potential criminal opportunities at places that can attract or ward off likely offenders. Police should work with or stimulate "place managers" to address problems at high-activity crime places (Felson, 1994). Place managers can include a wide range of individuals such as sales clerks, doormen, apartment managers, business owners, and neighbors. Some place managers, such as a school teacher or bar manager, look after settingsthat do not persist for the whole day (Felson, 2006). With the exception of short-term and superficial responses, all real changes at places must be enacted by place managers. Many of the alternative crime prevention strategies pursued by the police to deal with problem places involves the manipulation of property owners, business operators, and others to suppress local crime and disorder problems.

In their analysis of violence in bars in Cincinnati, Ohio, Madensen and Eck (2008) suggest that place-management decisions were very influential in determining whether or not crime occurs at a particular location. Like previous studies, they found very little support for the hypothesis that high-crime bars are simply the product of high-crime neighborhoods. Rather, Madensen and Eck (2008) reported that managers created environments at bars that suppressed or facilitated violence through business-related choices. The types of patrons that frequented the bars and the characteristics of the behavior settings were the product of management decisions such as bar themes; property characteristics; bar location; activities and entertainment; staff, training, and security; and market strategies. These decisions are interrelated and dynamic; violence inhibiting and facilitating decisions in one area can be mitigated or aggravated by decisions made in another area. For instance, a college bar hosting "hip-hop" night with dancing that brings large groups of intoxicated young men in close proximity to each other will be at far greater risk of violence when compared to a food-serving, wine-and-cigar bar that caters to more mature patrons. In the college bar, subsequent management choices about staffing, such as the presence of trained bouncers, and proactive decisions in dealing with disorderly patrons by halting the serving of alcohol or through their removal from the premises, will importantly influence the amount of violence the establishment experiences when the hip-hop event occurs.

Madensen (2007) developed a more general theory of place-management decisions and activities that can be applied to other types of facilities such as banks, retail stores, and even web-based businesses (figure 5.3). This perspective on the management of private businesses applies to the management of public places as well. For instance, Madensen (2007: 162–63) describes some of the relevant decisions that managers, such as elected officials and appointed public executives, make that influence the types and likelihood of crime and disorder problems

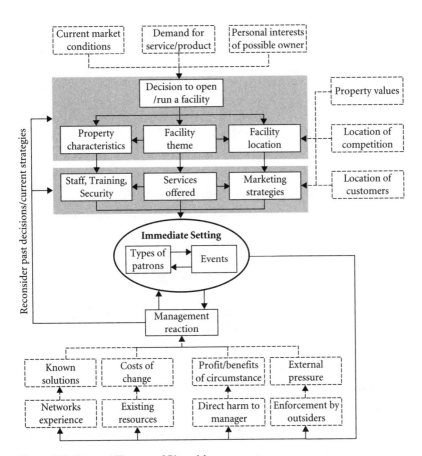

Figure 5.3. General Theory of Place Management
Source: Madensen (2007): 160.

at public parks. The theme of the park (e.g., national forest, playground, recreational) will influence property characteristics and the park location. Parks intended for families will have picnic areas, parks for children will have playgrounds, parks for teenagers will have basketball courts, and parks for the elderly will have sitting areas and shuffleboard (Madensen, 2007). Security features may include see-through fencing, locking public restrooms at night, road barricades, lighting, posted rules, and implementing curfews. If crime or disorder occurs in these locations, managers who have more experience or work with others who have successfully addressed these problems and managers who have access to greater resources (e.g., community or state funds) will have the ability to change these environments more quickly. Managers that are not negatively impacted (e.g., live elsewhere) and cannot be held accountable for the condition of the parks (e.g., appointed rather than elected public officials), will be less likely to aggressively respond to problems in these locations (Madensen, 2007).

In many cases, place managers will be proactive in dealing with crime and disorder problems and willing to work with the police to create safe environments. Sometimes, unfortunately, police officers need to force irresponsible or negligent parties to take action. Third-party policing, introduced in chapter 2, is defined as "police efforts to persuade or coerce organizations or non-offending persons, such as public housing agencies, property owners,parents, health and building inspectors, and business owners to take some responsibility for preventing crime or reducing crime problems" (Buerger and Green Mazerolle, 1998: 301). The police use a range of civil, criminal, and regulatory rules and laws to engage or force third parties into taking some crime control responsibility. The ultimate targets of third-party policing efforts are the people engaged in deviant and criminal behavior at the place, typically drug dealers, gang members, vandals, and petty criminals (Green, 1996). The engagement of place managers and the use of civil remedies can be important situational strategies used by police officers seeking to control crime hot spots. Research has revealed that third-party policing is an effective mechanism to control drug problems and is promising in controlling violent crime, disorderly youth, and property crime problems (Mazerolle and Ransley, 2006).

Problem-Oriented Policing at a Violent-Crime Hot Spot in Jersey City: A Case Study

To further illustrate the complexities and prospects of problem-oriented policing at crime spots, this section briefly describes the efforts made by Jersey City police officers to address violent-crime problems at one hot spot in the Jersey City Problem-Oriented Policing in Violent Places experiment (Braga, 1997: 361–78). The case study provides readers with a clearer sense for the dynamics and characteristic of a place that generate crime and disorder problems. It also demonstrates that a blend of situational prevention strategies and traditional enforcement actions are often necessary to deal with problem places.

The eastern section of Journal Square in Jersey City was a bustling hub for commuters; a central PATH (Port Authority Trans-Hudson) train station provided transportation to and fromNew York City, Newark, Hoboken, and other destinations in New Jersey. A bus stop, serviced by a multitude of routes, and a large taxi-stand area were present on the plaza in front of the PATH terminal. Adjacent to the entrance area of the train station, several restaurants and small businesses thrived off the large number of people frequenting the place. During all hours of the business day, the area was teeming with commuters and shoppers patronizing the many businesses of Journal Square. At night, the area was much quieter, but still maintained a steady flow of traffic. The intersection of Magnolia Avenue and Summit Avenue, located directly behind the PATH station, was comprised of fast-food restaurants, parking lots, and office buildings. Magnolia Avenue stretched east from the terminal and parking lots into a residential area. Summit Avenue crossed over the train tracks and was a major thoroughfare for automotive traffic to and from Journal Square.

During scanning phase, crime mapping revealed that the violent crime in the Journal Square East area clustered around the intersection of Magnolia and Summit avenues. Based on a cursory review of the incident reports and their own experiences at the place, the problem-solving officers identified the problems of the area as robberies of commuters as they left the PATH station to the parking lot or to the nearby residential area, and assaults arising from disputes between the disorderly homeless men that populated the area. During the analysis phase, a closer examination of the incident data revealed that the robberies of commuters were committed by the homeless men and groups of young males (notably Hispanic); the typical victims were younger males (between teens and early 30s). With the assistance of Rutgers University researchers, the Jersey City problem-solving officers conducted a series of interviews with key individuals in the Journal Square area to gain further insights on the problems of the place.

A lieutenant of the Port Authority Police (45-year-old white male and a veteran of 24 years), the agency responsible for law enforcement and security on PATH property, was interviewed. He believed the main problems of the Journal Square PATH station were robberies of commuters, drug selling, and groups of homeless individuals loitering in the terminal. The lieutenant regarded the terminal and the surrounding area as an opportunistic place for criminals. Features of the physical environment, such as poor lighting and "blind spots" that allowed criminals to conceal themselves from unsuspecting victims, were perceived to be associated with robbery at the place. However, the lieutenant felt strongly that the most important factor was simply the sheer volume of unsuspecting commuters using the place. The lieutenant compared the muggers to predators scanning a herd of cattle for suitable targets. The robbers looked for people with accessory bags that were easy to strong arm away from the victim or they preyed upon commuters who fell asleep and lost track of their belongings.

The Port Authority lieutenant identified homeless men and young males as the typical perpetrators of these crimes. Homeless men were viewed by the lieutenant as the largest source of problems in the area; these disorderly individuals panhandled, drank in public, insulted and threatened commuters, and urinated in the terminal. The drug selling at the place was viewed as sporadic. Residents from the surrounding streets bought drugs from sellers that worked in front of the PATH terminal. These sellers had been displaced from a nearby low-income hotel ("flop house") that burned down in 1993; this hotel was believed to attract many undesirables to the terminal such as drug addicts and homeless men. Port Authority and JCPD officers arrested the sellers when they observed the drug trade or received information about the illicit activity. Overall, the lieutenant thought the place was relatively quiet for a high-volume commuterterminal. He was very satisfied with the terminal as a place to work and felt very safe while on duty (he stated it was because he carried a firearm).

The manager of a Dunkin Donuts (27-year-old white male) located on the intersection of Magnolia Avenue and Summit Avenue was interviewed for his perspective on the problems of the place. The problems in and around his business were caused by the homeless people that loitered in the parking lot of the shop. These unsavory individuals drank in public, urinated in front of the glass windows of the store, harassed and insulted his patrons for money, assaulted each other, and vandalized the property of the store. The derelicts were present everyday and the manager placed calls to the police on a daily basis to disperse the group. Whenever the police left the area, the group reassembled shortly thereafter. The group ranged from approximately four or five people in the morning to as many as twenty-four during the later hours of the day.

The owner of the local liquor store (47-year-old Asian female) concurred with the manager of Dunkin Donuts that the homeless were a large problem. She stated that these individuals harassed her customers and often tried to shoplift alcohol from her establishment; she commented that recently a vagrant, armed with a knife, unsuccessfully attempted to rob a local bartender of a bottle of liquor. The homeless were believed to be responsible for violent crime in the area and had negative effects on the quality of life.

A homeless man (39-year-old black male) was conferred with about the problems of the place. He was originally from Newark, New Jersey, but viewed the Journal Square area as his home. He was present twenty-four hours a day, seven days a week. The area was attractive to him for a variety of reasons: there were many commuters and shoppers to beg money from, he enjoyed eating at the local Burger King and Dunkin Donuts, and he felt secure with his companions. His associates were his friends and guardians; he reported, "they look after me...sometimes they give me money and food." Although he claimed to receive threats by other homeless men on a daily basis, he perceived the area to be very safe and was not worried about becoming the victim of crime. He agreed that loitering, public drinking, and urination were problems of the area, but he blamed a lack of assistance and resources from society for these disorderly behaviors.

During the early stages of response development and implementation, the Jersey City police officers decided to focus their efforts on the problems occurring off the PATH property or, more succinctly, off the turf of the Port Authority Police. The Jersey City officers had a good rapport with the Port Authority Police and did not want to jeopardize a positive relationship by encroaching on their jurisdiction. As such, the Jersey City officers deferred responsibility for implementing responses to the problems to the Port Authority officers. Fortunately, the Port Authority police were willing partners and initiated several strategies to address robberies and disorder in the PATH terminal such as improved lighting in the areas leading to the parking lot, the removal of many benches frequented by the homeless, and increased traditional tactics by undercover Port Authority officers. This support allowed the Jersey City problem-solving officers to focus their efforts on preventing robberies of commuters leaving the PATH area and dealing with the homeless problem around the Magnolia and Summit intersection.

The robbery problem involving groups of young male perpetrators was resolved through traditional investigative methods. Early during the intervention period, the Jersey City problem solving officers rounded up fifteen juveniles and two adults known as the "Catch a Herb Crew." This robbery gang worked in small groups and selected vulnerable (physically weak in appearance; referred to as "Herbs" by the perpetrators) young males that frequented the Journal Square PATH station. The crew also perpetrated robberies in two other violent-crime hot spots inthe experiment. These individuals were charged with more than twenty robberies; the group was believed to be responsible for more than fifty robberies in the prior year. After this investigation ended, the officers continued to set up surveillances and follow suspicious persons around the place, but no further arrests were made over the course of the project.

The Jersey City officers also felt strongly that some of the opportunistic robberies and pick-pocketing at the terminal would not have occurred if the commuters were more wary of their surroundings. They met with Port Authority officers on educating the commuters and increasing awareness; the Jersey City officers provided their PATH counterparts with a box of crime prevention booklets and asked them to place the literature in locations that were easily accessible to the commuters (such as on top of newspaper vending machines).

The Jersey City officers believed many individuals in the troublesome homeless population were not of the "good people that had fallen under tough circumstances" variety. Rather, the Jersey City officers believe that particular individuals chose to reject society and exhibit antisocial behavior. Further, the officers did not have positive experiences using a social-service approach to addressing the homeless problem at another violent-crime hot spot in their caseload. As a result, the officers decided to reduce violence caused by disorderly homeless men by making the place as unattractive as possible. Since the problematic vagrants were constantly removed from the PATH station, the homeless usually congregated in the adjacent parking lots of Dunkin Donuts and Burger King near the Summit and Magnolia intersection. The officers soon discovered that abandoned buildings located at Summit Avenue and nearby West Street were used as "club houses." The officers entered the buildings and found two homeless men sleeping, numerous "beds," homemade furniture, cocaine vials, hypodermic needles, and large amounts of garbage. Finally, a twenty-foot-wide hole in a fence behind these buildings allowedthe vagrants to ascend from the train tracks (many slept under the Summit Avenue Bridge) into the area.

The officers worked with the managers of Dunkin Donuts and Burger King to address the problem of homeless loitering in the parking lots. According to the storeowners, the homeless perched upon a pile of timber or sat on the curbs. The square (6 inches by 6 inches) timber sections provided multiple seats for the vagrants (one officer commented the homeless resembled "a filthy crowd sitting on bleachers at a baseball game"). Based on recommendations made by the officers, the managers had the timbers removed. The Jersey City officers enlisted the assistance of the local JCPD Community Service Officer to bolster order maintenance activities at the place. During multiple daily patrols, the officers dispersed groups of loiterers and issued summons for public drinking. The officers also had a "No Public Drinking" sign posted on the southeast corner of the Magnolia and Summit intersection; this sign advised that persons consuming alcoholic beverages or carrying open containers in public were subject to a fine of up to five hundred dollars. The officers believed that forcing these disorderly individuals to leave the area on a routine basis was an effective response; regular moving and disruption of drinking were viewed as large inconveniences for these problematic persons. Summons for public drinking were not thought to be much of a deterrent because most homeless did not have any money and did not pay fines.

The officers identified the owner of the properties at Summit Avenue and West Street, with the assistance of the Tax Department, through tax records. The officers met with the owner and explained that the conditions of the properties were nuisances and contributed to the problems of the entire neighborhood. The owner explained that the real estate was in the process of foreclosure with a local bank; nevertheless, he agreed with the officers' assessment of the properties and promised to clean and secure the buildings. However, the buildings were never repaired by the owner. After several unsuccessful attempts to reach the owner, the officers requested the Environmental Compliance Division of the Incinerator Authority to issue notices of violation to the owner for maintaining properties with environmental hazards. The Environmental Division indicated that the Incinerator Authority had numerous problems with the owner in the past regarding other derelict properties in Jersey City; the violations were issued and the owner had ten days to comply. After more than ten days passed without any response or compliance noted, the Incinerator Authority boarded up the buildings and cleaned the waste around the properties; an abandoned automobile (another home for disorderly vagrants) was also removed. The owner of the property was billed for the cost of the work.

The gaping hole in the fence, in addition to providing a portal to the train tracks for the homeless, was a favorite spot for illegal dumpers. The mouth of the hole and the decline to the train tracks was littered with garbage and debris such as furniture, tires, large oil vats, and an oven. The vagrants left behind broken glass, trash, and human waste. The area was visibly filthy and the garbage gave off a stench that was unbearable for the residents of West Street during the summer months. At the request of the Jersey City officers, the Department of Public Works sent a clean-up crew that hauled much of the debris away and placed a large chain link fence. The Public Works Paints and Sign Division also placed a large "No Dumping" sign at the end of the street. These actions were believed by the officers to prevent many vagrants from traveling through the place to the PATH station. Further, the Jersey City problem-solving officers believed the fence removed an opportunity for illegal dumpers and the sign conveyed the message that "someone cared for the area."

During initial interviews for problem analysis, the officers received information that the disorderly homeless and other drug buyers purchased their narcotics from a first-floor apartment on Summit Avenue. According to the Jersey City officers, dealers at the apartment sold their product "twenty-four hours a day and seven days a week." The problem solving officers requested enforcement action by drug investigators assigned to Hudson County Prosecutor's Office. The Hudson County investigators made a series of controlled buys at the apartment, obtained a search warrant, and arrested three men. Several ounces of cocaine, a .32 caliber Harrington & Richardson revolver, 336 dollars, and numerous drug paraphernalia (such as syringes, vials, baggies, scale, and so on) were recovered. The Jersey City problem-solving officers believed that this operation dried up a major source of drugs at the place. Unfortunately, opportunistic minor drug selling remained around the PATH station over the course of the intervention period.

The problem-solving efforts of the Jersey City officers and their partners generated noteworthy violence-prevention gains in the Journal Square East area. Comparing the pre-test and post-test periods, robbery incidents decreased by 53 percent, assault incidents decreased by 10 percent, and total crime incidents decreased by nearly 13 percent in the Journal Square East hot spot area. In the control violent-crime hot spot that was matched to the Journal Square East hot spot, robbery incidents increased by 14 percent, assault incidents increased by 36 percent, and total incidents increased by 31 percent between the pre-test and post-test periods.

Crime Prevention Mechanisms Underlying Police Prevention Efforts at Crime Hot Spots

The important lesson for police practitioners and academics is that problem-oriented situational and enforcement policing interventions can change the criminal dynamics of crime hot spots in important ways. The rational choice perspective and routine activities theory provide useful frameworks to speculate on the theoretical mechanisms underlying these effects at problem places.

According to the rational choice perspective, offenders consider risks, effort, and rewards when contemplating criminal acts (Cornish and Clarke, 1986). Increased police presence and order-maintenance activities at places serve as powerful deterrents to criminal and disorderly conduct. In the Minneapolis hot spots patrol experiment, Sherman and Weisburd (1995) claimed evidence of place-specific "micro-deterrence" associated with increased police presence in hot spot areas (646). These tactics also increase the certainty of detection and apprehension at places, communicate that disorderly behavior will no longer be tolerated at places, and raise potential offenders' perceptions of risk at places (Cook, 1980; Zimring and Hawkins, 1973; also Koper, 1995). These perceptions of increased risks also influence the behavior of an array of would-be offenders.

Changes in the physical environment may discourage potential offenders from frequenting an area by altering criminal opportunities at a place. The presence of abandoned buildings, for instance, attracts offenders to places (Spelman, 1993). The abandoned building may serve as a location for muggers to conceal themselves while waiting for a victim to pass, a drinking spot for disorderly youth, or a space to stash or sell drugs. If the derelict building were secured, fewer potential offenders would enter the area because the necessary effort to commit crimes at the places would increase. Strategies to ameliorate physical incivilities (thereby changing site features and facilities) may diminish the number of easy opportunities at the place and, thus, discourage offenders from frequenting targeted places.

Complementing the rational choice perspective, routine activities theory focuses on the criminal event and posits that criminal events occur when potential offenders and suitable targets converge in space and time in the absence of a capable guardian (Cohen and Felson, 1979). The increased presence of police augments the level of guardianship in targeted places. Heightened levels of patrol prevent crimes by introducing the watchful eye of the police as a guardian to protect potential victims from potential offenders. According to the "broken windows" hypothesis, reductions in physical and social incivilities at places send clear signals to potential criminals that lawbreaking will no longer be tolerated. Some observers suggest that preventing disorder is the best way to prevent crimes in the city, particularly violent crimes such as robbery and stranger assaults (Wikstrom, 1995). Offenders make choices about the places they frequent based on cues at the site, and are likely to select places that emit cues where risks are low for committing crimes (Eck and Weisburd, 1995). Changing the perceptions of potential offenders by controlling disorder and changing easy criminal opportunities may reduce their numbers at the place. Therefore, since victims and offenders often share the same social milieus (Lauritsen, Sampson, and Laub, 1991; Garofalo, 1987), these changes will also reduce the number of potential victims at the place. Kleiman suggests that this phenomenon occurred in the reductions in violent crime and property crime from a crackdown on street-level heroin sales in Lynn, Massachusetts (1988: 23):

> A plausible explanation would be that street drug markets
> involve concentrations of both likely aggressors and attractive
> victims: attractive both because they have money and drugs
> worth stealing and because they are less likely than average to
> complain to thepolice. In addition, business disputes among
> drug dealers and between drug dealers and drug customers
> may result in violence rather than litigation. Breaking up the

drug market disperses potential victims and offenders making it less likely they will come in contact with one another.

In their book on restoring order in urban neighborhoods, Kelling and Coles (1996: 242–43) detail four elements of dealing with disorder that explain its potential crime prevention impact:

> First, dealing with disorder and low-level offenders informs police about, and puts them into contact with, those who have also committed index crimes, including the hard-core "six percent" of youthful offenders. Second, the high visibility of police actions and the concentration of police in areas characterized by high levels of disorder protect "good kids," while sending a message to 'wannabes' and those guilty of committing marginal crimes that their actions will no longer be tolerated.... Third, citizens begin to assert control over public spaces by upholding neighborhood standards for behavior, and ultimately move onto center stage in the ongoing processes of maintaining order and controlling crime. Finally, as problems of disorder and crime become the responsibility not merely of the police, but of the entire community...all mobilize to address them in an integrated fashion.

In the examples described in this chapter, regardless of the specific approach employed, problem-oriented interventions focused on problem places changed the relationships between offenders, targets, and guardians. Reduced crime rates followed these changes in the dynamics of problem places.

How Should Police Departments Deal with Problem Places?

Based on the available empirical evidence, we believe that police departments should strive to develop situational prevention strategies to deal with crime hot spots. Careful analyses of problems at crime hot spots seem likely to yield prevention strategies that will be well positioned to change the situations and dynamics that cause crime to cluster at specific locations. However, the existing research literature on the implementation of problem-oriented policing suggests that most police officers struggle to execute the model correctly (Read and Tilley, 2000; Scott, 2000). Even with these difficulties, adherence to the basic notions behind the approach seems to be useful in focusing police attention in crime hot spots.

Despite falling short of Goldstein's vision, the Jersey City and Lowell problem-oriented policing programs were still found to be effective in preventing crime at hot spot locations (Braga et al., 1999; Braga and Bond, 2008). Some scholars would describe the efforts of the Jersey City and Lowell police officers as "problem solving" rather than problem-oriented policing (Cordner, 1998). Problem solving is a "shallow" version of problem-oriented policing as these efforts are smaller in scope, involve rudimentary analysis, and lack formal assessments. According to Cordner (1998), problem solving better describes what an officer does to handle a particular dispute or drug house rather than initiatives to deal with problems of substantial magnitude like prostitution in a downtown area and thefts from autos in parking lots. Enforcement problem-oriented initiatives would also fit what we would consider shallow problem solving. When the complexities of crime problems at hot spots and the difficultiespolice officers experience in unraveling these problems and implementing individualized responses are considered, shallow problem solving can be a very practical way for police departments to prevent crimes at places.

We believe that police agencies should continue to develop their capacity to conduct more in-depth problem-oriented policing so their officers can go beyond the shallow problem solving that is currently practiced in the field. Unfortunately, we also believe that it is unlikely that police agencies will enhance their problem-solving efforts in the foreseeable future. There seems to be, at least, two obstacles (Braga and Weisburd, 2006). First, the hierarchical organizational structure of policing in itself tends to inhibit innovation and creativity. In their close examination of Compstat, Willis, Mastrofski, and Weisburd (2004) found that, while the program holds out the promise of allowing police agencies to adopt innovative technologies and problem-solving techniques, it actually hindered innovative problem solving while strengthening the existing hierarchy through the added pressure of increased internal accountability. Officers were reluctant to brainstorm problem-solving approaches during Compstat meetings for fear of undermining authority or the credibility of their colleagues. Moreover, the danger of "looking bad" in front of superior officers discouraged middle managers from pursuing more creative crime strategies with a higher risk of failure.

Second, the organizational culture of policing is resistant to this in-depth approach to problem solving. The community-policing movement that emerged in the 1980s stressed greater police recognition of the role of the community and emphasized "decentralization" and "debureaucratization" to empower rank-and-file officers to make decisions about how to better serve the neighborhoods to which they were assigned (Mastrofski, 1998; Skolnick and Bayley, 1986). Weisburd and his colleagues (2003) suggest that the popularity and rapid diffusion of Compstat programs across larger police departments in the United States during the 1990s could be interpreted as an effort to maintain and reinforce traditional police structures rather than an attempt to truly reform American policing. The rapid rise of Compstat within police agencies did not enhance their strategic problem-solving capacity at the beat level as Compstat departments were found to be reluctant to relinquish power that would decentralize some key elements of decision making such as allowing middle managers to determine beat boundaries and staffing levels, enhancing operational flexibility, and risk going beyond the standard tool kit of police tactics and strategies (Weisburd et al., 2003). The overall effect of the spread of Compstat, whether intended or not, was to reinforce the traditional bureaucratic model of command and control.

More generally, the type of in-depth problem solving that Goldstein and other problem-oriented policing advocates have proposed seems unrealistic in the real world of policing, especially at the street level where it is often envisioned. In the real world of police organizations, community and problem-oriented police officers rarely have the latitude necessary to assess and respond to problems creatively. As William Bratton (1998: 199) observed in his assessment of community policing in New York City at the beginning of his tenure, "street-level police officers were never going to be empowered to follow through." Compstat was offered as a solution to this problem, but the ability of the rank-and-file officer to make decisions changed little as middle managers were held accountable for achieving organizational goals of successful crime control (Willis, Mastrofski, and Weisburd, 2004). Of course, decentralizing decision-making power to line-level officers does not guarantee effective problem solving. In their assessment of problem solving in Chicago, a police department well known for its efforts to decentralize their organization to facilitate community policing, Skogan and his colleagues (1999) gave a failing grade ranging from "struggling" to "woeful" for problem-solving efforts in 40 percent of the beats they studied (231). Inadequate management, poor leadership and vision, lack of training, and weak performance measures were among the operational problems identified as affecting problem solving in the poorly performing beats (Skogan et al., 1999).

Conclusion

Policing crime hot spots represents an important advance in focusing police crime prevention practice. Since crime hot spots generate a bulk of urban crime problems, it seems commonsensical to address the conditions and situations that give rise to the criminal opportunities that sustain high-activity crime places. Focusing on changing places should lead the police to do more than just arrest offenders and increase enforcement. While arresting offenders remains a central strategy of the police and a necessary component of the police response to crime hot spots, it seems likely that altering place characteristics and dynamics will produce larger and longer-term crime prevention benefits.

We believe that the problem-oriented policing approach holds great promise in developing tailored responses to very specific recurring problems at crime hot spots. While it is difficult for police agencies to implement the "ideal" version of problem-oriented policing, we believe that even "shallow" problem solving better focuses police crime prevention efforts at crime hot spots. Implementing situational prevention strategies that reduce police reliance on aggressive enforcement strategies may also yield positive benefits for police-community relations. It is well known that unfocused and indiscriminate police enforcement efforts can have highly negative consequences for police-community relationships. We discuss ways to enhance community engagement and police legitimacy when pursuing hot spots policing strategies in the next chapter.

Enhancing Police Legitimacy through Community Engagement in Problem Places

6

Commissioner Edward F. Davis engaged the Ten Point Coalition [of activist black clergy] and Black Ministerial Alliance as key partners in implementing his vision of community policing in Boston. In April 2007, neighborhood clergy and Boston police officers walked the streets together in mostly minority neighborhoods of Grove Hall in Roxbury, the Bowdoin and Geneva sections of Dorchester, and the Franklin Hill and Franklin Field housing projects in Mattapan and Dorchester. As they went from door-to-door in these neighborhoods, local ministers introduced the officers to community members and encouraged ongoing dialogue between the police and the residents. While participating in the police-clergy neighborhood walks, Davis commented, "The basis for community policing is relationships. This isn't rocket science." The cornerstone of Davis' community policing efforts is known as the Safe Street Team initiative. Teams of officers are permanently assigned to gun violence hot spot areas, required to walk their beats, form working relationships with local businessmen and residents, and engage problem-oriented policing techniques in reducing violence.

At face value, these approaches seem to be generating some noteworthy violence prevention gains. According to FBI Uniform Crime Reports statistics recently released by the Boston Police, homicides declined nearly 11% and shootings fell more than 14% in 2007 when compared to 2006 figures.

—Braga, Hureau, and Winship, 2008: 170–71

The lessons learned from the community-policing movement of the 1980s and 1990s offer many important insights for the proper implementation of hot spots policing initiatives. We believe that these lessons suggest that police departments should move away from simple enforcement-based approaches to controlling crime hot spots and toward more collaborative, community problem-solving approaches to address crime hot spots. If the community is engaged appropriately, we believe that hot spots policing programs can enhance the legitimacy of the police in the eyes of the people they seek to protect and serve. In general, broad-based community policing initiatives have been found to reduce fear of crime and improve the relationships between the police and the communities they serve (Skogan and Frydl, 2004; Weisburd and Eck, 2004). Community-policing strategies that entail direct involvement of citizens and police, such as police community stations, citizen-contract patrol, and coordinated community policing, have been found to reduce fear of crime among residents and decrease individual concern about crime in neighborhoods (Brown and Wycoff, 1987; Pate and Skogan, 1985; Wycoff and Skogan, 1986).

In contrast to the methodologically rigorous evaluation research on the crime-control efficacy of hot spots policing presented in chapter 4, the research evidence on community perceptions of appropriate police behavior, procedural fairness and police legitimacy, and related topics presented here is still developing and, as such, not as scientifically strong. However, few observers of American policing would disagree with the statement that police-minority relations remain stressed by ongoing issues involving unwarranted stops, verbal abuse, brutality, and police corruption. As such, we feel that it is important to develop a *normative* dimension to our discussion of hot spots policing practices. It seems likely that overly aggressive and indiscriminant police crackdowns would produce some undesirable effects, such as increased resentment and fear of police, in targeted hot spot areas. The potential for negative effects needs to be drawn into our broader analysis of hot spots policing initiatives precisely because community reactions to police practices have normative significance to wider society. Indeed, the National Research

Council's Committee to Review Research on Police Policy and Practices concluded that police practices need to be evaluated in terms of their impact on the legitimacy of the police as well as their crime-control effectiveness (Skogan and Frydl, 2004).

The available research evidence suggests that community policing has the potential to enhance police legitimacy. Citizen support and cooperation is closely linked to judgments about the legitimacy of the police (Tyler, 2004). When citizens view the police as legitimate legal authorities, they are more likely to cooperate and obey the law (Tyler, 1990). Public judgments about the legitimacy of the police are influenced by their assessments of the manner in which the police exercise their authority (Tyler, 1990, 2004). The police generally obey the laws that limit their power (Skogan and Meares, 2004). However, minorities consistently express significantly lower confidence in the police when compared to whites (Tyler, 2004). Weitzer and Tuch (2006) suggest that neighborhood conditions, citizens' experiences with the police, and the media have created differences between white Americans and African Americans, Hispanics, and other minorities in their attitudes toward the police. Community policing has been a strategic innovation that has helped bridge the police "confidence gap" in minority communities. The available research evidence suggests that the approach improves citizens' judgments of police actions (Skogan, 2006). For example, over an eight-year period of community policing, Chicago residents' views of their police improved on measures of their effectiveness, responsiveness and-demeanor (Skogan and Steiner, 2004). Importantly, these improvements were shared among whites, African Americans and, to a lesser extent, Latinos (Skogan and Steiner, 2004).

While there is systematic research on the effects of community policing on citizen satisfaction with the police, there is a surprising lack of research assessing the effects of other police innovations on police-community relations. This is noteworthy for hot spots policing initiatives as many observers suggest a tension between the crime prevention effectiveness of focused police efforts and their potential harmful effects on police-community relations (Meares, 2006; Rosenbaum, 2006; Taylor,

2006; Weisburd and Braga, 2006). Legitimacy is linked to the ability of the police to prevent crime and keep neighborhoods safe. If the public's trust and confidence in the police is undermined, the ability of the police to prevent crime will be weakened by lawsuits, declining willingness to obey the law, and withdrawal from existing partnerships (Tyler, 1990, 2004). The political fallout from illegitimate police actions can seriously impede the ability of police departments to engage innovative crime-control tactics.

While residents in neighborhoods suffering from high levels of crime often demand higher levels of enforcement, they still want the police to be respectful and lawful in their crime control efforts (Skogan and Meares, 2004; Tyler, 2004). Residents do not want family members, friends, and neighbors to be targeted unfairly by enforcement efforts or treated poorly by overaggressive police officers. It is important to recognize that legitimate policing is not limited to the fair and respectful treatment of "good" community members. All too often community policing is defined in overly simplistic "good citizen" and "bad criminal" terms. Given high crime, arrest, and incarceration rates in certain neighborhoods, the police will routinely encounter community members who are, or have family or friends who are, former, current, and future offenders. As such, police officers should behave in a fair and respectful manner in all citizen contacts.

This chapter examines potential harmful effects of the concentration of police resources in specific hot spots that could lead citizens to question the fairness of these practices. Complaints about excessive force and police corruption are not uncommon in high-crime neighborhoods where police are sometimes viewed as an "occupying force" (Rosenbaum, 2006). We believe that police executives seeking to engage effective police crime prevention practices need to consider community perceptions of the "fairness" of the content of hot spots policing strategies and the behavior of the officers who are implementing them. Unfortunately, police-effectiveness studies have traditionally overlooked the effects of police practices upon citizen perceptions of police legitimacy (Tyler, 2000; 2001). Based on the available research evidence, we review the potential for problematic police practices in hot spots policing strategies and then discuss the key elements of community and problem-oriented policing programs that can be incorporated into hot spots programs to improve citizen support and cooperation.

Police Legitimacy and Focused Enforcement Efforts

As described in chapter 5, regardless of the approach employed, hot spots policing efforts have been found to generate crime prevention gains (Braga, 2001, 2005). Unfortunately, too little attention has been paid to the potential harmful effects of focused police action in hot spot areas. The concentration of police enforcement in specific hot spots could lead citizens to question the fairness of police practices. There is some evidence that residents of areas that are subject to focused police attention welcome the concentration of police efforts in problem places (McGarrell et al., 2001; Shaw, 1995). A separate examination of the Kansas City gun project (Sherman and Rogan, 1995a) found that the community strongly supported the intensive patrols and perceived an improvement in the quality of life in the treatment neighborhood (Shaw, 1995). The study did not, however, attempt to measure how the individuals who were stopped and searched by the police felt about the program.

Nonetheless, focused aggressive police-enforcement strategies have been criticized as resulting in increased citizen complaints about police misconduct and abuse of force in New York City (Greene, 1999). Order maintenance and "quality of life" policing strategies that seek to prevent more serious crimes by arresting offenders for minor crimes, such as public drinking and smoking marijuana in plain view, have been criticized as exacerbating already poor relationships between the police and minority communities (Golub, Johnson, and Dunlap, 2007; Harcourt and Ludwig, 2007). A recent examination of broken windows policing in high-activity crime places in Jersey City found that, while the approach reduced disorder and led to decreased citizen fear, aggressive street-level crackdowns on disorderly behavior were associated with increased citizen fear (Hinkle and Weisburd, 2008). While the study did not have data to explain why fear increased with increased police activity, Hinkle and Weisburd (2008) suggested that the explanation was direct and easy to understand. Walking on the street and observing police may make individuals feel safer, but if residents notice much greater police attention on the street block where they live, they are certain to be reminded of the problems that exist on their street. Additionally, seeing a sudden increase in police presence on their block may lead residents to infer that crime has increased and that their block is more dangerous and crime prone than in the past (Hinkle and Weisburd, 2008).

In a review of the benefits and consequences of police crackdowns, Scott (2004b) suggests that such tactics often heighten fear among offenders and residents. These findingspoint to the importance of "how" broken windows policing programs are implemented. Such programs must be geared not only to reduce disorder, but also to prevent increases in citizen fear that may accompany crackdowns and other intensive enforcement efforts associated with broken windows policing. Hinkle and Weisburd (2008) argue that the police must communicate with citizens and explain their actions. In essence, they need to gain legitimacy in the areas where they police.

Research also suggests that residents of many high-crime areas are very ambivalent about aggressive enforcement. Survey research suggests that many residents are willing to give up their civil liberties to achieve an enhanced sense of security (Rosenbaum, 1993). It is unclear, however, how long residents living in high-crime areas will tolerate aggressive enforcement actions.

> Residents will insist on aggressive enforcement up to the point
> where it directly affects them, their family, or their friends,
> who frequently end up in jail and prison or report being
> mistreated by the police. How much of this policing they will
> tolerate remains to be seen. Like other Americans, however,
> hot spots residents should have the opportunity to experience
> both safety and liberty and not be required to choose one or
> the other. This topic demands much more careful policy
> deliberation and research. (Rosenbaum, 2006: 254)

In his critical essay on limits of hot spots policing, Dennis Rosenbaum (2006) suggests that hot spots policing, because it has been operationally defined as aggressive enforcement in specific areas, runs the risk of weakening police-community relations. Rosenbaum (2006) argues that hot spots policing can easily become "zero tolerance" policing because this approach is easy for the police to adopt. Indiscriminate aggressive tactics can drive a wedge between the police and communities, as the latter can begin to feel like targets rather than partners.

> Because the police have chosen to focus on removing the "bad element" and serving as the "thin blue line" between "good" and "bad" residents, these strategies can pit one segment of the community against another, as the "good" residents are asked to serve as the informants and the "eyes and ears" of the police. Parents, siblings, and friends of gang members can feel a divided loyalty and be caught in the crossfire. (Rosenbaum, 2006: 253)

Policing strategies and tactics, unfortunately, vary by race and social class. Crime hot spots, illicit drug activity, and violent crime tend to cluster in low-income, minority neighborhoods. The pressure on the police to keep crime rates low is usually greatest in these hot spot areas and, therefore, these places receive increased police enforcement attention (Rosenbaum, 2006). Given the growing popularity of broken windows policing approaches to controlling urban crime problems (Kelling and Coles, 1996), low-income, minority residents often face increased levels of police-initiated contacts for minor offenses (such as loitering and public drinking) and traffic enforcement activities to reduce more serious crimes by searching for guns, drugs, and persons with outstanding warrants. Regrettably, the "hit rate" for these increased police-citizen contacts can be extremely low and the majority of persons who are inconvenienced (and sometimes offended) by these stops are innocent, low-income minority residents (Rosenbaum, 2006). Many of these citizens already tend to feel disenfranchised from government and do not have easy access to legal remedies when they feel mistreated or their civil liberties are being jeopardized.

Rosenbaum (2006) also raises the question of whether sustained enforcement efforts in minority communities will contribute to disproportionate minority confinement. Over the last two decades, the United States has imprisoned Americans at higher and higher rates. Spending on prisons has increased at more than double the rate of spending on education and health care (Hughes, 2006). The moral cost is that fully 2.3 million Americans every day are in prisons or jails (Sabol, Couture, and Harrison, 2007), institutions that are often dehumanizing and degrading. The disproportionate number of minority men affected by the unprecedented boom in U.S. incarceration rates between 1980 and 2000 has been well documented (e.g., Blumstein, 2002; Tonry, 1995). To many observers (Clear, 2007; Petersilia, 2003; Travis, 2005; Western, 2006), the large-scale cycle of arrest, removal, and return has damaged the familial and community relationships that hold neighborhoods together and worsened the prospects for employment, income, marriage, and responsible parenting for African American men, in particular.

Enforcement-oriented hot spots policing initiatives plausibly could generate negative effects on the rest of the criminal justice system. A recent evaluation of the adverse system side effects of Operation Sunrise, a widely publicized, geographically targeted drug enforcement strategy in Philadelphia, found that initiative strained the local judicial system by generated a high volume of arrests that resulted in a significant increase in fugitive defendants (Goldkamp and Vilcica, 2008). Short-term crime gains produced by particular types of hot spots policing initiatives could undermine the long-term stability of specific neighborhoods through the increased involvement of mostly low-income minority men in the criminal justice system.

Legal and Ethical Concerns

Police abuse and misconduct are also concentrated in neighborhoods with structural disadvantage, population mobility, minority residents, and other community factors (Kane, 2002). Rosenbaum (2006) observes that hot spots policing runs some risk of becoming abusive and/or corrupt policing in these high-crime neighborhoods. He suggests that, when officers feel the pressure to make arrests, seize drugs, and seize guns, some will be inclined to cut corners and, as a result, every officer's credibility will be compromised. According to a twenty-year prosecutor, "winking at questionable stops and arrests may serve to get major waves of contraband off the street for a while but it eventually begins to draw the ire of the judiciary and threatens the credibility of both the police and that of the prosecuting authorities" (Rosenbaum, 2006: 254). If not designed and managed properly, hot spots policing initiatives have the potential to exacerbate poor relations between the police and minority communities.

Police often complain that their hands are tied in doing something about criminals. While the extent of legal constraints on policing are the source of much debate (Bittner, 1967; Ohlin and Remington, 1993; Skogan and Frydl, 2004; Vollmer, 1933; Wickersham Commission, 1931; Wilson, 1950), it is clear that hot spots policing offers a target for police interventions that is less protected by traditional legal guarantees. The common law and our legal traditions have placed less concern over the rights of places than the rights of individuals. It is not that police can do what they like at places. Rather, the extent of constitutional and procedural guarantees has at times been relaxed where places are targeted.

When it is established that places are crime targets or deserve special protection, it becomes easier to legally justify enforcement in regard to individual offenders. For example, Dan Kahan and Tracey Meares (1998: 1172) note that law enforcement officials "needn't obtain a warrant or even have probable cause...to stop motorists at sobriety checkpoints or to search all individuals entering airports or government buildings." This means that at certain places, where issues of public safety are a central concern, it is possible to justify policing activities that would be unacceptable if carried out against individuals in other places. Places where crime is concentrated are often seen to meet this criterion, as is the case in many cities that have designated drug-market areas for special attention. Safe-school zones are another example of the identification of places that allow special activities by the police, in this case because of the vulnerability of potential victims.

The constitutional issues here are complex and do not simply justify intrusion in every case. Nonetheless, politicians, judges, and, indeed, ordinary citizens have an intuition that police should be allowed appropriate discretion to police certain places that exhibit specific problems, such as concentrated crime, when there is the support of residents. Hot spots policing, accordingly, provides a target for police that may lead to fewer legal constraints in terms of the development of crime prevention strategies.

The Need for Legitimate Police Crime Prevention Strategies

Policing minority communities always involves a delicate balance (Tyler, 2004). On the one hand, research suggests that the police benefit from the general willingness of members of a minority community to cooperate with them to report crimes, identify criminals, assist in investigations, and address conditions that might facilitate crime (Tyler et al., 2007). On the other hand, effective policing invariably involves tactics that bring the police into close and regular contact with community residents, contact that is often viewed by community residents as intrusive and unwarranted, leading minority citizens to doubt whether the police respect their rights and care about their well being (Tyler et al., 2007). Whether or not individuals have personal contact with police officers, their perceptions of the legitimacy of police have important consequences for police effectiveness (Skogan and Frydl, 2004; Tyler, 2004). Policing is far more difficult without the support of the public. Therefore, police effectiveness is powerfully influenced by the consequences of different tactical and policy choices for their legitimacy (Skogan and Frydl, 2004; Tyler, 2004).

In this discussion, we refer frequently to the idea of legitimacy as developed by New York University psychology professor Tom Tyler and his colleagues (see, e.g., Fagan and Tyler, 2005; Sunshine and Tyler, 2003; Tyler, 1990, 2004, 2006; Tyler et al., 2007; Tyler and Huo, 2002; Tyler and

Wakslak, 2004). In this body of work, legitimacy is regarded as a view among the members of the communities involved that legal authorities play an appropriate role in making and implementing rules governing public conduct. Obviously, legal authorities can shape public behavior by virtue of their ability to use force and communicate the risk of sanctioning for noncompliance. However, in democratic societies the authorities rely heavily upon public willingness to voluntarily defer because they view the conduct of the police and courts as reasonable and just. These ethical qualities distinguish legitimacy from coercion, and they reflect the idea that authorities have trust and confidence among the public; in other words, the view that people consider agents of social control to be acting on behalf of the community and exercising their authority in accord with principles of reasonable and appropriate conduct (Tyler et al., 2007). Such feelings create legitimacy—the view that authorities ought to be deferred to and obeyed. It is such legitimacy, in turn, that leads to public cooperation with the police, cooperation that is central to their ability to manage crime and social disorder within diverse communities.

In fact, recent studies suggest that the law and legal authorities currently lack general legitimacy among the American population. Public-opinion polls suggest that people are increasingly likely to say that they lack trust and confidence in the American justice system (Tyler, 1998). For example, fewer than one in four people express "quite a lot" of confidence in the criminal justice system, and more than one in three have "very little" confidence (U.S. Bureau of Justice Statistics, 1998). The same study also showed that more than two thirds of the public has only "some" or "very little" confidence in the courts. The highest levels of confidence are expressed in the police, but a majority of the public still indicates lacking confidence in the police (Tyler et al., 2007).

There is a longstanding racial divide in public confidence in the police and the courts (Skogan and Frydl, 2004; Bobo and Johnson, 2004; Weitzer and Tuch, 2006). For over four decades, minority group members have expressed far lower levels of confidence in the justice system and in legal authorities compared to whites (Garofalo, 1977; Hindelang,

1974; Huang and Vaughn, 1996; Schumann et al., 1997). In this regard, it is important to note as well that minority police also express less confidence than white police officers that the police will deal impartially with minorities (Weisburd, Greenspan, et al., 2001). One group of researchers notes that:

> ... [c]oncern about police behavior toward racial minorities is
> an enduring feature of 20th century American politics and
> public policy. Hardly a week goes by without a newspaper or
> television account of an incident where police officers are
> alleged to have treated a person who is in a minority group
> badly, with the subtext that the person's race accounted for the
> mistreatment. (Mastrofski et al., 1998: 1)

Minority group concerns are varied and include racial profiling (Cole, 1999; Kennedy, 1997; Harris, 1999; Hagan, Shedd, and Payne, 2005), the excessive use of force (Locke, 1995; Skolnick and Fyfe, 1993; Worden, 1995), the perceived gap in the willingness of legal authorities to protect the minority community (Kennedy, 1997), and the degree to which people should be detained for minor crimes (Kelling and Coles, 1996; Wilson and Kelling, 1982).

A growing body of research suggests that self-regulatory social-control approaches that rely upon the encouragement of deference-based legitimacy are often more effective than is sanction-based compliance (Tyler, 2004, 2006; Tyler and Fagan, 2008). Rule following, especially in the long-term, depends upon creating and maintaining legitimacy and that legitimacy matters during particular personal experiences with legal authorities. When dealing with people, police officers focus not only upon displays of force, but upon establishing their "legitimate right to intervene" in a particular situation (Reiss, 1971: 46). When legitimacy is higher, people are more likely to voluntarily defer to the police (Tyler and Huo, 2002). When legitimacy is low, officers are more likely to have to use physical force introducing "the risk of injury to both the arrested person and the officer" (Reiss, 1971: 60). Interestingly, Reiss (1971) finds that 73 percent of injuries to officers occur when the officers are interfered with, and interference most typically comes from people other than the parties involved in the immediate situation—from bystanders or family members. "When such persons question the legitimacy of police intervention and a police officer reacts to control their behavior, more serious conflict may ensue as each party attempts to gain control of the situation. This results more often in injury to the officer" (Reiss, 1971: 60).

The importance of gaining active cooperation from the public in the effort to fight crime and disorder has also become more central to discussions of law and policing (Tyler et al., 2007). Research suggests that the police have difficulty maintaining social order and managing crime without the active cooperation of people within the affected communities (Sampson and Bartusch, 1998; Sampson, Raudenbush, and Earls, 1997). This includes people acting as individuals, people who report crime, who work in neighborhood groups, and who attend neighborhood meetings.

Police Behavior and Legitimacy

It is obviously important to understand the factors that shape police legitimacy. One central focus of past research has been upon the strategies used by the police to manage crime (see, for example, Braga, 2008). However, studies consistently suggest that public views about the police and the law are not simple reflections of the crime rate (Meares, 2004; Tyler, 2004). Recent discussions of policing acknowledge the important role that policing strategies have in shaping crime, but argue that attention needs to be given to a larger framework within which the influence of police actions on police legitimacy in the eyes of the public is also studied (Skogan and Frydl, 2004). Such concerns have fueled a series of reforms in the manner in which legal authorities act, including community policing and neighborhood courts (Fagan and Malkin, 2003).

Research suggests that the public evaluates police not only in terms of the ability of the police to fight crime (Moore, 2002; Moore and Braga, 2003). People are also sensitive to the manner through which the police exercise their authority. As a consequence, the procedural justice of police actions is central to police legitimacy and policies such as racial profiling which are not evaluated to be just undermine police legitimacy (Fagan, 2002; Tyler and Wakslak, 2004). The issue of police behavior is very important in shaping the views of the public. Studies in the United States emphasize that both whites and minority group members focus on the manner in which the police exercise their authority both when making general evaluations of the legitimacy of the police (Sunshine and Tyler, 2003) and when reacting to personal experiences with the police (Tyler and Huo, 2002).

The procedural justice literature provides a related set of findings that suggests that situational clues and framing effects may be important in affecting a person's evaluation of a situation. Previous research on a variety of law enforcement issues establishes that legal institutions gain and preserve legitimacy through adherence to procedural fairness norms (Tyler, 2003, 2004, 2005). That is, judgments about the fairness of the manner in which these actors exercise their authority influence evaluations of legitimacy of the police and other legal actors in critically important ways. Such procedural justice judgments are found to both shape reactions to personal experiences with legal authorities (Paternoster et al., 1997; Tyler, 1990; Tyler and Huo, 2002) and to be important in assessments based upon the general activities of the police (Tyler, 1990; Sunshine and Tyler, 2003; Tyler and Fagan, 2008). In both instances, citizens view the police and courts as less legitimate when they personally experience or vicariously become aware of instances of unfair, disrespectful, or unethical treatment—in other words, procedural injustice (Tyler et al., 2007). Accordingly, experiences with the law and legal actors will shape attributions of the legitimacy of those actors and the institutions they represent.

There are many examples that illustrate this dynamic. For instance, respectful and polite treatment by police reduces perceptions of racial profiling (Tyler and Wakslak, 2004), and such treatment combined with officer efforts to explain the reasons for their actions translates into feelings of citizen satisfaction with police more generally (Skogan and

Harnett, 1997; Tyler and Huo, 2002). These legitimacy gains, in turn, translate into higher levels of respect for law andcooperation with law enforcement efforts. A large social science literature now examines these relationships and corroborates these findings in numerous distinct contexts (Tyler, 2003; Tyler et al., 1997). Conversely, the lack of just legal and political procedures is found to motivate collective actions, such as riots, and to encourage people to become committed to crimes and even to extreme acts of terrorism (Krueger and Maleckova, 2003; McCauley, 2002).

In summary, studies of personal encounters with the police consistently document that post-experience feelings are determined by the fairness in which the problem was handled (Tyler, 2001). The National Research Council's Committee to Review Police Policy and Practices identifies four dimensions of fairness in police-citizen interactions (Skogan and Frydl, 2004). First, the citizens need to have meaningful participation in interactions. Importantly, citizens must have the ability to explain situations and communicate with the police. Second, citizens need to feel that the police officers were neutral in their assessments of situations by using objective indicators to make decisions rather than personal views. Third, citizens must feel that they were treated with respect and dignity by the police during interactions. Fourth, police officers need to inspire trust in the citizenry. If people believe authorities care about their well-being and are considerate of their needs and concerns, they view procedures as fairer. Police can encourage the public to view them as trustworthy by explaining their decisions and accounting for their conduct.

Regardless of the specific approach employed or tactics engaged, hot spots policing will generate an increased amount of police-citizen contacts in very small areas. Police behavior in these areas will greatly influence the amount of support and involvement from community members residing in crime hot spot areas. To maximize their ability to manage crime problems in these places, police managers should strive to ensure fair police-citizen interactions and the development of strong partnerships with community members. While the work is difficult, long-term community engagement efforts can pay large dividends in improving the quality of police-community relationships and collaborative crime prevention efforts.

The Importance of Community Policing in Addressing Problem Places

Community-based efforts to prevent crime require simultaneous investments in the physical and social infrastructure of local neighborhoods (Bursik and Grasmick, 1993; Sampson and Lauritsen, 1994). Given the nature of American society, most of these investments will probably have to come from the neighborhoods themselves—that is, residents must come together and join forces with the criminal justice system to establish and maintain social order (Sampson, 2002). Community-based crime prevention efforts rely upon a vision of community based on shared values for a safe and healthy environment (Kahan and Meares, 1998; Sampson, 1999; Sampson, Raudenbush, and Earls, 1997). Divisive policies that separate residents and institutions by race and class work against a community-based approach (Sampson, 2002). Police departments obviously play an important role in community-based crime prevention and need to engage strategies that bring them closer to the community and its values.

When dealing with crime problems in hot spot locations, police departments should adopt what Ralph Taylor (2001, 2006) calls a "community co-production model" rather than drift toward overly aggressive arrest-based strategies. Dealing with social and physical disorder is rooted in a tradition of stable relationships with the community and responsiveness to local concerns (Taylor, 2006). Community co-production requires the police to build partnerships with other organizations and the community, which brings its own set of challenges (Crawford, 1997; Rosenbaum, 2002). Nonetheless, a sole commitment to increasing arrests is not the most powerful approach to community crime prevention and, according to many observers (e.g., Taylor, 2006), and may undermine relationships in low-income, urban minority com-

CRIME

munities where co-production is most needed and distrust between the police and citizens is most profound.

As described earlier in this chapter, inappropriate applications of hot spots policing initiatives seem very likely to generate negative police-community relations and, in the long run, will undermine the ability of the police to manage problem places in high-crime neighborhoods. We believe that police department should strive to engage a community co-production model when developing and implementing hot spots policing programs. Ideally, police departments should have a solid commitment to the community-policing philosophy before experimentation with more aggressive hot spots policing initiatives.

Community policing is not a specific set of programs; communities with different problems and varied resources to bring to bear against them will implement different strategies (Skogan, 2006). However, as an organizational strategy, the community-policing *process* leaves setting priorities and the means of achieving them largely to residents and the police that serve in the neighborhood. We believe that a strategic focus on crime hot spots has the potential to improve the crime-and-disorder reduction goals of community policing initiatives and can help the police develop relationships with community members residing in areas that need them the most. The three core, and densely interrelated, elements of community policing are citizen involvement, decentralization, and problem solving (Skogan, 2006). In this section, we consider each of these elements in the context of hot spots policing programs.

Citizen Involvement

Order within communities is an important outcome of informal social processes beyond formal social-control activities such as policing (see Bursik and Grasmick, 1993; Sampson, 2002); thus, it is important to stimulate community involvement in hot spots policing initiatives. Among other benefits, citizen participation can improve police-community relations, increase the legitimacy of police operations, reduce fear, and decrease crime and disorder (Eck and Rosenbaum, 1994). More indirectly, community involvement can help rebuild the social and organizational fabric of neighborhoods that previously been given up for lost, enabling residents to contribute to maintaining order in their community (Sampson, Raudenbush and Earls, 1997; Skogan, 2006). Moreover, residents involved in crime prevention efforts can increase the level of guardianship in communities (Cohen and Felson, 1979), discourage crime by properly managing places (Felson, 1995), and maintain conditions and crime-control gains once the police have ceased or reduced their actions in the hot spot area.

Community-policing initiatives require that the police form partnerships with citizens and community-based organizations to set priorities and develop crime prevention tactics. While listening to community concerns will generate a wider range of problems that need to be dealt with, the concentration of crime and disorder problems at particular problem places in larger neighborhood environments will naturally be part of the discussion. The identification of crime and disorder hot spot locations can be a collaborative process that adds to the legitimacy of the hot spots policing initiative. In meetings with residents, officers can bring crime maps as points of discussion for the development of community crime prevention plans and, in consultation with community members, identify specific hot spot locations and collaborate on crime prevention plans to address these places. Dealing with hot spot locations in a collaborative and transparent way has great potential to improve police-community relations and enhance overall police legitimacy.

It is important to engage the community throughout the process of developing, implementing, and assessing the effectiveness of police crime prevention plans. The Kansas City Gun Project (Sherman and Rogan, 1995a) and its replication in Indianapolis (McGarrell et al., 2001) examined the gun violence–prevention effects of proactive patrol and intensive enforcement of firearms laws in targeted areas via safety frisks during traffic stops, plain view searches and seizures, and searches incident to arrests on other charges. Aggressive enforcement efforts, such as this approach, have the potential to generate negative public opinion of police action. Indeed, some observers question the fairness and intrusiveness of aggressive law enforcement approaches and caution that street searches, especially of young men and minorities, look like police harassment (Moore, 1980; Kleck, 1991). The police managers involved in these projects secured community support before and during the interventions through a series of meetings with community members. The police departments also stressed to their officers that they needed to treat citizens with respect and explain the reasons for the stop. Effective police management (leadership, supervision, and maintaining positive relationships with the community) seems to be the crucial factor in securing community support for aggressive, but respectful, policing (Davis and Mateu-Gelabert, 1999; McGarrell et al., 2001).

Despite its acknowledged importance, community involvement remains a problem area in the development of police crime prevention programs. True police-community partnerships are scarce and there are numerous problems in stimulating community involvement (see, e.g., Grinc, 1994; Rosenbaum, 1994; Buerger, 1994; Weisburd and McElroy, 1988). Experience has revealed that it is very difficult to get citizens involved in police-community crime prevention efforts. This is especially true in disadvantaged neighborhoods that could benefit the most from such partnerships. Sadd and Grinc (1994) suggest that a lack of community involvement in poorer neighborhoods arises from generations of residents that have faced the brunt of police abuse and past experiences with seemingly endless government programs designed to improve the quality of their lives. Thus, in their examination of the Community Patrol Officer Program in New York City, Weisburd and McElroy (1988) noted that community police officers were often confronted with settings of severe social disorganization, and that such disorganization was not easily transformed into the kind of community organization envisioned by the community problem-solving philosophy.

In the Jersey City Problem-Oriented Policing in Violent Places experiment, problem-solving officers experienced much difficulty in engaging residents and business owners in the crime hot spots. Persistent presence in the crime hot spot and constant outreach to community members were necessary to thaw the initial cold reception experienced by the problem-solving officers. In his qualitative process evaluation, Braga (1997) described the community, with the exception of a few interested individuals at most places, as generally apathetic. High levels of distrust, suspicion, and even fear, of the police characterized interactions at these particular locations. The Jersey City problem-solving officers expressed frustration over the reluctance of these community members to "improve their own neighborhoods" (Braga, 1997: 167). Certain officers believed that a preponderance of criminals lived at the places, therefore their apathy was viewed as rational. Either the residents were involved in criminal activity and did not want to assist the police, or they were fearful of reprisals from their neighbors.

The Jersey City problem-solving officers tried to overcome the lack of enthusiasm and communication by attending block meetings and talking to residents during their regular patrols. The situation improved slightly over the course of the experiment (Braga, 1997). The officers believed that their constant presence, noticeable reductions in disorder, and efforts to open lines of communication caused some residents to trust specific officers (those responsible for the particular place) and to believe that this program was not an effort that would "just disappear" like past police initiatives. Throughout the intervention period, the officers encouraged the neighborhood residents to share information with the police concerning illicit behaviors in the neighborhood and to participate in police efforts to reclaim the neighborhood from drug sellers (Braga, 1997). After many appearances at the place, the officers made progress in gaining the trust of the residents. At the beginning of the program, the residents spoke about problems in vague terms to the officers; for example, they offered benign information such as "there are drug sellers on the corner." Once key drug sellers were arrested and physical changes occurred, the residents provided the officers with very specific and enlightening information, such as "John Doe stashes his drugs in the hubcap of the blue station wagon parked on the corner." (Braga, 1997: 210).

While the involvement of community members increased over the course of the experiment, police-community relations in the violent-crime hot spots were complex and sometimes quite fragile. David Bayley (1988), in his critical review of community policing, anticipated that close relations with the community could "undermine the determination of the police to take strong enforcement action when it is needed" (227). The Jersey City problem-solving officers sometimes felt pressured by cooperative community members to overlook obvious violations and crimes to maintain good relations (Braga, 1997). For instance, at one hot spot location, the officers set up routine surveillances of the drinking and drug activity in front of a troublesome apartment building and made arrests when appropriate. The community members in the hot spot area were very supportive of arrests of people they did not know, but became upset when someone they knew was apprehended. The assistant resident manager of the building had been very helpful giving the officers information on illicit activity and rallying the support of the residents, but she tried to use this relationship to her own advantage. When the officers arrested her friend in front of the building on narcotics-possession charges, the assistant manager pressured them to release him because "he's a good guy, not part of the problem." Nonetheless, the officers arrested him because it was their job; the assistant manager became very upset and the action alienated her and other residents who provided very good information. These situations were not common, but made the officers very uncomfortable. This issue was viewed as highly counterproductive to working with the community in particular, and problem solving in general (Braga, 1997).

It is important for police to recognize that relationships with the community are dynamic and can evolve over time as issues arise and new residents and businesses move in and out of places. Nonetheless, sustained community-engagement efforts can generate positive effects over the long term. Wesley Skogan (2006), however, reported some encouraging findings from a thirteen-year study of community policing in Chicago. After community policing was implemented in 1993, crime and fear dropped in the city's predominately African American neighborhoods. Skogan (2006) also found that residents in black-majority communities were very enthusiastic about community policing and turned out in large numbers for beat meetings, neighborhood problem-solving projects, and supportive rallies. Unfortunately, by most measures, things grew worse for the city's growing Latino population. Long-time Latino residents in racially integrated neighborhoods did well, but newer Latino residents of predominately Spanish-speaking neighborhoods experienced higher levels of crime and disorder problems (Skogan, 2006). Very few residents of Latino-majority communities participated in beat meetings and other community problem-solving initiatives. Clearly additional outreach by the Chicago police was needed to engage this newer population of citizens.

In many police crime prevention projects, community members serve as an information source rather than as "partners" or "co-producers" of public safety (see, e.g., Capowich and Roehl, 1994; Sadd and Grinc, 1994; Braga, 1997). Buerger (1994: 271) suggests that the "police establishment assigns to the community a role that simply enhances the police response to crime and disorder." Often, officers gain extra sets of "eyes and ears" on illegal street activities, while the officers' authority and sovereignty over service provision remain essentially unchanged from their traditional role in police-citizen transactions (Braga, 1997).

Research, however, suggests that many citizens are comfortable in these passive roles. For example, the evaluators of the eight city Innovative Neighborhood Oriented Policing (INOP) programs collected data that strongly suggest that community members did not want to become involved in community problem-solving efforts (Sadd and Grinc, 1994). Across all eight INOP cities, the most frequently reported explanation for a lack of citizen involvement in community-policing efforts was fear of retaliation from local drug dealers and gang members. Similarly, at three violent-crime hot spots in the Jersey City Problem-Oriented Policing in Violent Places experiment, community members who were perceived by local drug sellers and illicit loiterers as too cooperative with the police had multiple threats made on their lives (Braga, 1997). One particularly disturbing example is described here.

Although residents appreciated the improvements, the illicit users of the place were not pleased and they showed their disapproval by trying to intimidate the resident manager. At the end of February, the resident manager was threatened by an unidentified male (presumed to be involved with the apartment that held drug parties) that "we will kill you if you call the cops on us again." On June 13, two bullets were fired through the window of the manager's office. Luckily, the attack was at night when he was not present. (Braga, 1997: 471)

Sometimes, it is simply too risky for community members to participate actively in partnerships with the police in very violent places. After community members were not publicly responsive to his requests for assistance, a Jersey City problem-solving officer was not discouraged and tried a different approach. As Braga (1997: 493) describes, the officer reasoned, "these people won't talk to me now because there are too many knuckle heads (disorderly youths and drug sellers) watching my conversations.... I can't say I blame them, they need to live here." He then slipped his business card into some residents' mailboxes so they could contact him at their own convenience (during safer times). After receiving the business card, one resident did call the Jersey City officer and privately met with him on a regular basis in a coffee shop some distance away from his home (Braga, 1997). The resident routinely shared information with the officer on the criminal dynamics of the place and key criminal operators in the area. These conversations greatly enriched the officer's plans to address the problems in the violent crime hot spot. As "information sources" rather than "partners," citizens seem to reap the benefits of having a mechanism to address their concerns without changing their routine activities. In other words, they are able to go about their daily business without additional tasks or suffering the repercussions of being perceived as a community activist or working with the police.

In practice, police officers tackling particular problem places should, at the very least, strive to develop the level of community involvement that facilitates the development and implementation of fair and effective responses. Sometimes, key community members will not want to participate in police efforts to control crime. In these situations, police may want to consider the use of civil remedies to induce some participation. Civil remedies are procedures and sanctions specified by civil statutes and regulations that can be used to prevent crime and disorder problems. As Green Mazerolle and Roehl (1998) describe, civil remedies generally aim to persuade or coerce non-offending third parties to take responsibility and action to prevent or end criminal or nuisance behavior. Such approaches can include using nuisance and drug-abatement statutes to require landlords and property owners to maintain drug- and nuisance-free properties through repair requirements, fines, padlocks, securing entries/exits, and property forfeiture (Green Mazerolle and Roehl, 1998).

Fortunately, community members often do want to assist the police in some capacity. For very serious crime problems that threaten the viability of a community, organized groups may be very aggressive in seeking appropriate police action. For example, the Ten Point Coalition of activist black clergy played an important role in organizing Boston communities suffering from gang violence (see Winship and Berrien, 1999; Braga and Winship, 2006). In 1992, the Ten Point Coalition formed after gang members invaded the Morningstar Baptist Church, where a slain rival gang member was being memorialized, and attacked mourners with knives and guns. In the wake of that watershed moment, the Ten Point Coalition decided to respond to violence in their community by reaching out to drug-involved and gang-involved youth and by organizing within Boston's black community. The Ten Point clergy came to work closely with the Boston Centers for Youth and Families streetworkers program to provide at-risk youth with opportunities such as summer and after-school jobs, job-skills training, educational assistance, and substance abuse counseling.

Although the Ten Point coalition was initially very critical of the Boston law enforcement community, the two groups eventually forged a strong working relationship. Ten Point clergy and others involved in this faith-based organization accompanied police officers on home visits to the families of troubled youth and also acted as advocates for youth in the criminal justice system. These home visits and street work by the clergy were later incorporated into Operation Ceasefire's portfolio of gang violence-reduction interventions (Braga et al., 2001; Kennedy, Piehl, and Braga, 1996). Ten Point clergy also provided a strong moral voice at the gang forums in the presentation of Operation Ceasefire's anti-violence message. More recently, black clergy have been key community partners in the Boston Police Department's Safe Street Team hot spots policing initiative (Braga, Hureau, and Winship, 2008).

While they were not involved in Operation Ceasefire until after the strategy had been designed and implemented, the Ten Point Coalition played a crucial role in framing a discussion that made it much easier to speak directly about the nature of youth violence in Boston. Members of the Ceasefire Working Group could speak with relative safety about the painful realities of minority male offending and victimization, "gangs," and chronic offenders. The Ten Point clergy also made it possible for Boston's minority community to have an ongoing conversation with Boston's law enforcement agencies on legitimate and illegitimate means to control crime in the community. The clergy supported Operation Ceasefire's tight focus on violent youth but condemned any indiscriminate, highly aggressive law enforcement sweeps that put nonviolent minority youth at risk of being swept into the criminal justice system. Before the Ten Point developed its role as an intermediary, Boston's black community viewed past attempts of law enforcement agencies to monitor violent youth as illegitimate. As Christopher Winship and Jenny Berrien (1999) observe, the Ten Point Coalition evolved into an institution that provides an umbrella of legitimacy for the police to implement their violence-prevention plans. With the Ten Point's approval of and involvement in Operation Ceasefire, the community supported the approach as a legitimate youth violence-prevention campaign.

In their article on the relationship between the Chicago Police Department and predominately African American churches on the West Side of Chicago, Meares and Brown Corkran (2007) noted the significance of this collaboration in building the community's capacity to resist crime, and, through the integration of key community institutions in the partnership, to complete other community-building goals and urban-renewal projects of residents. Like Boston, the initial relationship between the black community and the police was tense and characterized by mistrust. However, the ongoing connection between the police and church leaders led to noteworthy improvements in West Side residents' perceptions of the legitimacy of the local police in particular and local government in general (Meares and Brown Corkran, 2007). While churches played key roles in the Boston and Chicago experiences, other community institutions can obviously be engaged to build public trust, reduce crime, and support urban renewal.

Decentralization

A key idea in the community policing movement is to devolve authority and responsibility further down the organizational hierarchy (Kelling and Moore, 1988; Skogan, 2006; Skogan and Hartnett, 1997). The decentralization of decision making is intended to encourage the more rapid development of local responses to locally defined problems. Indeed, by 1999, a national survey of police departments found that assigning officers geographically had become the norm in cities with populations over 250,000 (U.S. Bureau of Justice Statistics, 2001). These fixed geographic areas are typically larger than places, such as beats or neighborhoods. However, a specificpolice-management focus on hot spot areas naturally places the police in close contact with residents and users of very small geographic areas that suffer from high-levels of crime and are in desperate need of additional police attention. In a community policing framework, hot spots policing can increase the interaction and communication with community members in places that most need police attention. In turn, this allows police officers to build an awareness of local problems specific to these places and enhances likelihood of the necessary citizen involvement in the development and implementation of responses.

Community policing advocates stress that more responsibility for identifying and responding to local problems should be delegated to individual patrol officers and their sergeants who have the flexibility to develop preventive strategies that deal with the wide range of problems specific to the communities they serve (Greene, 2000; Skogan, 2006; Skogan and Hartnett, 1997). As described earlier in this chapter, the key initiative in the Boston Police Department's revitalized community policing efforts is known as the Safe Street Team initiative. Teams of Boston police officers are permanently assigned to violent-crime hot spot areas and required to use foot patrol in these places, form working relationships with local businessmen and residents, and engage problem-oriented policing techniques in reducing violence (Braga, Hureau, and Winship, 2008). A sergeant and a team of six patrol officers are explicitly charged with working with local residents to identify and deal with problems that cause violence and other crime and disorder problems to cluster at these specific places. While a formal evaluation has not yet been completed, preliminary research findings suggest that the Safe Street Teams have been effective in reducing violence in the targeted hot spots and improved community perceptions of the Boston Police Department (Braga, Hureau, and Winship, 2008).

As a result of their permanent assignment to specific hot spot locations in Boston, these decentralized problem-solving teams focused on local problems have made solid inroads with communities that have long felt disconnected from the Boston Police Department. A recent newspaper story on the efforts of one Safe Street Team assigned to Codman Square in Boston's Dorchester neighborhood describes how the officers' local efforts have brought them closer to the community. As Cynthia Loesch, president of the Codman Square Neighborhood Council, discusses in the article:

> ...a group of Safe Streets officers meet weekly with the
> B.O.L.D. Teens program at Codman Square Health Center. The
> officers—who often attend meetings in civilian clothes and
> sometimes in their free time—plan recreational events, like a
> recent bowling outing to Hyde Park. Mostly, Loesch said, they
> have been able to break down barriers to trust on both sides.

"The young people are getting to know that the officers have kids and families and are normal," she said. "The officers benefit from it too. They view the neighborhood differently and I like that idea. That is true violence prevention and community policing." (Forry, 2008: 1)

Assigning specific hot spot areas to sergeants and patrol officers can also ensure that these high-activity crime places receive the attention that they deserve. In the Jersey City DMAP and Violent Places experiments, a strong treatment dosage was ensured by assigning individual responsibility to sergeants and line-level officers for dealing with very specific hot spot locations (Braga et al., 1999; Weisburd and Green, 1995). Individual assignments and routine contact with supervisors on progress made certain that the sergeants and officers were focused on controlling their places.

Problem Solving

Problem-oriented policing initiatives can proceed without a commitment to community policing (Eck and Spelman, 1987; Goldstein, 1990; Skogan, 2006). However, community-policing initiatives often use problem-oriented policing as an important process in dealing with local community concerns proactively. The best problem-solving programs encourage officers to respond creatively to the problems they encounter (Eck, 2006). The search for appropriate responses to local problems may well be "non-police" in nature and require the assistance of other municipal agencies, community-based organizations, and residents. At face value, problem-oriented policing initiatives seem well positioned to generate positive community reactions to police intervention as the approach focuses on dealing with specific crime and disorder problems that cause ongoing concern to affected community members.

As the previous chapter argues, problem-oriented policing strategies that change the criminal opportunity structure at hot spots reduce crime through prevention rather than simply arrest and prosecution. Certainly, arrests hold offenders accountable for their crimes and should remain an important tool in the police crime-control toolbox. However, arrest is not the only mechanism through which crime problems can be addressed. An over-reliance on arrests in specific places can exacerbate already strained police-community relationships.

Situational strategies that modify the underlying conditions, situations, and dynamics that cause crime to cluster at specific places can be viewed as "harm-reduction" strategies and generate positive community perceptions. In addition to ameliorating disorderly conditions that generate crime problems and reducing victimization, preventive strategies reduce the need to arrest, prosecute, and incarcerate offenders. For instance, over the course of the late 1980s and continuing into the 1990s, the law enforcement "war" on street-level crack cocaine markets were associated with the dramatic increase in the incarceration of mostly minority, low-income young men (see, e.g., Clear, 2007; Tonry, 1995; Western, 2006). Traditional drug-enforcement strategies engaged by police departments played an important role in increasing the number of African American young men who were subsequently processed in state, local, and federal criminal justice systems and faced very stiff penalties for selling crack. To many observers, the removal of these young men through arrest, prosecution, and incarceration strategies generated highly negative views of the police and criminal justice system in the eyes of many minority community members (Kennedy, 1997; Weitzer and Tuch, 2006).

In taking a problem-oriented policing approach to dealing with street-level drug markets, the attributes of a place are viewed as key factors in explaining the existence of an illicit drug market at a specific location (Braga, 2008; Weisburd and Green, 1994, 1995). By modifying the underlying conditions, dynamics, and situations that promote drug dealing in hot spots, police can disrupt local drug markets without an overreliance on routine heavy enforcement to control street-level drug sales. Situational crime prevention and problem-oriented policing suggest an approach to policing that may lead to less coercive and, in the long term, more humane crime prevention practices. In dealing with problem places, it is often necessary for police to expand their toolbox to take into account the fact that their targets are places and not people. The civil law rather than law enforcement is often the most successful method for interrupting crime at place (Green Mazerolle and Roehl, 1998). As Cheh has observed (1991: 1329), "Police and prosecutors have embraced civil strategies not only because they expand the arsenal of weaponsavailable to reach anti-social behavior, but also because officials believe that civil remedies offer speedy solutions that are unencumbered by the rigorous constitutional protections associated with criminal trials."

Whatever the reason for the shift in tactics from ones that rely on the criminal law to ones that rely on civil or administrative law, the end result is crime prevention strategies that are less reliant on traditional law enforcement practices that often lead to the arrest and imprisonment of offenders. Successful crime prevention programs at crime hot spots need not lead to high numbers of arrests, especially if strategies are implemented that discourage offenders from frequenting the area. In this sense, hot spots policing offers an approach to crime prevention that can increase public safety while decreasing the human and financial costs of imprisonment for Americans. If hot spots policing were to become the central focus of police, rather than the arrest and apprehension of offenders, we would likely see at the same time a reduction of prison populations and an increase in the crime prevention effectiveness of the police.

Finally, it is important to note that community perceptions of police departments may be de-coupled from police effectiveness in crime prevention. As discussed earlier, citizens judge the legitimacy of police departments on more than their ability to manage crime problems and hold offenders accountable for committing crimes. Even when engaging a problem-oriented policing approach to dealing with crime hot spots, police need to pay specific attention to developing positive relationships with community members in these places independent of the crime prevention strategies employed to deal with crime and disorder concerns. In the Jersey City Problem-Oriented Policing in Violent Places study, interviews with residents and business owners revealed that, despite significant reductions in crime and disorder incidents and calls, community perceptions improved in only seven of the twelve treatment hot spot areas (Braga, 1997).

The evaluation of the Lowell Police Department's Policing Crime and Disorder Hot Spots program also suggests that the problem of improving police-community relations may be need to be addressed through an additional set of actions and programs beyond the strategies implemented to control crime and disorder at the targeted places. While the main impact evaluation found that the intervention significantly reduced citizen calls for service and indicators of social disorder in the targeted hot spots (Braga and Bond, 2008), an analysis of key community-member data suggested that these crime-reduction strategies did not have the desired effects on police-community relationships (Braga and Bond, 2009). Community members noticed improvements in the level of disorder and increased police presence in the Lowell crime and disorder hot spot areas. Unfortunately, community members did not experience significant changes in the style of policing, the willingness of the police to work with citizens on problems, and the demeanor of the police. Indeed, consistent with the problem-oriented policing approach, the problem of improving police-community relations at specific places needs to be carefully analyzed and a portfolio of appropriate strategies that are logically linked to the underlying conditions and dynamics needs to be developed and implemented.

Conclusion

Much of this book is about improving police performance in preventing crime by taking a more strategic approach that better fits the nature of urban crime problems. To many, such as former NYPD Commissioner and former LAPD Chief William Bratton (1998), the most important mission and valued product of policing is obvious: it is reduced crime. Without doubt, reducing crime and criminal victimization is the single most important contribution that the police are expected to make to society's well-being. Citizens and their representatives want efficient and effective crime prevention. However, it is certainly not the only dimension of police performance and it seems self-evident that improved police performance is also, and perhaps most fundamentally, a normative and political question (Moore and Braga, 2004). When police use public authority to pursue crime-control goals, citizens become interested in how much authority was used and to what important effect, and in how justly and fairly it was deployed (Moore, 2002). Unfortunately, many individual citizens, particularly members of minority groups, hold a reasonable, experience-based belief that they are subjected to higher levels of police scrutiny and receive lower levels of police services.

The concentration of crime at specific hot spot locations within neighborhoods provides an important opportunity for police to make connections with citizens who are most vulnerable to victimization and experience fear and diminished quality of life as a result of ongoing and intense crime and disorder problems. Regrettably, these community members are often the same people who view the police with suspicion and question the legitimacy of police efforts to control crime in their neighborhoods. In this sense, residents and business owners in high-activity crime places represent "hot spots" of community dissatisfaction with and mistrust of the police. If police departments are concerned with improving their relationships with community members, the residents and business owners in hot spot locations seem like a logical place to start. Like crime, poor police-community relationships are not evenly spread throughout city environments. If the police can win the hearts and minds of long-suffering community members in hot spot areas, it seems likely to produce larger impacts on the overall legitimacy of police departments in the city than developing stronger relationships with community members in more stable neighborhoods who are more likely to already have generally positive perceptions of police services.

As in the case of understanding the effectiveness of police strategies, the potential impact of police crime prevention efforts in problem places on citizen perceptions of legitimacy may depend in good part on the types of strategies used and the context of the hot spots affected.

Unfocused and indiscriminate enforcement actions seem likely to produce poor relationships between the police and community members residing in hot spot areas. We believe that the police should adopt alternative approaches to controlling hot spots that do not rely solely on one-dimensional intensive enforcement. Of course, arresting criminal offenders is a central part of the police function and should remain an important tool in an array of responses to crime hot spots. Our summary of the available research evidence suggests situational problem-oriented policing actions that engage community members and alleviate disorderly conditions can generate both crime prevention gains and positive citizen perceptions of the police. Hot spots policing programs infused with community and problem-oriented policing principles hold great promise in improving police legitimacy in the eyes of community members living in places suffering from crime and disorder problems.

Conclusion

Improving Policing by Focusing on Problem Places

In this book, we argue that hot spots policing can be an efficient and effective way for police departments to prevent and control crime and disorder. Hot spots policing should be privileged over traditional methods of crime prevention because it is rooted in an evidence-based model of police practices, seeks to change crime places rather than criminal offenders, and for its potential to improve police legitimacy among community members. We present our summary arguments for hot spots policing below and then discuss some of operational changes necessary in American police departments to take advantage of the tremendous opportunities for crime prevention in focusing on problem places.

Engaging an Evidence-Based Model for Police Crime Prevention

Police crime prevention policy and practices are often far from objective (Sherman and Eck, 2002). Instead of being based on scientific evidence, police crime prevention efforts are sometimes driven by political ideology, anecdotal evidence, and program favorites of the month. The introduction of hot spots policing as a method of dealing with crime brings a strong scientific basis for action to policing. Scientific principles are applied in hot spots policing by engaging analytical approaches and interventions based on sound criminological theory and evidence, just as decisions made by doctors are supposed to be based on medical science (Eck, 2006; Sherman, 1998). Indeed, the hot spots policing approach could be viewed as what David Bayley calls "smarter law enforcement" (1998: 174).

At the heart of the evidence-based model is the notion that "we are all entitled to our own opinions, but not to our own facts" (Sherman, 1998: 4). Use of opinions instead of facts to guide crime prevention policy and practice has a greater chance to result in harmful or unintended negative effects or not work at all, waste scarce public resources, and divert policy attention from the real priorities of the day (McCord, 2003; Welsh and Farrington, 2000). Within an evidence-based paradigm, drawing conclusions based on facts calls attention to a number of fundamental issues such as the validity of the evidence; methods used to locate, appraise, and synthesize evidence; and implementation (Welsh, 2006). Clearly, not all evaluations are created equal and not all research reviews conduct an exhaustive search and consider the validity of study findings.

A series of rigorous evaluations of the crime prevention effectiveness of hot spots policing, detailed in chapter 4, provides a solid scientific evidence base for practitioners, policymakers, and academics to consider. Three independent reviews of evaluation research conducted for the U.S. Congress, U.S. National Research Council, and Campbell Collaboration Crime and Justice Group found hot spots policing to be effective in preventing crime (see Braga, 2001, 2005; Sherman, 1997; Sherman and Eck, 2002; Skogan and Frydl, 2004; Weisburd and Eck, 2004). Strong evidence of crime prevention gains associated with the hot spots policing approach can be found in five randomized controlled experiments and three quasi-experimental evaluations conducted in Houston, Texas; Jersey City, New Jersey; Kansas City, Missouri; Lowell, Massachusetts; Minneapolis, Minnesota; and St. Louis, Missouri. Importantly, when crime displacement was measured, these crime prevention gains were generated without displacing offenders to nearby locations. Moreover, this body of evaluation research suggests that a diffusion of crime-control benefits to nearby areas was more likely than crime displacement.

Police have used science as a tool of policing for decades, most obviously in forensics. The specific methods and tools used by the police to address crime hot spots should be rooted in scientific principles to maximize the potential crime prevention benefits in targeted places. When implemented to control crime hot spots, problem-oriented policing can be seen as a mechanism to make police crime prevention policy and practice into an applied social science with strong prospects of generating crime-control gains. As John Eck (2006: 123) observes, the four principles laid out by Goldstein (1979) form the basic empirical principles of any scientific inquiry: (1) define problems with specificity, (2) study problems in depth, (3) conduct a broad search for solutions, and (4) focus on outcomes. As discussed in chapter 5, there is a growing body of research evidence demonstrating the crime prevention value of the problem-oriented policing approach (Sherman and Eck, 2002; Skogan and Frydl, 2004; Weisburd et al., 2010). Even when not fully implemented, limited problem-solving efforts have demonstrated crime-control gains (Braga and Weisburd, 2006). Relative to one-dimensional patrol and offender-based arrest strategies, problem-oriented policing brings an evidence-based practice to addressing the problem of crime hot spots.

While scientific evidence can point police in the right direction, the adoption and implementation of particular police crime prevention efforts needs to be balanced by the experience-based knowledge and wisdom held by practitioners on local normative values, political contexts, and operational environments. Blindly following scientific evidence without equally considering reality-based experience makes little sense in the complex world of policing and crime. And it also may have the unintended effect of limiting the ability of police to innovate by privileging research evidence, and the slow development of knowledge by the scientific method, over the common sense practical experience necessary to deal with new and evolving crime problems. As Mark Moore (2006: 335–36) suggests in his critique of evidence-based policing:

Science alone cannot answer important questions that are central to the development of effective clinical practice. Science, by itself, cannot tell us how to divide up the world of practical problems we see in front of us in a way that is amenable to their solution. Science, by itself, cannot necessarily suggest the particular intervention that should be tried to deal with a given problem. Science, by itself, cannot tell us in what terms we ought to evaluate the interventions we make. For all this work, we need the experience of practitioners as well as the experiments of science.

If our vision of evidence-based policing going forward is one the embraces these aspects of science, I am all for it. If our vision is one that seeks to privilege a certain kind of science and a particular kind of scientist, I am against it. The world of crime and policing is far too important, far too complex, and far too urgent to leave entirely in the hands of scientists. We need a great deal of practical wisdom as well as rigorous and responsive science to move the field forward.

Changing Places, Not People

As the empirical evidence reviewed in this book confirms, crime is highly concentrated in a small number of hot spot- places that are generally stable targets for intervention over time. According to Harvard sociologist Robert Sampson, the idea of crime hot spots suggests a crime prevention response that in the end may be more effective than policies that simply target individuals or families (Sampson, 2002: 243). By proactively responding to neighborhoods and places that disproportionately generate crimes, Sampson suggests that proactive place-based strategies can more effectively stave off crime epidemics and their spatial diffusion when compared to crime prevention strategies that target people. Having said that crime is concentrated among a few places, it is also important to note that crime is also concentrated among a few offenders, a fact pointed out in research by Wolfgang, Figlio, and Sellin (1972) more than thirty years ago. In their classic study of nearly ten thousand boys in Philadelphia, Wolfgang, Figlio, and Sellin (1972) revealed that the most active 6 percent of delinquent boys were responsible for more than 50 percent of all delinquent acts committed.

There is some evidence to suggest that crime may be more concentrated at places than among offenders. In the prestigious Police Foundation Ideas in Policing series, Weisburd (2008) presented some preliminary analyses that tried to make this comparison using crime incidents from Seattle over the 1989 to 2002 time period. The results suggested that when using targets as a criterion, places were indeed a more efficient focus than offenders. Using this approach, the analysis revealed that on average about 1,500 street segments accounted for 50 percent of the crime each year during the study period. During the same period, 6,108 offenders were responsible for 50 percent of the crime each year. Simply stated, the results suggest that the police have to approach four times as many targets to identify the same level of overall crime when they focus on people as opposed to places.

As we discussed in chapter 1, the stability of police targets is an important consideration in developing police practices. If there is high instability of crime across time at a unit of analysis, then police strategies will be less efficient. For example, let us say that criminals vary in offending greatly over time with a very high peak in one time period and very low activity in subsequent periods. Investment of resources in incarceration of such offenders may have little real crime prevention benefit, though of course it may satisfy important considerations of just punishments for criminals. Similarly, if it is very hard to identify and track targets for crime prevention initiatives, the efficiency of strategies will also be challenged.

There is perhaps no more established fact in criminology than the variability and instability of offending across the life course. A primary factor in this variability is the fact that most offenders age out of crime, often at a relatively young age (Blumstein et al., 1986; Wolfgang, Thornberry, and Figlio, 1987; Gottfredson and Hirschi, 1990; Tracy and

Kempf-Leonard, 1996; Laub and Sampson, 2003). But there is also evidence of strong instability in criminal behavior for most offenders even when short time periods are observed. Hot spots of crime, as we have detailed in this volume, evidence very strong stability of offending over relatively long periods of time (Weisburd et al., 2004). This stability in turn suggests that hot spots policing will not only be more efficient in terms of the number of targets but also in the application of police strategies to specific targets. Places, simply put, are not moving targets. A police strategy that is focused on very high-crime-rate hot spots is not likely to be focusing on places that will naturally become cool a year later. The stability of crime at place across time makes crime places a particularly salient focus for investment of police resources.

Crime hot spots are not moving targets in another important sense in that, unlike offenders, they stay in one place. The American Housing Survey from the United States Census Bureau shows that Americans move once every seven years (American Housing Survey Branch 2005). It is reasonable to assume that offenders move even more often than this. Studies have often noted the difficulty of tracking offenders for survey research (Wolfgang, Thornberry, and Figlio, 1987; Laub and Sampson 2003), and it is a common experience of the police to look for an offender and find that he or she no longer lives at the last known address. Hot spots policing provides a target that stays in the same place. This is not an insignificant issue when considering the investment of police resources in crime prevention.

Most criminological research focuses on why some people become persistent offenders and offender-focused crime prevention efforts attempt, often with considerable difficulties, to do something about individual motivations to commit crime (see, e.g., Farrington, Ohlin, and Wilson, 1986; Visher and Weisburd, 1998). Prevention efforts focused on people as individuals might work, with enough time, money, and commitment. However, as Eck (2000) observes, by the time a crime problem comes to the attention of the police, the questions of why people offend are no longer directly relevant for police operations. The most pressing concerns for the police are why offenders are committing crimes at particular places, selecting particular targets, and committing crimes at specific times. While police officers are important entry points to social services for many people, they are best positioned to prevent crimes by focusing on the situational opportunities for offending rather than attempting to manipulate socioeconomic, family, and individual conditions that are the subjects of much criminological inquiry and the primary focus of other governmental agencies. Interventions that deal with the "root causes" of crime are usually beyond the scope of most police crime prevention efforts. Interventions that deal with opportunities for crime and how likely offenders, potential victims, and others make decisions based on perceived opportunities have greater utility in designing effective policing crime prevention programs (Eck, 2000; Felson and Clarke, 1998).

Hot spots policing is an intervention that maximizes the ability of the police to prevent crime by changing criminal opportunities at high-activity crime places. Research suggests that simply increasing police presence and visibility in crime hot spots can generate short-term positive crime prevention gains. Changing crime-generating features, dynamics, and situations in hot spot areas can generate even greater crime prevention impacts that could have longer-term impacts at the place and the surrounding neighborhood. Managing and eliminating problems in crime hot spots could, in turn, create safer neighborhoods that could attract economic investments, businesses, and homeowners. In this way, robust hot spots policing programs could serve as an important first step in "tipping" neighborhoods characterized by, and producing, fear and crime to neighborhoods characterized by safe street conditions (Gladwell, 2000).

Increasing Prospects for Police Legitimacy

In contrast to the strong scientific evidence on the crime prevention effectiveness of hot spots policing programs and the promising scientific evidence on crime prevention value of problem-oriented policing, there is far less rigorous evidence on the prospects of procedural fairness, consensus building, and transparency in improving community perceptions of the legitimacy of police actions. Practical experience and the available research evidence are strong enough, however, to observe that inappropriate police actions, such as excessive force, disrespectful treatment, and indiscriminant enforcement, have undesirable impacts on police-community relations. In short, there are more and less desirable ways to address crime and disorder problems in hot spot areas. Normative assessments of planned actions can be helpful in avoiding community backlash when concentrating police resources in small places.

Hot spots policing represents an approach to crime prevention that not only has the potential to generate strong crime prevention gains, but also, if implemented properly, increase police legitimacy in the eyes of community members. As described in chapter 6, the police need active public cooperation, not simply political support and approval, to control crime and maintain order. Cooperation increases not only when the police are viewed as effective in preventing crime and maintaining order but when citizens see the police as legitimate authorities who are entitled to be obeyed (Tyler and Fagan, 2008). Legitimacy judgments are shaped by public views about the fairness of the processes the police use when dealing with members of the public (Tyler, 1990; Tyler et al., 2007). We believe that hot spots policing programs should be developed and implemented by police managers with the ideas of legitimacy and fairness in mind.

Minority residents tend to view the police with distrust and suspicion (Weitzer and Tuch, 2006). These views are driven by years of poor police service. At certain times and in certain places in U.S. history, African Americans, in particular, have been subjected to high levels of arrest, abusive and corrupt behavior, and physical brutality by the police. More recently, ongoing poor relations between minorities and the police have been highlighted in the debate over racial profiling (Fagan and Davies, 2000; Harris, 1999). As Lawrence Sherman (2002) observes, "counteracting this legacy may require more public accountability for the processes by which police select crime-prevention strategies and risk factor targets" (395).

A police focus on crime hot spots can be correlated with race, but the correlation is a coincidence rather than a cause. Public concern over racial profiling is often the result of poorly delineated *offender* profiles rather than more precisely drawn *offense* profiles such as risk analyses that identify particular high-activity crime places in need of attention (Sherman, 2002). The concentration of crime in space and time provides an important opportunity for consensus building and transparency in target selection that can go far in bringing the police closer to the communities they seek to serve. Within a community policing framework, hot spots policing initiatives can be framed as collaborative exercises where the police and community jointly review crime maps and select particular places for focused attention. In these settings, police and community members can also discuss the range of strategies that might be adopted to address targeted crime hot spots.

Consensus and transparency, coupled with a tight focus on high-crime locations, can enhance the legitimacy of police intrusions that are necessary to intercept criminals for violating "risk laws," such as those against carrying guns or driving while intoxicated. Increasing police presence and police-citizen contacts in high-activity places can be important strategies to reduce gun violence and drunk driving fatalities (Sherman, 1992b; Sherman and Rogan, 1995a). To maintain the legitimacy of these important enforcement activities in crime hot spot areas, police need to pay attention to what Tom Tyler and others call "procedural justice" in their interactions with citizens (Tyler, 1990; Tyler et al., 2007; Tyler and Fagan, 2008). Traffic and pedestrian stops need to be viewed as procedurally fair by citizens subjected to the police intrusion. Fair policing requires police officers to treat citizens with respect and dignity throughout the interaction, to explain that their intrusion on the citizen's activities was based on neutral and objective criteria, and to allow citizens the opportunity to explain their behavior.

The particular strategies selected to address crime hot spots can obviously either enhance or undermine police legitimacy. Overly aggressive and indiscriminate arrest-based strategies are more likely to generate community concern and poor relations. Unfortunately, zero-tolerance approaches that advocate full enforcement of all laws, no matter how minor, to reduce serious crimes have been engaged by police departments from Australia to Arizona (Sherman, 2002). Zero-tolerance approaches are a perversion of the tight focus of broken windows policing on controlling disorderly behavior to prevent more serious crimes (Wilson and Kelling, 1982). Zero-tolerance strategies seem to generate more harm in disadvantaged communities already suffering from serious crime and disorder problems as evidenced by studies suggesting elevated complaints against the police and increased arrests and subsequent incarceration of young minority men (Greene, 1999; Harcourt and Ludwig, 2007). Given our review on community reactions to police behavior and actions, we strongly believe that police agencies need to move away from one-dimensional intensive enforcement efforts to control crime hot spots.

Approaches that seek to change the underlying conditions that generate and sustain crime hot spots, such as situational crime prevention and problem-oriented policing, seem well positioned to reduce harm and increase police legitimacy. Situational strategies can provide an opportunity for local residents and business owners to be involved in the prevention effort. Collaboration and cooperation between police and community members can improve relationships and generate mutual feelings of trust (Skogan, 2006). Since these approaches seek to prevent crime by removing or blocking criminal opportunities, fewer community members are subjected to injury and property loss. Equally important, the police are less reliant on making arrests in doing something about crime at a place. Fewer arrests lead to smaller numbers of people involved with the criminal justice system. New research suggests that the large-scale cycle of arrest, removal, and return of individuals damages the stability of familial and community relationships, disrupts neighborhood life, and erodes the capacity of neighborhoods for self-regulation (Clear, 2007; Western, 2006). Changing criminogenic conditions, such as the characteristics of a place that cause it to be a good spot to sell drugs, can have very desirable effects for the police and the community. Such activities should be at the core of hot spots policing.

Operational Changes Necessary to Implement Hot Spots Policing

To many observers, police departments, like other institutions, are self-interested and generally try to respond to demands in their environments in ways that benefit themselves by acquiring resources, domain, and other forms of support (Mastrofski, 1998; Scott, 1987). In this book, we present hot spots policing as a clear example that, when police practice is harnessed to applied science, it results in better prospects for desired outcomes. *If* hot spots policing is implemented properly, the approach has good prospects for reducing crime. In practice, however, there are many aspects of police organizations and the larger societal environments in which they operate that can relegate hot spots policing to the periphery of police operations.

In the organizational-change literature (Scott, 1987; Ritti and Mastrofski, 2002), there is a tension between the actions that a technical-rational model suggests are needed in changing police organizations, compared to what an institutional model suggests will drive the manner in which police organizations do actually change. The former suggests that police organizations will search for and adopt those things that are most efficient and effective in accomplishing core technical goals, such as preventing crime. The latter suggests that police organizations will do what is *au courant* within the policing industry or will respond to pressures from powerful stakeholders who are consequential for the success of the organization and its leaders. Institutional-model theory suggests that the organization will be less concerned with making the innovation, such as hot spots policing, technically effective than simply doing things that will satisfy powerful stakeholders or give the appearance of innovation.

At present, there is little research evidence on which of these perspectives on organizational change best captures the adoption of recent innovations in police departments. A handful of studies on community policing and Compstat illustrate just how difficult it is to get police organizations to transform themselves within the framework of the technical-rational model (e.g., see Mastrofski, 2006; Willis, Mastrofski, and Weisburd, 2007). These studies do suggest conditions that could make a technical-rational model more applicable in the adoption of hot spots policing. Willis, Mastrofski, and Weisburd (2007) argue that there is the need for greater environmental support for a *focused* mission for local police in the United States and the need to establish reliable and well-understood crime-control technologies that the police will employ. If police departments are supported by communities, political representatives, and other stakeholders in controlling crime as a central mission, and police leaders have faith that hot spots policing generates crime prevention benefits, we believe that the approach will be adopted in a technically effective manner.

It is important to note that crime hot spots have indeed always been a concern for the police. Police departments are usually geographically organized and police officers are dispatched to particular addresses in response to emergency calls for service. With the widespread adoption of community policing and the diffusion of management innovations such as Compstat, police pay more attention to ongoing crime and disorder problems that are manifested at particular places within communities. Given the enduring and expanding role of place in policing, we focus the remainder of this section on what must change in order for police departments to take maximum advantage of the opportunities for crime prevention that are offered by hot spots policing approaches.

Developing Place-Based Data Systems for Analysis and Intervention

Throughout this book, our position has been more radical than simply advocating that police add a new strategy to the basket of police interventions. For hot spots policing to succeed, police must expand their unit of analysis for understanding and doing something about crime. In particular, police departments should be as concerned about the places where crime is committed as they are about the people who are committing crime. As Lawrence Sherman has quipped, "Why aren't we thinking more about 'wheredunit' rather than 'whodunit'?" (Sherman 1995: 37). Policing today continues to place people at the center of police practices. David Weisburd (2008) has elsewhere characterized this traditional focus of police departments as "people-based policing." This is reflected in how data are collected, as well as how the police are organized. Hot spots policing demands a fundamental change in the structure of police efforts to do something about crime and other community problems.

For example, police data has developed historically out of a system that was focused on offenders and their characteristics. Indeed, the addition of a place-based identifier was not initially a source of much concern in incident, arrest, or police call databases. In the late 1980s, researchers who tried to analyze the locations of crime using police databases were often frustrated by an inability to identify where a crime occurred (see, e.g., Harries, 1999; Weisburd and McEwen, 1997). There were often multiple names given to similar addresses, some based on the actual address and some on the names given to stores or other institutions at that address. Such name identifiers often included scores of possible permutations, and address identifiers often failed to identify whether the address was in the south, north, east, or west of cities with such designations. Over the last decade, police have become much better at identifying where the crime is located, in part because of significant advances in records-management systems and in part because of advances in geographic-information systems. But it is striking how police in most jurisdictions have failed to go very much beyond the simple identification of an address in their data systems.

In the case of arrest databases, it is common to collect data on age, gender, and often education and other demographic characteristics of offenders. But it is rare for such databases to tell us much about the nature of the places that are the context of police activities. A successful program of hot spots policing would require that the police routinely capture rich data about places. We should know as much about the places that are hot spots of crime as we do about offenders who commit crimes. Such data should be regularly available to police when they decide to focus interventions on specific places. The failure to collect such data routinely, or to gain such data from other agencies, limits the ability of police to develop effective place-based policing strategies.

Carolyn Block and Lynn Green (1994) have already suggested the importance of such databases in what they have called a GeoArchive. The Illinois Criminal Justice Information Authority developed the GeoArchive as an extensive geographic database of community and law enforcement data. A variety of data are collected including: street-map data, official crime data (calls for service, arrests, offender characteristics, victim characteristics), corrections data (the addresses of persons released on probation or parole), landmark data (parks, schools, public transportation, liquor stores, abandoned buildings), and population information (Block, 1997). Several other municipalities and police departments have also recognized the importance of robust place-based data systems to focus prevention efforts appropriately. For instance, the Redlands, California, police department integrates cutting-edge technology to map community, family, school, and peer-group risk and protective factors. This enables the department to focus limited community and police resources on the most problematic areas where the greatest potential for change exists (Harries, 1999). These types of information-gathering efforts can be invaluable to police officers and others in analyzing urban crime problems and developing appropriate interventions at the local, district, or citywide level.

The availability of robust place-based data systems can also be used to minimize the potential threat of spatial crime displacement as a result of hot spots policing interventions. As described earlier, criminals are most likely to displace to locations that have the same attributes as the place that the target of opportunity-blocking crime prevention measures. Police can use place-based data systems to identify likely nearby targets of displaced offenders based on a search for areas with similar attributes to the targeted location. For instance, if police focus on disorderly drug selling emanating from an abandoned building, crime analysts and street officers could search the place-based data system for similar locations close to the targeted place and monitor potential changes in criminal acts. Such proactive monitoring and response could also maximize potential diffusion of crime-control benefits in areas surrounding the targeted hot spot.

The failures of traditional person-centered policing to develop data sources relevant for place-based policing is also evidenced in the lack of interest of police executives in knowing where the police are (Weisburd, 2008). While technologies for tracking the whereabouts of police, often termed automated-vehicle-locator technologies, have been available for decades, not a single police agency in the country has used these technologies to try to understand the routine relationships between police patrol and crime. We need to know not only where crime is but also where the police are. This information would allow us to identify how police presence affects crime at place and to design more effective patrol strategies. The Police Foundation has begun an innovative program in collaboration with the Dallas Police Department with this aim in mind (Weisburd, 2008). But it is in some sense indicative of the failure of police to take a place-based approach that this technology has only now begun to be applied to practical crime prevention.

As with most technologies, the functionality and sophistication of crime mapping and geographic-information systems is continually being enhanced and expanded. Recent advances include the use of high definition or 3-D crime mapping to understand the distribution of crimes across specific buildings, parking lots, and other facilities on a street block or the location of repeat crimes on specific floors and at specific units in multilevel buildings (Rengert, Mattson, and Henderson, 2001). Research on repeat victimization has led to experimentation with "prospective mapping" to predict the location of future crimes based on the notion that future targets are likely to be nearby people or places with characteristics similar to the original target (Johnson and Bowers, 2004). A detailed discussion of defining hot spots and the various ways in which crime-mapping technology can be deployed to identify hot spots, repeat-victim addresses, and other identifiable risks is beyond the scope of this discussion. Many texts and reports are available on the current state-of-the-art crime mapping and geographic analysis of crime (see Harries, 1999; Eck, Chainey, and Cameron, 2005; Clarke and Eck, 2005).

While dealing with crime hot spots is a very productive way to reduce crime, we also think it is important to offer a word of caution in the overreliance on place-based systems in identifying, analyzing, and responding to crime problems. Practitioners and scholars value computerized mapping as a powerful tool for identifying crime problems and developing crime-control and prevention programs. However, police officers need to remember that examining the spatial distribution of official crime data is only one way to look at crime problems. To some observers, crime mapping can stifle creativity in analyzing problems. As Gloria Laycock suggests (as quoted in Scott, 2000: 104):

> Mapping, however, is actually a bit of a red herring. It can even be unhelpful. I worry that people are becoming obsessed with maps and their pretty colors, without thinking much about what information they contain or what can be learned from them. The technology itself becomes fascinating, rather than the knowledge gained from it. So technology can at times inhibit the development of problem-oriented policing because it stops people from thinking.

In his extensive work on the characterization of societal problems such as crime, Malcolm Sparrow (2008) cautions against the temptation to define and analyze problems along one dimension as harms come in a multitude of different shapes. Too often, in problem-oriented policing ventures, police agencies fail to use analytic methods beyond the traditional hot spot analysis. Goldstein (1990) decries the narrowness of using this one analytical approach. He pointed out that not only did the police tend to rely on one analytic approach; worse, they relied on one standard tactical response—*directed patrol*—whenever this analysis showed a concentration. Directed patrol meant flooding the particular area at the relevant times with uniformed patrol in order to suppress the "crime problem" (Sparrow, 2008).

Sparrow (2008) further argues that the best way to define problems is not so much about the dimensionality of consequences but about the shape of the problem itself, and the dimensions that best show how it is concentrated. For example, many cities have problems with delinquent groups, particularly youth violence fueled by conflicts between gangs (Braga, Kennedy, and Tita, 2002; Curry, Ball, and Fox, 1994). The resulting crime and disorder problems often exhibit geographic concentration, and mapping can identify such hot spots of youth violence. However, such analyses reveal nothing about the violent youth groups, or their conflict networks, that exist across the city. Identifying gangs and understanding the nature of their conflicts could be instrumental in preventing or responding to flare-ups of violence. Interventions focused on serious offenders, violent groups, patterns of conflict, and weapons all hold promise for reducing violence, including violence manifested in hot spots. The well-known Operation Ceasefire "pulling levers" intervention in Boston strategically focused law enforcement, social service, and community-based agencies on disrupting ongoing conflicts among rival street gangs (Kennedy, Piehl, and Braga, 1996; Kennedy, 2006). This response was mostly grounded in social-network analyses of antagonistic relationships among gangs and gang members. Ceasefire intervention was associated with a 63 percent reduction in youth homicide in Boston (Braga et al., 2001) and has been replicated with similar success elsewhere (Kennedy, 2006; McGarrell et al., 2006).

We believe that hot spots policing represents a potent response to the crime problem and police departments should be organized to take a place-based approach to crime. However, it is also important for police agencies to recognize that a place-only lens on crime problems could limit their understanding of certain types of crime problems and yield interventions that may not be well tailored to the underlying conditions and dynamics that generate and sustain the problem. Effective problem analysis is rooted in creativity, insight, and imagination (Braga, 2008; Goldstein, 1990) and this requires a variety of problem frames and dimensions to be considered and a varied set of analytic methodologies to be engaged.

Maintaining a Focus on Problem Solving at Crime Hot Spots

In policing crime hot spots, there must be a shift from arresting and prosecuting offenders to reducing the opportunities for crime at place. The idea that police are too focused on law enforcement is not a new one, and indeed was a central concern of Herman Goldstein when he introduced the idea of problem-oriented policing in 1979. Goldstein and others have for almost three decades tried to influence the police to be less focused on arrest and prosecution of individual offenders and more focused on solving crime problems. But these calls have at best been only partially heeded by the police, and there is much evidence that law enforcement and arrest of offenders remains the primary tool of policing even in innovative programs (Braga and Weisburd, 2006). But why should we be surprised? In a police culture in which person-based policing is predominant, it is natural for police officers to continue to focus on offenders and their arrest.

Hot spots policing provides an opportunity to finally shift this emphasis, because it places the crime hot spot rather than the offender at the center of the crime prevention equation. It changes the central concern of police to improving places rather than simply processing offenders. Success in this context must be measured not in terms of how many arrests the police make but in terms of whether places become safer for the people who live, visit, or work in such places. As noted in chapter 5, dealing with the underlying conditions, situations, and dynamics that generate crime hot spots requires the expansion of the toolbox of policing far beyond traditional law enforcement. In this context, hot spots policing requires a "problem-oriented" approach. Police need to be concerned not only about places, offenders, and victims but also about potential nonpolice guardians. If the goal of the police is to improve safety at crime hot spots, then it is natural in hot spots policing to be concerned with what Eck and others have termed "place managers" (Eck, 1994; Eck and Wartell, 1996). "Third-party policing" (Mazerolle and Ransley, 2005) is also a natural part of hot spots policing. But, more generally, hot spots policing brings the attention of the police to the full range of people and contexts that are part of the crime problem.

Police departments should engage a problem-oriented approach to address the underlying problems that generate and sustain crime hot spots. Problem analysis and the wide search for appropriate responses can yield a powerful blend of traditional and alternative strategies to control crime hot spots. Research and practical experience suggests that problem-oriented policing can be difficult for officers to implement in the ways envisioned by Herman Goldstein. Fortunately, research also suggests that even when problem solving is limited it can generate crime prevention effects (Braga and Weisburd, 2006). We believe this surprising finding underscores the robustness of the problem-oriented policing model. It also makes a strong argument for police departments to adopt the approach.

It is beyond the scope of this book to tackle all the internal and external administrative arrangements necessary to facilitate effective problem-oriented policing in crime hot spots. Many other texts provide more than adequate coverage of these important issues (see, e.g., Braga, 2008; Clarke and Eck, 2005; Eck and Spelman, 1987; Goldstein, 1990; Sparrow, Moore, and Kennedy, 1990; Scott, 2000). In the near term, police departments need to improve crime-analysis capabilities, measure the performance of implemented responses, and secure productive partnerships with a wide range of criminal justice, social service, and community-based partners. There are also important changes in management that need to happen, such as redefining the role of line-level officers, exercising strong leadership, improving supervision, and decentralizing decision-making authority.

Organizing Police Departments for Place-Based Management

While there are jurisdiction-wide specialized units, such as homicide or internal-affairs units, the majority of officers and detectives within police departments are usually organized by geography. Unfortunately, the geographic organization of policing today fails to recognize the importance of places in developing police strategies. By arranging police in large precincts and beats, the police have assumed that the common denominator of crime is found at large geographic levels. While it might be argued that precincts and beats are seldom fit for even larger geographic units such as communities, they are particularly ill fitted for hot spots policing. Perhaps police should consider dividing patrol according to microplaces that have similar crime levels and developmental trends over time. Such a reorganization of police around places would focus strategic thinking and resources on solving common problems.

The reorganization of police for hot spots policing might also take other forms, but it is clear that today's precincts or beats do not take into account what we now know about the geographic distribution of crime, its concentration at relatively small crime places, and the stability of crime over time at a small number of hot spot locations. Although a long list of management and policy issues would need to considered, it might not be too difficult for police executives and scholars to imagine a set of administrative arrangements for officers and detectives organized at larger areal units, such as precincts and districts, which would allow for a place-based reorganization of police services. For instance, all crime hot spots in an entire jurisdiction could be placed under the responsibility of a single command structure. While the development of an organizational structure for place-based policing is beyond the scope of this book, we feel that this is an area that is ripe for future research study.

In the absence of place-based reorganization of police, we believe that the Compstat process, described in chapter 2, could be instrumental in implementing and managing a robust hot spots policing program. The Compstat system has become a highly influential administrative innovation that has diffused widely across American police departments (Weisburd et al., 2003). Indeed, it seems to be setting the standard for police management generally, and particularly for the use of performance measurement in systems of internal accountability. Moore and Braga (2003: 446–47) identify some of the features that make this measurement system behaviorally powerful in driving the New York Police Department:

- The measurement system aligns with organizational units so that the managers of those units can be held accountable for their performance.
- The measures are simple, objective, reliably calculated and continuous so that changes in performance can be observed over time within an operational unit, and across units that are roughly similar.

- The measures are closely aligned with what external overseers want and expect from the organization, with any important value that the organization is trying to produce, and with a goal that the organization itself wants to produce.
- The system holds managers to account frequently enough to capture their attention.
- The managers think that their current standing and pay, as well as their future promotional opportunities, depend on performing well with respect to these measures.
- The reviews of performance are public so that everyone can see how well a particular manager has done.
- There are many managers in comparable situations so that comparisons can be made across managers as well as for a particular manager over time.

These features combine to give the Compstat system great behavioral power. The managers in the department work hard, and demand that others work hard, to produce results that the system will record as favorable. Given the power of the system, Moore (2002) observes that it is particularly important that one pay close attention to what the system recognizes as valuable, what it ignores, and how managers subject to the system are likely to respond, since that will determine whether the system drives the organization toward high levels of performance or not.

Each precinct commander is held publicly accountable for levels of serious crime in his precinct (Silverman, 1999, 2006). The precinct commander's crime statistics are reviewed in the context of crime rates in immediately adjacent precincts so that he cannot reduce crime in his precinct simply by driving it to neighboring precincts. Crime mapping and hot spots analyses are usually an important part of the process of identifying, understanding, and responding to crime problems within precinct (Silverman, 1999, 2006). Special attention is also focused on particular crime problems that seem to be troublesome within the larger overall pattern of serious crime. If the Compstat system reveals a crime problem that is getting worse in a precinct, or not improving as much as top management thinks it should, the precinct commander is questioned about his *plans* for dealing with the problem (Moore and Braga, 2003). He is often peppered with questions about whether he is or is not making use of particular activities such as the use of warrant squads, or increased use of fingerprinting, or arrests for weapons offenses that top management thinks might be helpful in dealing with the problem. The system seems to hold managers accountable for an *outcome* of policing as well as *processes* (Moore and Braga, 2003).

As Moore (2002) observes, this part of the system has two important features. First, to some degree, it softens the harsh "strict liability" aspects of the system. Precinct commanders are held accountable for reducing crime. However, they can also get credit if they have a thoughtful plan for dealing with crime problems that have not been resolved. A thoughtful plan is one that makes sense, and/or one that takes advantage of processes and activities that are favored by top management (Moore, 2002). In essence, the Compstat system was constructed to enforce tightly aligned internal and external accountability. The system followed the organizational structure so that individual managers could be called to account for specific results, and the results they achieved were believed to be important to their career prospects. Second, because the system focuses some attention on plans and processes for achieving results as well as the results themselves, the system has some capacity to support innovation and organizational learning about what works to produce outcomes as well as the outcomes themselves (Moore, 2002). If a manager's plan for dealing with a problem is innovative, and if it works, there is come capacity for the system to capture that idea for the future. If a manager is faced with a problem that he cannot seem to solve, top management has a chance to suggest ideas, and through that device, to spread innovations through the department.

Moore (2002) also notes some of the potential weaknesses of Compstat in driving organizational change. First, even though the system is capturing one important dimension of value to be produced by the police, it is not capturing all the relevant valued dimensions. It does not, for instance, capture levels of fear in the community, or their perceptions of the quality of service they receive. Second, while the system focuses on results, it does not concentrate much attention on the resources used to produce those results. In this regard, the system equates the crime-reduction effect of policing with the "profit" earned by policing. The "profitability" of policing cannot be observed until the value of the resources used in policing is subtracted from the value of the effects produced (Moore, 2002).

Third, although the system allows precinct commanders to talk about their special efforts to deal with serious crime problems, it provides little room for them to talk about problem-solving efforts focused on noncrime problems, and the quality of the engagement between the police and community groups in identifying and responding to the concerns of the community. Weisburd and his colleagues (2003) suggest that Compstat departments, relative to police departments without a Compstat process, seem to find it more difficult to implement effective problem-solving tactics and are less successful in adopting innovations that demand significant change in the philosophy and practice of policing.

No system can do everything that is valuable, of course. Skilled management often depends on making choices about what particular things to concentrate on, and then living with a system that is at best an imperfect reflection of what one is really trying to achieve (Moore, 2002). In this spirit, we suggest that police departments should implement a Compstat-like accountability system for managing their hot spots policing programs that puts a premium on problem-oriented policing and community policing in addressing crime hot spots. The Lowell Policing Crime and Disorder Hot Spots experiment provides an example of such an approach (Braga and Bond, 2008, 2009).

Former Lowell Police Superintendent Edward F. Davis assigned ultimate responsibility for the implementation of the problem-oriented policing intervention at the treatment crime and disorder hot spots to the captains that managed Lowell's three police sectors. After receiving their assigned treatment hot spots, the captains were required to submit a report for each place that identified specific problems that generated repeat citizen calls for service, detailed the results of their problem analyses, and listed situational and enforcement responses that were logically linked to the underlying conditions that gave rise to these problems. Within each sector, lieutenants and sergeants spent time analyzing official data sources and discussing problems with community members.

The captains were held accountable for the implementation of the problem-oriented policing interventions through Compstat-like monthly meetings with the command staff. At each monthly meeting, the LPD Crime Analysis Unit presented simple trend analyses of citizen calls for service in each of the treatment hot spots to determine whether identified crime and disorder problems were being positively impacted. If the data revealed that calls for service were decreasing in their hot spots, Superintendent Davis praised the captains and their officers for their hard work and asked them to explain why they believed their actions were producing the desired effects, how their strategies were affecting the identified problems at their places, and what else could be done to keep calls for service decreasing. If the analysis revealed that the number of citizen calls for service had remained the same or increased, Superintendent Davis peppered the captains with questions about their plans for dealing with recurring problems in the hot spot areas (e.g., whether or not they were making use of particular activities such as increased order-maintenance approaches and alleviating identified physical-disorder problems). The meetings also served as a venue for the command staff, captains, and other officers to explore and share ideas on plausibly effective prevention strategies for persistent problems in the treatment places.

While the performance-measurement-accountability principles were borrowed from the well-known Compstat management process (Moore and Braga, 2003; Silverman, 1999), the activities at the monthly meetings represented an ongoing scanning, analysis, response, and assessment process. The routine measurement and review of strategies in the treatment places served as an important mechanism to ensure that there was a strong treatment dosage for the experiment. Police officers are generally known to be resistant to operational and strategic changes (Guyot, 1979) and often oppose restrictions imposed on them when participating in field experiments. The monthly meetings were designed to ensure that the captains and their officers were implementing the problem-oriented policing program and adhering to the requirements of the experimental research design. While some observers suggest that standard department-wide Compstat systems may stifle the creativity of the problem-oriented policing process (Weisburd et al., 2003), the LPD monthly meetings were explicitly focused on implementing the approach by addressing local community concerns as measured by trends in citizen calls for service in the treatment hot spot areas, holding police managers accountable for dealing with identified problems, and serving as a venue to enhance the creativity of implemented responses through open discussion and idea sharing.

Concluding Remarks

In this book, we have tried to establish that hot spots policing increases the crime prevention effectiveness of police departments. As we have illustrated, basic research suggests that crime is concentrated at very small geographic units of analysis, such as street segments or small groups of street blocks. Such crime hot spots offer stable targets for police interventions, as contrasted with the constantly moving targets of criminal offenders. Evaluation research provides solid experimental evidence for the effectiveness of hot spots policing and contradicts the assumption that such interventions will just move crime around the corner. Indeed, the evidence available suggests that such interventions are much more likely to lead to a diffusion of crime-control benefits to areas nearby. Crime hot spots also provide a focus for policing that can reduce legal barriers to police strategies and lessens the long-term social and moral consequences of traditional police activities that simply seek to arrest people.

Research accordingly suggests that it is time for police to shift from person-based policing to hot spots policing. While such a shift is largely an evolution in trends that have begun over the last few decades, it will nonetheless demand radical changes in data collection in policing, in the organization of police activities, and particularly in the overall world view of the police. It remains true today that police officers see the key work of policing as catching criminals. It is time to change that world view so that police understand that the key to crime prevention is in ameliorating crime at problem places.

NOTES

INTRODUCTION

1. The Gross Domestic Product per capita was used to compare 2 billion U.S. dollars in 1974 to its relative worth in 2007. To arrive at an estimate of 13 billion U.S. dollars value in 2007, we used an Internet calculation tool available at http://www.measuringworth.com/uscompare/ (accessed December 30, 2008).

2. Operations researchers have long worked with police agencies to design computerized software tools, such as Hypercube, to help planners improve police services by optimizing the deployment of response units given service levels in particular areas. These programs calculate a number of variables such as travel times, workloads, and preventive patrol frequencies. This provides police planners with the information they need to achieve various goals, such as reduction of response times and balancing workloads among response units. See Larson, 1972; Gau and Larson, 1988; McKnew, 1983; Sacks, 2003.

3. Pierce, Spaar, and Briggs (1988) performed a similar set of analyses in Boston during the early to mid-1980s. They noted that a relatively small proportion of street addresses in Boston produced a disproportionate amount of police work. For instance, Pierce and his colleagues noted that street address locations producing 5 or more requests in a given year represented only 18 percent of all potential address but accounted for 75 percent of the total demand for police services. Similarly, street addresses producing

50 or more requests in a given year represented less than 1 percent of all potential addresses, but accounted for nearly 24 percent of the total demand for police services. Pierce, Spaar, and Briggs (1988) also examined street intersections and block faces and reported that locations with 50 or more requests per year represented only 7 percent of intersections and block faces but accounted for 53 percent of calls for service to the police. Pierce, Spaar, and Briggs (1988: 6–31) concluded that "These findings strongly suggest that by identifying patterns of repetitive requests for assistance, police departments could locate areas at high risk of experiencing future problems. Thus, police departments are in a position to develop strategic plans to help ameliorate the underlying problems that contribute to long-term repetitive requests for assistance from specific locales."

CHAPTER 2

1. It should be noted that a few early criminologists did examine the "micro" idea of place as discussed here (see Shaw and Myers, 1929). However, interest in micro places was not sustained and did not lead to significant theoretical or empirical inquiry.

CHAPTER 3

1. Collective efficacy is generally defined as "social cohesion among neighbors combined with their willingness to intervene on behalf of the common good" (Sampson, Raudenbush, and Earls, 1997: 918).

CHAPTER 4

1. It is important to note that experiments sometimes do not include pre-test measurement. Some experimental designs simply randomize subjects to treatment and control groups and then measure outcomes for each group in the post-test period only.

2. There are other quasi-experimental approaches that suggest the potential for gaining higher levels of internal validity. For example, a regression continuity design (see Berk, 2008; Ludwig and Miller, 2007) takes advantage of treatments that are administered at a certain specific cutting point in the

data to see whether the expected regression line below and above the data are similar. Such designs are still uncommon in criminology.

3. In 2001, an earlier systematic review identified 588 distinct abstracts and the full-text reports, journal articles, and books for 43 abstracts were acquired (Braga, 2001). The search results of the earlier review were included in the 2003 review (Braga, 2005).

4. "Zero tolerance" is a policy whereby law enforcement officials do not tolerate any disorder, especially public-order offences such as vagrancy, disorderly conduct, or soliciting for prostitution.

5. Property crime incidents experienced a significant increase while property crime calls for service did not significantly change in the treatments' catchment areas relative to controls. The research team viewed this result as an artifact of the experiment rather than a substantive finding (Braga et al., 1999, 567–69).

6. Only one study, the Kansas City Gun Study (Sherman and Rogan, 1995a), reported the necessary information to properly calculate a program effect size. Two studies, the St. Louis Problem-Oriented Policing in Three Drug Market Locations Study (Hope, 1994) and the Beenleigh, Australia, Calls for Service Project (Criminal Justice Commission, 1998), did not report the necessary information to calculate program effect size. As described in the Campbell review (Braga, 2005), the Houston Beat Program (Caeti, 1999) did not use appropriate statistical methods to estimate program effects and, unfortunately, an accurate effect size could not be calculated.

7. Call data are suggested to be more reliable measures of crime and crime-related activity than incident data or arrest data (Pierce, Spaar, and Briggs, 1988; Sherman et al., 1989). Most notably, citizen calls for service are affected less heavily by police discretion than other official data sources (Warner and Pierce, 1993). Therefore, call data are regarded as "the widest ongoing data collection net for criminal events in the city" (Sherman, Buerger, and Gartin, 1989: 35; but see Klinger and Bridges, 1997).

8. While meta-analysis seeks to convert effect sizes to standardized metrics, there are ongoing debates regarding the appropriate statistical methods for such conversions (see e.g., Guevara, Berlin, and Wolf, 2004). This is particularly the case when drawing from published studies that may not include sufficient data for computing exact standardized effect sizes. In turn, such computations become particularly complex when dealing with non-normal distributions

such as that used in analyses conducted by Braga et al. (1999). For example, Braga (2005) uses a p-value approach to estimate the effect size of the Braga et al. (1999) in his Campbell review. While this approach is commonly used in converting effect sizes in normal distribution tests, there has been concern in recent writings that it may have an upwards bias for the Poisson distribution and exaggerate effect sizes (Guevara, Berline, and Wolf, 2004). Weisburd et al. (2007) used a much more conservative approach relying on an odds ratio to estimate treatment effects in the Braga et al (1999) study. Weisburd et al. (2008) reports a smaller effect size (ES = 0.198, p = 0.031). While the effect size reported by Weisburd et al. (2008) is based on raw numbers from the original study and thus is not sensitive to the conversion difficulties of the p-value approach in the case of a Poisson distribution, it provides a downward estimate of the effect size from the study because it fails to take into account the fully randomized block design of the study. In this regard the p value of the original study is several times lower than the p value that is associated with the odds-ratio method.

Campbell reviews are updated on an ongoing basis and the next iteration of the hot spots policing meta-analysis will consider the alternative effect sizes for the Braga et al. (1999) study as well as add effect sizes to the meta-analysis for new studies (e.g., Braga and Bond, 2008). Given the continuing strong evidence for hot spots policing in primary studies (see also Braga and Bond, 2008), it is unlikely that the controversy over the effect size of the Jersey City problem-oriented policing study would change the overall conclusion that hot spots policing programs are effective in reducing crime and disorder.

9. Since the distribution of effect sizes was found to be heterogeneous, the Campbell review used a random-effects meta-analytic model to calculate the mean effect size for all studies. Q = 20.53, df = 5, p = 0.001, random-effects variance component (v) = 0.09184. The random-effects variance component reported here was calculated using the method of moments technique and the overall results do not differ substantively when the full information maximum-likelihood technique is used (Mean ES = 0.322, SE = 0.0135, p = 0.0168, variance component = 0.06737). Using a fixed-effects model, the mean effect size for the key outcome measures is smaller, but remains statistically significant (Mean ES = 0.197, SE = 0.069, p = 0.0042).

10. As described in the Campbell review (Braga, 2005), the modest difference between the mean effect sizes reported by the fixed-effects and random-effects models suggests a possible relationship between study size and effect size with the smaller studies having the large effects. This is often seen as evidence of "publication bias" (i.e., unpublished studies not included in review) that requires a "trim-and-fill" analysis to estimate how many studies have not been observed and adjust for missing effect sizes (see, e.g., Duval and Tweedie, 2000). A trim-and-fill analysis was considered overly conservative in this meta-analysis for two reasons. First, this review includes unpublished studies. Second, there is strong reason to believe that the relationship between sample size and effect size also reflect implementation problems. As described earlier, the RECAP experiment, which accounts for two studies (commercial places and residential places) with large weights in this analysis, suffered from serious implementation problems that influenced the evaluation findings (inadequate intervention at treatment places; see Buerger, 1993). When a trim-and-fill analysis is run on these data, the random effects model does not generate substantive changes to the findings reported here.

11. The Q-statistic was statistically significant ($Q = 13.6365$, df = 3, p = 0.0034). Therefore, a random-effects meta-analytic model was used (v = 0.182234).

12. Since the reported outcome measures in each study were not statistically independent effects, a mean effect size and inverse variance weight for each study was calculated based on all reported outcome measures within each study. The Q-statistic revealed that this distribution of effect sizes was homogeneous and, as such, a fixed-effects meta-analytic model was used ($Q = 7.55$, df = 5, p = 0.183).

13. The Q-statistic revealed that this distribution of effect sizes was homogeneous and, as such, a fixed-effects meta-analytic model was used ($Q = 3.08$, df = 3, p = 0.379).

14. None of these effect-size distributions were heterogeneous; therefore, the Campbell review used fixed-effects meta-analytic models to estimate mean effect sizes. When RECAP was included, the Q statistic was not statistically significant for disorder calls ($Q = 6.5341$, df = 5, p = 0.2577), violence calls ($Q = 4.97$, df = 4, p = 0.2901), and property calls ($Q = 8.42$, df = 4, p = 0.0773). When "hard" crime calls for service were included in the RECAP meta-analysis, the results did not change for violence calls ($Q = 5.37$, df = 5,

p = 0.3725) and property calls (Q = 8.51, df = 5, p = 0.1303). When RECAP was not included, the Q-statistic was not statistically significant for disorder calls (Q = 3.1933, df = 3, p = 0.3628), violence calls (Q = 2.023, df = 2, p = 0.3637), and property calls (Q = 5.589, df = 2, p = 0.0611). When "hard" crime calls for service were included in the meta-analysis without RECAP, the results did not change for violence calls (Q = 2.267, df = 3, p = 0.5189) and property calls (Q = 5.617, df = 3, p = 0.1318).

CHAPTER 5

1. In the case of *Terry v. Ohio* (1968), the Supreme Court upheld the right of the police officers to conduct brief threshold inquiries of suspicious persons when they have reason to believe that such persons may be armed and dangerous to the police or others. In practice, this threshold inquiry typically involves a safety frisk of the suspicious person.

REFERENCES

Agnew, R. (1992). "Foundation for a General Strain Theory of Crime and Delinquency." *Criminology* 30:47–84.

Agnew, R. (1999). "A General Strain Theory of Community Differences in Crime Rates." *Journal of Research in Crime and Delinquency* 36:123–55.

Akers, R. (1973). *Deviant Behavior: A Social Learning Approach.* Belmont, Calif.: Wadsworth.

American Housing Survey Branch. (2005). *American Housing Survey for the United States: 2005.* Washington, D.C.: U.S. Census Bureau, Housing and Economic Statistics Division.

Anderson, D., and K. Pease. (1997). "Biting Back: Preventing Repeat Burglary and Car Crime in Huddersfield." In: R. V. Clarke (ed.), *Situational Crime Prevention: Successful Case Studies.* 2nd ed. New York: Harrow and Heston.

Barker, M., J. Geraghty, B. Webb, and T. Key. (1993). *The Prevention of Street Robbery.* Police Research Prevention Group Series Paper No. 44. London: Home Office.

Barr, R., and K. Pease. (1990). "Crime Placement, Displacement, and Deflection." In: M. Tonry and N. Morris (eds.), *Crime and Justice: A Review of Research* 12. Chicago: University of Chicago Press.

Baumer, E., J. Lauritsen, R. Rosenfeld, and R. Wright. (1998). "The Influence of Crack Cocaine on Robbery, Burglary, and Homicide Rates: A Cross-City,

Longitudinal Analysis." *Journal of Research in Crime and Delinquency* 35:316–40.

Bayley, D. (1988). "Community Policing: A Report from the Devil's Advocate." In: J. R. Greene and S. D. Mastrofski (eds.), *Community Policing: Rhetoric or Reality?* New York: Praeger.

———. (1994). *Police for the Future.* New York: Oxford University Press.

Bennett, T., and R. Wright. (1984). *Burglars on Burglary.* Franborough, Hants, U.K.: Gower.

Berk, R. (2008). "Recent Perspectives on the Regression Discontinuity Design." Working paper 01010. Philadelphia: University of Pennsylvania, Departments of Criminology and Statistics.

Bichler, G., and R. V. Clarke. (1997). "Eliminating Pay Phone Toll Fraud at the Port Authority Bus Terminal in Manhattan." In: R. V. Clarke (ed.), *Preventing Mass Transit Crime.* Crime Prevention Studies 6. Monsey, N.Y.: Criminal Justice Press.

Biron, L. L., and C. Ladouceur. (1991). "The Boy Next Door: Local Teen-Age Burglars in Montreal." *Security Journal* 2:200–4.

Bittner, E. (1967). "The Police on Skid Row: A Study of Peacekeeping." *American Sociological Review* 32:699–715.

———. (1970). *The Functions of the Police in Modern Society.* New York: Aronson.

Block, C. R. (1997). "The GeoArchive: An Information Foundation for Community Policing." In: D. Weisburd and J. T. McEwen (eds.), *Crime Mapping and Crime Prevention.* Crime Prevention Studies 8. Monsey, N.Y.: Criminal Justice Press.

———, M. Dabdoub, and S. Fregly (eds.) (1995). *Crime Analysis through Computer Mapping.* Washington, D.C.: Police Executive Research Forum.

———, and L. Green. (1994). *The GeoArchive Handbook: A Guide for Developing a Geographic Database as an Information Foundation for Community Policing.* Chicago: Illinois Criminal Justice Information Authority.

Block, R., and C. R. Block. (1995). "Space, Place and Crime: Hot Spot Areas and Hot Places of Liquor-Related Crime." In: J. Eck and D. Weisburd (eds.), *Crime and Place.* Crime Prevention Studies 4. Monsey, N.Y.: Criminal Justice Press.

Blumstein, A. (2000). "Disaggregating the Violence Trends." In: A. Blumstein and J. Wallman (eds.), *The Crime Drop in America*. New York: Cambridge University Press.

———. (2002). "Prisons: A Policy Challenge." In: J. Q. Wilson and J. Petersilia (eds.), *Crime*. Oakland, Calif.: ICS Press.

———, J. Cohen, J. Roth, and C. Visher (eds.) (1986). *Criminal Careers and Career Criminals*. Washington, D.C.: National Academy Press.

Bobo, L. D., and D. Johnson. (2004). "A Taste for Punishment: Black and White Americans' Views on the Death Penalty and the War on Drugs." *DuBois Review* 1:151–80.

Boggs, S. L. (1965). "Urban Crime Patterns." *American Sociological Review* 30:899–908.

Braga, A. A. (1997). "Solving Violent Crime Problems: An Evaluation of the Jersey City Police Department's Pilot Program to Control Violent Places." PhD diss., Rutgers University. Ann Arbor, Mich.: University Microfilms International.

Braga, A. A. (2001). "The Effects of Hot Spots Policing on Crime." *Annals of the American Academy of Political and Social Science* 455:104–25.

———. (2005). "Hot Spots Policing and Crime Prevention: A Systematic Review of Randomized Controlled Trials." *Journal of Experimental Criminology* 1:317–42.

———. (2008). *Problem-Oriented Policing and Crime Prevention*. 2nd ed. Monsey, N.Y.: Criminal Justice Press.

———, and B. J. Bond. (2008). "Policing Crime and Disorder Hot Spots: A Randomized Controlled Trial." *Criminology* 46:577–608.

———, and B. J. Bond. (2009). "Community Perceptions of Police Crime Prevention Efforts: Using Interviews in Small Areas to Evaluate Crime Reduction Strategies." In: J. Knutsson and N. Tilley (eds.), *Evaluating Crime Reduction*. Crime Prevention Studies 24. Monsey, N.Y.: Criminal Justice Press.

———, and R. V. Clarke. (1994). "Improved Radios and More Stripped Cars in Germany: A Routine Activities Analysis." *Security Journal* 5:154–59.

———, D. Hureau, and C. Winship. (2008). "Losing Faith? Police, Black Churches, and the Resurgence of Youth Violence in Boston." *Ohio State Journal of Criminal Law* 6:141–72.

————, D. M. Kennedy, and G. Tita. (2002). "New Approaches to the Strategic Prevention of Gang and Group-Involved Violence." In: C. R. Huff (ed.), *Gangs in America*. 3rd ed. Newbury Park, Calif.: Sage.

————, D. M. Kennedy, E. J. Waring and A. M. Piehl. (2001). "Problem-Oriented Policing, Deterrence, and Youth Violence: An Evaluation of Boston's Operation Ceasefire." *Journal of Research in Crime and Delinquency* 38:195–225.

————, and D. L. Weisburd. (2006). "Problem-Oriented Policing: The Disconnect Between Principles and Practice." In: D. L. Weisburd and A. A. Braga (eds.), *Police Innovation: Contrasting Perspectives*. New York: Cambridge University Press.

————, D. L. Weisburd, E. J. Waring, L. Green Mazerolle, W. Spelman, and F. Gajewski. (1999). "Problem-Oriented Policing in Violent Crime Places: A Randomized Controlled Experiment." *Criminology* 37:541–80.

————, and C. Winship. (2006). "Partnership, Accountability, and Innovation: Clarifying Boston's Experience with Pulling Levers." In: D. L. Weisburd and A. A. Braga (eds.), *Police Innovation: Contrasting Perspectives*. New York: Cambridge University Press.

Brantingham, P. J., and P. L. Brantingham. (1975). "Residential Burglary and Urban Form." *Urban Studies* 12:273–84.

————, and P. L. Brantingham. (1981). "Notes on the Geometry of Crime." In: P. J. Brantingham and P. L. Brantingham (eds.), *Environmental Criminology*. Beverly Hills, Calif.: Sage.

————, and P. L. Brantingham. (1982). "Mobility, Notoriety and Crime: A Study of Crime Patterns in Urban Nodal Points." *Journal of Environmental Systems* 11:89–99.

————, and P. L. Brantingham. (1990). "Situational Crime Prevention in Practice." *Canadian Journal of Criminology* (January): 17–40.

————, and P. L. Brantingham (eds.) (1991). *Environmental Criminology*. 2nd ed. Prospect Heights, Ill.: Waveland Press.

————, and P. L. Brantingham. (1999). "A Theoretical Model of Crime Hot Spot Generation." *Studies on Crime and Crime Prevention* 8:7–26.

Bratton, W. (1998). *Turnaround: How America's Top Cop Reversed the Crime Epidemic*. New York: Random House.

Bright, J. A. (1969). *The Beat Patrol Experiment*. London, U.K.: Home Office Police Research and Development Branch (unpublished).

Brisgone, R. (2004). "Report on Qualitative Analysis of Displacement in a Prostitution Site. In: D. L. Weisburd, L. Wyckoff, J. Ready, J. E. Eck, J. Hinkle, and F. Gajewski (eds.), *Does Crime Just Move Around the Corner? A Study of Displacement and Diffusion in Jersey City, New Jersey.* (Final Report submitted to the U.S. Department of Justice, National Institute of Justice).

Brown, L., and M. Wycoff. (1987). "Policing Houston: Reducing Fear and Improving Service." *Crime and Delinquency* 33:71–89.

Buerger, M. (ed.) (1992). *The Crime Prevention Casebook: Securing High Crime Locations.* Washington, D.C.: Crime Control Institute.

———. (1993). "Convincing the Recalcitrant: Reexamining the Minneapolis RECAP Experiment." PhD diss., Rutgers University. Ann Arbor, Mich.: University Microfilms International.

———. (1994). "The Limits of Community." In: D. Rosenbaum (ed.), *The Challenge of Community Policing: Testing the Promises.* Thousand Oaks, Calif.: Sage.

———, E. Cohn, and A. Petrosino. (1995). "Defining the 'Hot Spots of Crime': Operationalizing Theoretical Concepts for Field Research." In: J. Eck and D. Weisburd (eds.), *Crime and Place.* Crime Prevention Studies 4. Monsey, N.Y.: Criminal Justice Press.

———, and L. Green Mazerolle. (1998). "Third-Party Policing: A Theoretical Analysis of an Emerging Trend." *Justice Quarterly* 15:301–28.

Burney, E. (1990). *Putting Street Crime in its Place: A Report to the Community/Police Consultative Group for Lambeth.* London: Goldsmith's College.

Bursik, R., and H. Grasmick. (1993). *Neighborhoods and Crime: The Dimensions of Effective Community Control.* Lexington, Mass.: Lexington Books.

Caeti, T. (1999). "Houston's Targeted Beat Program: A Quasi-Experimental Test of Patrol Strategies." PhD diss., Sam Houston State University. Ann Arbor, Mich.: University Microfilms International.

Campbell, D., and J. Stanley. (1966). *Experimental and Quasi-Experimental Designs for Research.* Chicago: Rand McNally.

Capone, D. L., and W. Nichols. (1976). "Urban Structure and Criminal Mobility." *American Behavioral Scientist* 20:199–213.

Capowich, G., and J. Roehl. (1994). "Problem-Oriented Policing: Actions and Effectiveness in San Diego." In: D. Rosenbaum (ed.), *The Challenge of Community Policing: Testing the Promises.* Thousand Oaks, Calif.: Sage.

Carroll, J., and F. Weaver. (1986). "Shoplifters' Perceptions of Crime Opportunities: A Process-Tracing Study." In: D. Cornish and R. V. Clarke (eds.), *The Reasoning Criminal: Rational Choice Perspectives on Offending.* New York: Springer-Verlag.

Carter, R. L., and K. Hill. (1976). "The Criminal's Image of the City and Urban Crime Patterns." *Social Science Quarterly* 57:597–607.

Caulkins, J. (1992). "Thinking About Displacement in Drug Markets: Why Observing Change of Venue Isn't Enough." *Journal of Drug Issues* 22:17–30.

Chaiken, J. (1978). "What is Known about Deterrent Effects of Police Activities." In: J. A. Cramer (eds.), *Preventing Crime.* Beverly Hills, Calif.: Sage.

Chaiken, J., M. Lawless, and K. Stevenson. (1974). *The Impact of Police Activity on Crime: Robberies on the New York City Subway System.* Santa Monica, Calif.: Rand.

———, M. Lawless, and K. Stevenson. (1975). "The Impact of Police Activity on Crime: Robberies on the New York City Subway System." *Urban Analysis* 3:173–205.

Cheh, M. (1991). "Constitutional Limits on Using Civil Remedies to Achieve Criminal Law Objectives: Understanding and Transcending the Criminal-Civil Law Distinction." *Hastings Law Journal* 42:1325–413.

Clarke, R. V. (1980). "Situational Crime Prevention: Theory and Practice." *British Journal of Criminology* 20:136–47.

———. (1983). "Situational Crime Prevention: Its Theoretical Basis and Practical Scope." In: M. Tonry and N. Morris (eds.), *Crime and Justice: An Annual Review of Research*, vol. 4. Chicago: University of Chicago Press.

———. (1990). "Deterring Obscene Phone Callers: Preliminary Results of the New Jersey Experience." *Security Journal* 1:143–48.

———. (ed.). (1992). *Situational Crime Prevention: Successful Case Studies.* Albany, N.Y.: Harrow and Heston.

———. (1995). "Situational Crime Prevention." In: M. Tonry and D. Farrington (eds.), *Building a Safer Society: Strategic Approaches to Crime Prevention.* Chicago: University of Chicago Press.

———. (ed.) (1997). *Situational Crime Prevention: Successful Case Studies.* 2nd ed. Albany, N.Y.: Harrow and Heston.

———. (1998). "Defining Police Strategies: Problem Solving, Problem-Oriented Policing and Community-Oriented Policing." In: T. O'Connor

Shelley and A. C. Grant (eds.), *Problem-Oriented Policing: Crime-Specific Problems, Critical Issues, and Making POP Work*. Washington, D.C.: Police Executive Research Forum.

———, and D. Cornish. (1972). *The Controlled Trial in Institutional Research.* London: H.M. Stationary Office.

———, and J. E. Eck. (2003). *Become a Problem-Solving Crime Analyst in 55 Small Steps.* London: Jill Dando Institute of Crime Science.

———, and J. E. Eck. (2005). *Crime Analysis for Problem Solvers in 60 Small Steps.* Washington, D.C.: U.S. Department of Justice, Office of Community Oriented Policing Services.

———, and J. E. Eck. (2007). *Understanding Risky Facilities.* Problem-Oriented Guides for Police, Problem Solving Tools Series 6. Washington, D.C.: U.S. Department of Justice, Office of Community Oriented Policing Services.

———, S. Field and G. McGrath. (1991). "Target Hardening of Banks in Australia and the Displacement of Robberies." *Security Journal* 2:84–90.

———, and M. Felson. (1993). "Introduction: Criminology, Routine Activity, and Rational Choice." In: R. V. Clarke and M. Felson (eds.), *Routine Activity and Rational Choice.* Advances in Criminological Theory 5. New Brunswick, N.J.: Transaction Press.

———, and H. Goldstein. (2003). "Thefts from Cars in Center-City Parking Facilities: A Case Study in Implementing Problem-Oriented Policing." In: J. Knutsson (ed.), *Problem-Oriented Policing: From Innovation to Mainstream.* Crime Prevention Studies 15. Monsey, N.Y.: Criminal Justice Press.

———, and P. Mayhew. (1988). "The British Gas Suicide Story and Its Criminological Implications." In: M. Tonry and N. Morris (eds.), *Crime and Justice: A Review of Research*, vol. 10. Chicago: University of Chicago Press.

———, and G. McGrath. (1990). "Cash Reduction and Robbery Prevention in Australian Betting Shops." *Security Journal* 1:160–63.

———, and D. Weisburd. (1990). "On the Distribution of Deviance." In: D. M. Gottfredson and R. V. Clarke (eds.), *Policy and Theory in Criminal Justice.* Aldershot, U.K.: Avebury.

———, and D. Weisburd. (1994). "Diffusion of Crime Control Benefits: Observations on the Reverse of Displacement." *Crime Prevention Studies* 2:165–84.

Clear, T. R. (2007). *Imprisoning Communities: How Mass Incarceration Makes Disadvantaged Neighborhoods Worse*. New York: Oxford University Press.

Clifton Jr., W. (1987). *Convenience Store Robberies in Gainesville, Florida: An Intervention Strategy by the Gainesville Police Department*. Gainesville: Gainesville Police Department. Photocopy.

Cloward, R., and L. Ohlin. (1960). *Delinquency and Opportunity*. Glencoe, Ill.: Free Press.

Cohen, L. E., and M. Felson. (1979). "Social Change and Crime Rate Trends: A Routine Activity Approach." *American Sociological Review* 44:588–605.

Cook, P. J. (1980). "Research in Criminal Deterrence: Laying the Groundwork for the Second Decade." In: N. Morris and M. Tonry (eds.), *Crime and Justice: An Annual Review of Research*, vol. 2. Chicago: University of Chicago Press.

———, and J. Laub. (2002). "After the Epidemic: Recent Trends in Youth Violence in the United States." In M. Tonry (ed.), *Crime and Justice: A Review of Research*, vol. 29. Chicago: University of Chicago Press.

Cook, T., and D. Campbell. (1979). *Quasi-Experimentation: Design and Analysis Issues for Field Settings*. Boston: Houghton Mifflin Company.

Cordner, G. (1998). "Problem-Oriented Policing Vs. Zero Tolerance." In: T. O'Connor Shelley and A. C. Grant (eds.), *Problem-Oriented Policing: Crime-Specific Problems, Critical Issues, and Making POP Work*. Washington, D.C.: Police Executive Research Forum.

———, and E. P. Biebel. (2005). "Problem-Oriented Policing in Practice." *Criminology and Public Policy* 4:155–80.

Cornish, D. (1994). "The Procedural Analysis of Offending and Its Relevance for Situational Prevention." In: R. V. Clarke (ed.), *Crime Prevention Studies*, vol. 3. Monsey, N.Y.: Criminal Justice Press.

———, and R. V. Clarke (eds.) (1986). *The Reasoning Criminal: Rational Choice Perspectives on Offending*. New York: Springer-Verlag.

———, and R. V. Clarke. (1987). "Understanding Crime Displacement: An Application of Rational Choice Theory." *Criminology* 25:933–47.

Cole, D. (1999). *No Equal Justice: Race and Class in the American Criminal Justice System*. New York: Free Press.

Costanzo, C. M., W. C. Halperin, and N. Gale. (1986). "Crime Mobility and the Directional Component in Journeys to Crime." In: R. M. Figlio, S. Hakim, and G. F. Rengert (eds.), *Metropolitan Crime Patterns*. Monsey, N.Y.: Criminal Justice Press.

Crawford, A. (1997). *The Local Governance of Crime: Appeals to Community and Partnership*. Oxford, U.K.: Oxford University Press.

Criminal Justice Commission. (1998). *Beenleigh Calls for Service Project: Evaluation Report*. Brisbane, Queensland: Criminal Justice Commission.

Cromwell, P. F., J. N. Olson, and D. W. Avary. (1991). *Breaking and Entering: An Ethnographic Analysis of Burglary*. Newbury Park, Calif.: Sage.

Crow, W. J., and J. L. Bull. (1975). *Robbery Deterrence: An Applied Behavioral Science Demonstration—Final Report*. La Jolla, Calif.: Western Behavioral Sciences Institute.

Crowell, N., and A. Burgess (eds.) (1996). *Understanding Violence against Women*. Washington, D.C.: U.S. National Academy Press.

Cullen, F., and P. Gendreau. (2000). "Assessing Correctional Rehabilitation: Policy, Practice, and Prospects." In: Julie Horney (ed.), *Policies, Processes, and Decisions of the Criminal Justice System*. Criminal Justice 2000, vol. 3. Washington, D.C.: U.S. Department of Justice, National Institute of Justice.

Curry, G. D, R. Ball, and R. Fox. (1994). *Gang Crime and Law Enforcement Record Keeping*. Washington, D.C.: National Institute of Justice.

Dahman, J. S. (1975). *Examination of Police Patrol Effectiveness*. MacLean, Va.: Mitre Corp.

Davis, R. C., and P. Mateu-Gelabert. (1999). *Respectful and Effective Policing: Two Examples in the South Bronx*. New York: Vera Institute of Justice.

Decker, J. (1972). "Curbside Deterrence: An Analysis of the Effect of a Slug Rejectory Device, Coin View Window, and Warning Labels on Slug Usage in New York City Parking Meters." *Criminology* 10:127–42.

Deutsch, S., and F. Alt. (1977). The Effect of Massachusetts' Gun Control Law on Gun-Related Crimes in the City of Boston." *Evaluation Quarterly* 1:543–68.

Duffala, D. C. (1976). "Convenience Stores, Robbery, and Physical Environmental Features." *American Behavioral Scientist* 20:227–46.

Duval, S., and R. Tweedie. (2000). "A Nonparametric 'Trim and Fill' Method of Accounting for Publication Bias in Meta-Analysis." *Journal of the American Statistical Association* 95:89–98.

Eck, J. E. (1983). *Solving Crimes: The Investigation of Burglary and Robbery.* Washington, D.C.: Police Executive Research Forum.

———. (1992). "Drug Trips: Drug Offender Mobility." Paper presented at the annual meeting of the American Society of Criminology, New Orleans, November.

———. (1993a). "Alternative Futures for Policing." In: D. Weisburd and C. Uchida (eds.), *Police Innovation and Control of the Police.* New York: Springer-Verlag.

———. (1993b). "The Threat of Crime Displacement." *Criminal Justice Abstracts* 25:527–46.

———. (1994). "Drug Markets and Drug Places: A Case-Control Study of the Spatial Structure of Illicit Dealing." Unpublished PhD diss., University of Maryland, College Park.

———. (1997). "Preventing Crime at Places." In: University of Maryland, Department of Criminology and Criminal Justice (eds.), *Preventing Crime: What Works, What Doesn't, What's Promising.* Washington, D.C.: Office of Justice Programs, U.S. Department of Justice.

———. (2000). "Problem-Oriented Policing and Its Problems: The Means Over Ends Syndrome Strikes Back and the Return of the Problem-Solver." Cincinnati, Ohio: University of Cincinnati. (Unpublished manuscript.)

———. (2002). "Preventing Crime at Places." In: L. Sherman, D. Farrington, B. Welsh, and D. L. MacKenzie (eds.), *Evidence-Based Crime Prevention.* New York: Routledge.

———. (2003). "Police Problems: The Complexity of Problem Theory, Research and Evaluation." In: J. Knutsson (ed.), *Problem-Oriented Policing: From Innovation to Mainstream.* Crime Prevention Studies 15. Monsey, N.Y.: Criminal Justice Press.

———. (2006). "Science, Values, and Problem-Oriented Policing: Why Problem-Oriented Policing?" In: D. L. Weisburd and A. A. Braga (eds.), *Police Innovation: Contrasting Perspectives.* New York: Cambridge University Press.

———, S. Chainey, and J. Cameron. (2005). *Mapping Crime: Understanding Hot Spots.* Washington, D.C.: U.S. Department of Justice, National Institute of Justice.

———, J. Gersh, and C. Taylor. (2000). "Finding Hot Spots through Repeat Address Mapping." In: V. Goldsmith, P. McGuire, J. Mollenkopf, and

T. Ross (eds.), *Analyzing Crime Patterns: Frontiers of Practice*. Thousand Oaks, Calif.: Sage.

————, and E. Maguire. (2000). "Have Changes in Policing Reduced Violent Crime? An Assessment of the Evidence." In: A. Blumstein and J. Wallman (eds.), *The Crime Drop in America*. New York: Cambridge University Press.

————, and D. Rosenbaum. (1994). "The New Police Order: Effectiveness, Equity, and Efficiency in Community Policing." In: D. Rosenbaum (ed.), *The Challenge of Community Policing: Testing the Promises*. Thousand Oaks, Calif.: Sage.

————, and W. Spelman. (1987). *Problem-Solving: Problem-Oriented Policing in Newport News*. Washington, D.C.: National Institute of Justice.

————, and J. Wartell. (1996). *Reducing Crime and Drug Dealing by Improving Place Management: A Randomized Experiment*. Report to the San Diego Police Department. Washington, D.C.: Crime Control Institute.

————, and J. Wartell. (1998). "Improving the Management of Rental Properties with Drug Problems: A Randomized Experiment." In: L. Mazerolle and J. Roehl (eds.), *Civil Remedies and Crime Prevention*. Crime Prevention Studies 9. Monsey, N.Y.: Criminal Justice Press.

————, and D. Weisburd. (1995). "Crime Places in Crime Theory." In: J. Eck and D. Weisburd (eds.), *Crime and Place*. Crime Prevention Studies 4. Monsey, N.Y.: Criminal Justice Press.

Ekblom, P. (1987). *Preventing Robberies at Sub-Post Offices: An Evaluation of a Security Initiative*. Home Office Crime Prevention Unit Paper No. 9. London: H.M. Stationery Office.

Engstad, P. A. (1975). "Environmental Opportunities and the Ecology of Crime." In: R. A. Silverman and J. J. Teevan (eds.), *Crime in Canadian Society*. Toronto: Butterworths.

Fagan, J. (2002). "Law, Social Science and Racial Profiling." *Justice Research and Policy* 4:104–29.

————, and G. Davies. (2000). "Street Stops and Broken Windows: Terry, Race and Disorder in New York City," *Fordham Urban Law Journal* 28:457–504.

————, and V. Malkin. (2003) "Theorizing Community Justice through Community Courts." *Fordham Urban Law Journal* 30:857–953.

————, and T. R. Tyler. (2005). "Legal Socialization of Children and Adolescents." *Social Justice Research* 18:217–42.

Farrell, G. (1995). "Preventing Repeat Victimization." In: M. Tonry and D. Farrington (eds.), *Building a Safer Society: Strategic Approaches to Crime Prevention*. Crime and Justice Series 19. Chicago: University of Chicago Press.

————. (2005). "Progress and Prospects in the Prevention of Repeat Victimization." In: N. Tilley (ed.), *Handbook of Crime Prevention and Community Safety*. London: Willan Publishing.

————, W. Buck, and K. Pease. (1993). "The Merseyside Domestic Violence Prevention Project." *Studies on Crime and Crime Prevention*, vol. 2. Stockholm: Scandinavian University Press.

————, and K. Pease. (1993). *Once Bitten, Twice Bitten: Repeat Victimization and Its Implications for Crime Prevention*. Crime Reduction Research Series Paper 5. London: Home Office.

————, and W. Sousa. (2001). "Repeat Victimization and Hot Spots: The Overlap and Its Implication for Crime Control and Problem-Oriented Policing." In: G. Farrell and K. Pease (eds.), *Repeat Victimization*. Crime Prevention Studies 12. Monsey, N.Y.: Criminal Justice Press.

————, W. Sousa, and D. Lamm Weisel. (2002). "The Time-Window Effect in the Measurement of Repeat Victimization: A Methodology for its Examination, and an Empirical Study." In: N. Tilley (ed.), *Analysis for Crime Prevention*. Crime Prevention Studies 13. Monsey, N.Y.: Criminal Justice Press.

Farrington, D. P. (1983). "Offending from 10 to 25 Years of Age." In: K. Van Dusen and S. A. Mednick (eds.), *Prospective Studies of Crime and Delinquency*. Boston: Kluwer-Nijhoff.

————, L. Ohlin, and J. Q. Wilson. (1986). *Understanding and Preventing Crime*. New York: Springer-Verlag.

————, and A. Petrosino. (2001). "The Campbell Collaboration Crime and Justice Group." *Annals of the American Academy of Political and Social Science* 578:35–49.

————, and B. Welsh. (2005). "Randomized Experiments in Criminology: What Have We Learned in the Last Two Decades?" *Journal of Experimental Criminology* 1:9–38.

Feeney, F. (1986). "Robbers as Decision-Makers." In: D. Cornish and R. V. Clarke (eds.), *The Reasoning Criminal: Rational Choice Perspectives on Offending.* New York: Springer-Verlag.

Felson, M. (1994). *Crime and Everyday Life.* Thousand Oaks, Calif.: Pine Forge.

———. (2006). *Crime and Nature.* Thousand Oaks, Calif.: Sage.

———, and R. V. Clarke. (1998). *Opportunity Makes the Thief: Practical Theory for Crime Prevention.* Crime Prevention and Detection Series Paper 98. London: Home Office.

———, et al. (1996). "Redesigning Hell: Preventing Crime and Disorder at the Port Authority Bus Terminal." In: R. V. Clarke (ed.), *Preventing Mass Transit Crime.* Crime Prevention Studies 6. Monsey, N.Y.: Criminal Justice Press.

Fielding, H. ([1751] 1977). *An Enquiry into the Causes of the Late Increase of Robbers.* Montclair, N.J.: Patterson-Smith.

Forrester, D., M. Chatterton, and K. Pease. (1988). *The Kirkholt Burglary Prevention Project.* Home Office Crime Prevention Unit Paper 13. London: Home Office.

———, S. Frenz, M. O'Connell, and K. Pease. (1990). *The Kirkholt Burglary Prevention Project: Phase II.* Home Office Crime Prevention Unit Paper 23. London: Home Office.

Forry, W. (2008). "BPD's Safe Streets Deployment Getting High Marks after First Year." *Dorchester Reporter,* August 14:1.

Friedman, J., S. Hakim, and J. Weinblatt. (1989). "Casino Gambling as a 'Growth Pole' Strategy and its Effects on Crime." *Journal of Regional Science* 29:615–23.

Frisbie, D., G. Fishbine, R. Hintz, M. Joelsons, and J. B. Nutter. (1977). *Crime in Minneapolis: Proposals for Prevention.* St. Paul, Minn.: Governor's Commission on Crime Prevention and Control.

Fritsch, E. J., T. Caeti, and R. W. Taylor. (1999). "Gang Suppression through Saturation Patrol, Aggressive Curfew, and Truancy Enforcement: A Quasi-Experimental Test of the Dallas Anti-Gang Initiative." *Crime & Delinquency* 45:122–39.

Gabor, T. (1990). "Crime Displacement and Situational Prevention: Toward the Development of Some Principles." *Canadian Journal of Criminology* 32:41–74.

———, M. Baril, M. Cusson, E. Elie, M. Le Blanc, and A. Normandeau. (1987). *Armed Robbery: Cops, Robbers, and Victims.* Springfield, Ill.: Charles C. Thomas.

Garofolo, J. (1977). *Public Opinion about Crime: The Attitudes of Victims and Nonvictims in Selected Cities.* Washington, D.C.: Government Printing Office.

———. (1987). "Reassessing the Lifestyle Model of Criminal Victimization." In: M. Gottfredson and T. Hirschi (eds.), *Positive Criminology.* Newbury Park, Calif.: Sage.

Gau, S., and R. Larson. (1988). "Hypercube Model with Multiple-Unit Dispatches and Police-Patrol-Initiated Activities." MIT Operations Research Center Working Paper #OR 188–88.

Gill, M., and K. Pease. (1998). "Repeat Robbers: How Are They Different?" In: M. Gill (ed.), *Crime at Work: Studies in Security and Crime Prevention.* Leicester, U.K.: Perpetuity Press.

Gladwell, M. (2000). *The Tipping Point: How Little Things Can Make a Big Difference.* Boston: Little, Brown.

Goldkamp, J. S., and E. R. Vilcica. (2008). "Targeted Enforcement and Adverse System Side Effects: The Generation of Fugitives in Philadelphia." *Criminology* 46:371–410.

Goldstein, H. (1979). "Improving Policing: A Problem-Oriented Approach." *Crime & Delinquency* 25:236–58.

———. (1990). *Problem-Oriented Policing.* Philadelphia, Pa.: Temple University Press.

Golub, A., B. D. Johnson, and E. Dunlap. (2007). "The Race/Ethnicity Disparity in Misdemeanor Marijuana Arrests in New York City." *Criminology and Public Policy* 6:131–64.

Gottfredson, M., and T. Hirschi. (1990). *A General Theory of Crime.* Stanford, Calif.: Stanford University Press.

Grandjean, C. (1990). "Bank Robberies and Physical Security in Switzerland: A Case Study of the Escalation and Displacement Phenomena." *Security Journal* 1:155–59.

Green, L. (1996). *Policing Places with Drug Problems.* Thousand Oaks, Calif.: Sage.

Green Mazerolle, L., and J. Roehl. (1998). "Civil Remedies and Crime Prevention: An Introduction." In: L. Green Mazerolle and J. Roehl (eds.),

Civil Remedies and Crime Prevention. Crime Prevention Studies 9. Monsey, N.Y.: Criminal Justice Press.

Greenberg, S. W., and W. M. Rohe. (1984). "Neighborhood Design and Crime: A Test of Two Perspectives." *Journal of the American Planning Association* 49:48–61.

Greene, J. A. (1999). "Zero Tolerance: A Case Study of Police Practices and Policies in New York City." *Crime & Delinquency* 45:171–81.

Greene, J. R. (2000). "Community Policing in America: Changing the Nature, Structure and Function of the Police." In: J. Horney, R. Peterson, D. MacKenzie, J. Martin, and D. Rosenbaum (eds.), *Policies, Processes and Decisions of the Criminal Justice System.* Criminal Justice 2000 Series, vol. 3. Washington, D.C.: U.S. National Institute of Justice.

Greenwood, P., J. Chaiken, and J. Petersilia. (1977). *The Investigation Process.* Lexington, Mass.: Lexington Books.

Grinc, R. (1994). "'Angels in Marble:' Problems in Stimulating Community Involvement in Community Policing." *Crime & Delinquency* 40:437–68.

Groff, E., D. L. Weisburd, and N. Morris. (2009). "Where the Action Is at Places: Examining Spatio-Temporal Patterns of Juvenile Crime at Places Using Trajectory Analysisand GIS." In: D. L. Weisburd, W. Bernasco, and G. Bruinsma (eds.), *Putting Crime in its Place: Units of Analysis in Geographic Criminology.* New York: Springer.

Guerry, A. M. (1833). *Essai sur la statistique morale de la France.* Paris: Crochard.

Guevara, J. P., J. Berlin, and F. Wolf. (2004). "Meta-Analytic Methods for Pooling Rates when Follow-up Duration Varies: A Case Study." *BMC Medical Research Methodology* 4:4–17.

Guyot, D. (1979). "Bending Granite: Attempts to Change the Rank Structure of American Police Departments." *Journal of Police Science and Administration* 7:253–84.

Hagan, J., C. Shedd, and M. Payne. (2005). "Race, Ethnicity and Youth Perceptions of Criminal Injustice." *American Sociological Review* 70:381–407.

Hale, C. (1982). "Patrol Administration." In: B. Gamire (ed.), *Local Governmental Police Management.* 2nd ed. Washington, D.C.: International City Management Association.

Hannan, T. H. (1982). "Bank Robberies and Bank Security Precautions." *Journal of Legal Studies* 11:83–92.

Harcourt, B. (1998). "Reflecting on the Subject: A Critique of the Social Influence of Deterrence, the Broken Windows Theory, and Order-Maintenance Policing New York Style." *Michigan Law Review* 97:291–389.

———. (2001). *Illusion of Order: The False Promise of Broken Windows Policing*. Cambridge, Mass.: Harvard University Press.

———, and J. Ludwig. (2007). "Reefer Madness: Broken Windows Policing and Misdemeanor Marijuana Arrests in New York City, 1989–2000." *Criminology and Public Policy* 6:165–82.

Harries, K. (1999). *Mapping Crime: Principle and Practice*. Washington, D.C.: National Institute of Justice, U.S. Department of Justice.

Harris, D. (1999). "The Stories, the Statistics, and the Law: Why 'Driving While Black' Matters." *Minnesota Law Review* 84:265–325.

Hawkins, J. D., M. Arthur, and R. Catalano. (1995). "Preventing Substance Abuse." In: M. Tonry and D. Farrington (eds.), *Building a Safer Society: Strategic Approaches to Crime Prevention*. Chicago: University of Chicago Press.

Hawley, A. (1944). "Ecology and Human Ecology." *Social Forces* 23:398–405.

———. (1950). *Human Ecology: A Theory of Urban Structure*. New York: Ronald Press.

Hay, R., and R. McCleary. (1979). "On the Specification of Box-Tiao Time Series Models for Impact Assessment: A Comment on the Recent Work of Deutsch and Alt." *Evaluation Quarterly* 3:277–314.

Heckman, J., and J. Smith. (1995). "Assessing the Case for Social Experiments." *Journal of Economic Perspectives* 9:85–110.

Hesseling, R. (1994). "Displacement: A Review of the Empirical Literature." *Crime Prevention Studies* 3:197–230.

Hindelang, M. J. (1974). "Public Opinion Regarding Crime, Criminal Justice, and Related Topics." *Journal of Research in Crime and Delinquency* 11:101–16.

———, M. Gottfredson, and J. Garofalo. (1978). *Victims of Personal Crime: An Empirical Foundation for a Theory of Personal Victimization*. Cambridge, Mass.: Ballinger.

Hinkle, J., and D. L. Weisburd. (2008). "The Irony of Broken Windows Policing: A Micro-Place Study of the Relationship between Disorder, Focused Police Crackdowns, and Fear of Crime." *Journal of Criminal Justice* 36:503–12.

Hirschi, T. (1969). *Causes of Delinquency*. Berkeley and Los Angeles: University of California Press.

Holmes, T., and R. Rahe. (1967). "The Social Readjustment Rating Scale." *Journal of Psychosomatic Research* 11:213–18.

Homel, R., and J. Clark. (1994). "The Prevention of Violence in Pubs and Clubs." *Crime Prevention Studies* 3:1–46.

Hope, T. (1994). "Problem-Oriented Policing and Drug Market Locations: Three Case Studies." *Crime Prevention Studies* 2:5–32.

Hough, M., and N. Tilley. (1998). *Getting the Grease to Squeak: Research Lessons for Crime Prevention*. Crime Detection and Prevention Series Paper 85. London: Home Office.

Huang, W. S. W., and M. S. Vaughn. (1996). "Support and Confidence: Public Attitudes toward the Police." In: T. J. Flanagan and D. R. Longmire (eds.), *Americans View Crime and Justice: A National Public Opinion Survey*. Thousand Oaks, Calif.: Sage.

Hughes, K. (2006). *Justice Expenditure and Employment in the United States, 2003*. Washington, D.C.: U.S. Department of Justice, Bureau of Justice Statistics.

Hunter, A., and T. Baumer. (1982). "Street Traffic, Social Integration, and Fear of Crime." *Sociological Inquiry* 52:122–31.

Hunter, R. (1988). "Environmental Characteristics of Convenience Store Robberies in the State of Florida." Paper presented at the annual meeting of the American Society of Criminology, Chicago.

———, and C. R Jeffrey. (1992). "Preventing Convenience Store Robbery through Environmental Design." In: R. Clarke (ed.), *Situational Crime Prevention: Successful Case Studies*. Albany, N.Y.: Harrow and Heston.

Jang, S. J., and B. Johnson. (2001). "Neighborhood Disorder, Individual Religiosity, and Adolescent Use of Illicit Drugs: A Test of Multilevel Hypotheses." *Criminology* 39:109–44.

Johnson, E., and J. Payne. (1986). "The Decision to Commit a Crime: An Information-Processing Analysis." In: D. Cornish and R. Clarke (eds.), *The Reasoning Criminal: Rational Choice Perspectives on Offending*. New York: Springer-Verlag.

Johnson, S., and K. Bowers. (2004). "The Burglary as Clue to the Future: The Beginnings of Prospective Hot-Spotting." *European Journal of Criminology* 1:237–55.

——, and K. Bowers. (2007). "Burglary Prediction: The Roles of Theory, Flow, and Friction." In: G. Farrell, K. Bowers, S. Johnson, and M. Townsley (eds.), *Imagination for Crime Prevention: Essays in Honour of Ken Pease*. Crime Prevention Studies 21. Monsey, N.Y.: Criminal Justice Press.

Kahan, D., and T. L. Meares. (1998). "The Coming Crisis of Criminal Procedure." *Georgetown Law Journal* 86:1153–84.

Kane, R. (2002). "The Social Ecology of Police Misconduct." *Criminology* 40:867–96.

Kansas City Police Department. (1978). *Response Time Analysis: Executive Summary*. Washington, D.C.: U.S. Department of Justice.

Kelling, G., and C. Coles. (1996). *Fixing Broken Windows: Restoring Order and Reducing Crime in Our Communities*. New York: Free Press.

——, T. Pate, D. Dieckman and C. Brown. (1974). *The Kansas City Preventive Patrol Experiment: A Technical Report*. Washington, D.C.: Police Foundation.

——, and M. H. Moore. (1988). "From Political to Reform to Community: The Evolving Strategy of Police." In: J. Greene and S. Mastrofski (eds.), *Community Policing: Rhetoric or Reality?* New York: Praeger.

Kennedy, D. M. (2006). "Old Wine in New Bottles: Policing and the Lessons of Pulling Levers." In: D. L. Weisburd and A. A. Braga (eds.), *Police Innovation: Contrasting Perspectives*. New York: Cambridge University Press.

——, and M. H. Moore. (1995). "Underwriting the Risky Investment in Community Policing: What Social Science Should Be Doing to Evaluate Community Policing." *Justice System Journal* 17(3): 271–90.

——, A. M. Piehl, and A. A. Braga. (1996). "Youth Violence in Boston: Gun Markets, Serious Youth Offenders, and a Use-Reduction Strategy." *Law and Contemporary Problems* 59:147–97.

Kennedy, R. (1997). *Race, Crime and the Law*. New York: Pantheon.

Kleck, G. (1991). *Point Blank: Guns and Violence in America*. New York: Aldine de Gruyter.

Kleiman, M. (1988). "Crackdowns: The Effects of Intensive Enforcement on Retail Heroin Dealing." In: M. Chaiken (ed.), *Street-Level Drug Enforcement: Examining the Issues*. Washington, D.C.: National Institute of Justice.

Klinger, D., and G. Bridges. (1997). "Measurement Error in Calls-for-Service as an Indicator of Crime." *Criminology* 35:705–26.

Klockars, C. (1985). "Order Maintenance, the Quality of Urban Life, and Police: A Different Line of Argument." In: W. Geller (ed.), *Police Leadership in America: Crisis and Opportunity.* New York: Praeger.

Koper, C. (1995). "Just Enough Police Presence: Reducing Crime and Disorderly Behavior by Optimizing Patrol Time in Crime Hot Spots." *Justice Quarterly* 12:649–72.

Krueger, A. B., and J. Maleckova. (2003). "Education, Poverty and Terrorism: Is There a Causal Connection?" *Journal of Economic Perspectives* 17:119–44.

Kube, E. (1988). "Preventing Bank Robbery: Lessons from Interviewing Robbers." *Journal of Security Administration.* 11:78–83.

Landes, W. M. (1978). "An Economic Study of U.S. Aircraft Hijacking, 1961–1976." *Journal of Law and Economics* 21:1–32.

Larson, R. (1972). *Urban Police Patrol Analysis.* Cambridge: MIT Press.

Laub, J., and R. Sampson. (2003). *Shared Beginnings, Divergent Lives: Delinquent Boys to Age 70.* Cambridge, Mass.: Harvard University Press.

Lauritsen, J., R. Sampson, and J. Laub. (1991). "The Link between Offending and Victimization among Adolescents." *Criminology* 29:265–92.

LaVigne, N. G. (1991). "Crimes of Convenience: An Analysis of Criminal Decision-Making and Convenience Store Crime in Austin, Texas." Master's thesis, University of Texas, Austin.

Laycock, G. (1985). *Property Marking: A Deterrent to Domestic Burglary?* Crime Prevention Unit Paper 3. London: Home Office.

———, and C. Austin. (1992). "Crime Prevention in Parking Facilities." *Security Journal* 3:154–60.

LeBeau, J. (1987). "The Methods and Measures of Centrography and the Spatial Dynamics of Rape." *Journal of Quantitative Criminology* 3:125–41.

Leigh, A., T. Read, and N. Tilley. (1996). *Problem-Oriented Policing: Brit POP.* Crime Prevention and Detection Series Paper 75. London: Home Office.

Lenz, R. (1986). "Geographical and Temporal Changes among Robberies in Milwaukee." In: R. M. Figlio, S. Hakim, and G. F. Rengert (eds.), *Metropolitan Crime Patterns.* Monsey, N.Y.: Criminal Justice Press.

Levine, J. P. (1975). "The Ineffectiveness of Adding Police to Prevent Crime." *Public Policy* 23:523–45.

Lewin, K. (1947). "Group Decisions and Social Change." In: T. Newcomb and E. Hartley (eds.), *Readings in Social Psychology.* New York: Atherton Press.

Lipsey, M. (1990). *Design Sensitivity: Statistical Power for Experimental Research*. Thousand Oaks, Calif.: Sage.

———. (1992). "Juvenile Delinquency Treatment: A Meta-Analytic Inquiry." In: T. D. Cook, H. Cooper, D. Codray, H. Hartman, L. Hedges, R. Light, T. Louis, and F. Mosteller (eds.), *Meta-Analysis for Explanation: A Casebook*. New York: Sage.

———, and D. Wilson. (1993). *Practical Meta-Analysis*. Thousand Oaks, Calif.: Sage.

Locke, H. G. (1995). "The Color of Law and the Issue of Color: Race and the Abuse of Police Power." In: W. A. Geller and H. Toch (eds.), *And Justice for All: Understanding and Controlling Police Abuse of Force*. Washington, D.C.: Police Executive Research Forum.

Loeber, R., and D. Farrington. (1998). *Serious and Violent Juvenile Offenders: Risk Factors and Successful Interventions*. Thousand Oaks, Calif.: Sage.

Loftin, C., and R. Hill. (1974). "Regional Subculture and Homicide: An Examination of the Gastil-Hackney Thesis." *American Sociological Review* 39:714–24.

Ludwig, J., and P. Cook. (2000). "Homicide and Suicide Rates Associated with the Implementation of the Brady Handgun Violence Prevention Act." *Journal of the American Medical Association* 284:585–91.

———, and D. Miller. (2007). "Does Head Start Improve Children's Life Chances? Evidence from a Regression Discontinuity Design." *Quarterly Journal of Economics* 122:159–208.

MacKenzie, D. L. (2000). "Evidence-Based Corrections: Identifying What Works." *Crime & Delinquency* 46:457–71.

Madensen, T. D. (2007). "Bar Management and Crime: Toward a Dynamic Theory of Place Management and Crime Hot Spots." Unpublished PhD diss., University of Cincinnati, Ohio.

———, and J. E. Eck. (2008). "Violence in Bars: Exploring the Impact of Place Manager Decision-Making." *Crime Prevention and Community Safety* 10:111–25.

Maguire, M. (1988). "Searchers and Opportunists: Offender Behavior and Burglary Prevention." *Journal of Security Administration* 11:70–77.

Mamalian, C., N. LaVigne, and E. Groff. (1999). *The Use of Computerized Crime Mapping by Law Enforcement: Survey Results*. NIJ Research Preview.

Washington, D.C.: U.S. Department of Justice, National Institute of Justice.

Maple, J. (1999). *The Crime Fighter: How You Can Make Your Community Crime Free*. New York: Broadway.

Martinson, R. (1974). "What Works? Questions and Answers about Prison Reform." *The Public Interest* 35:22–54.

Mastrofski, S. D. (1998). "Community Policing and Police Organization Structure." In: J. P. Brodeur (ed.), *How to Recognize Good Policing: Problems and Issues*. Thousand Oaks, Calif.: Sage.

———. (2006). "Community Policing: A Skeptical View." In: D. L. Weisburd and A. A. Braga (eds.), *Police Innovation: Contrasting Perspectives*. New York: Cambridge University Press.

———, R. B. Parks, C. DeJong, and R. E. Worden. (1998). "Race and Every-Day Policing: A Research Perspective." Paper delivered at the 12th International Congress on Criminology. Seoul, South Korea, August.

———, and R. Ritti. (2000). "Making Sense of Community Policing: A Theoretical Perspective." *Police Practice and Research* 1:183–210.

Matthews, R. (1990). "Developing More Effective Strategies for Curbing Prostitution." *Security Journal* 1:182–87.

Mawby, R. I. (1977). "Defensible Space: A Theoretical and Empirical Appraisal." *Urban Studies* 14:169–79.

Mayhew, P. (1979). "Defensible Space: The Current Status of a Crime Prevention Theory." *Howard Journal of Penology and Crime Prevention* 18:150–59.

———. (1981). "Crime in Public View: Surveillance and Crime Prevention." In: P. J. Brantingham and P. L. Brantingham (eds.), *Environmental Criminology*. Beverly Hills, Calif.: Sage.

———, R. V. Clarke, and J. M. Hough. (1980). "Steering Column Locks and Car Theft." In: R. V. Clarke and P. Mayhew (eds.), *Designing Out Crime*. London: H.M. Stationery Office.

Mayhew, P., R. V. Clarke, A. Sturman, and M. Hough. (1976). *Crime as Opportunity*. Home Office Research Study 34. London: H.M. Stationary Office.

Mazerolle, L., J. F. Price, and J. Roehl. (2000). "Civil Remedies and Drug Control: A Randomized Field Trial in Oakland, California." *Evaluation Review* 24:212–41.

Mazerolle, L., and J. Ransley. (2005). *Third-Party Policing*. Cambridge, U.K.: Cambridge University Press.

———. (2006). "The Case for Third-Party Policing." In: D. L. Weisburd and A.A. Braga (eds.), *Police Innovation: Contrasting Perspectives*. New York: Cambridge University Press.

Mazerolle, L., and W. Terrill. (1997). "Problem-Oriented Policing in Public Housing: Identifying the Distribution of Problem Places." *Policing: An International Journal of Police Strategies and Management* 20:235–55.

McCauley, C. (2002). "Psychological Issues in Understanding Terrorism and the Response to Terrorism." In: C. Stout and K. Schwab (eds.), *The Psychology of Terrorism*. Volume 3. *Theoretical Understandings and Perspectives*. Westport, Conn.: Praeger.

McCord, J. (2003). "Cures that Harm: Unanticipated Outcomes of Crime Prevention Programs." *Annals of the American Academy of Political and Social Science* 587:16–30.

McGarrell, E., S. Chermak, A. Weiss, and J. Wilson. (2001). "Reducing Firearms Violence through Directed Police Patrol." *Criminology and Public Policy* 1:119–48.

———, S. Chermak, J. Wilson, and N. Corsaro. (2006). "Reducing Homicide through a 'Lever-Pulling' Strategy." *Justice Quarterly* 23:214–29.

McKnew, M. A. (1983). "An Approximation to the Hypercube Model with Patrol Initiated Activities: An Application to Police." *Decision Sciences* 14:408–18.

Meares, T. L. (2004). "Mass Incarceration: Who Pays the Price for Criminal Offending?" *Criminology and Public Policy* 3:295–302.

———. (2006). "Third-Party Policing: A Critical View." In: D. L. Weisburd and A. A. Braga (eds.), *Police Innovation: Contrasting Perspectives*. New York: Cambridge University Press.

———, and K. Brown Corkran. (2007). "When 2 or 3 Come Together." *William and Mary Law Review* 48:1315–87.

Merry, S. F. (1981). "Defensible Space Undefended: Social Factors in Crime Prevention through Environmental Design." *Urban Affairs Quarterly* 16:397–422.

Merton, R. K. (1968). "Social Structure and Anomie." *American Sociological Review* 3:672–82.

Meyer, J., and B. Rowan. (1977). "Formal Structure as Myth." *American Journal of Sociology* 83:340–63.

Moffitt, T. (1993). "Adolescence-Limited and Life-Course Persistent Antisocial Behavior: A Developmental Taxonomy." *Psychological Review* 4:674.

Moore, M. H. (1980). "The Police and Weapons Offenses." *Annals of the American Academy of Political and Social Science* 455:92–109.

———. (2002). *Recognizing Value in Policing*. Washington, D.C.: Police Executive Research Forum.

———. (2006). "Improving Police through Expertise, Experience, and Experiments." In: D. L. Weisburd and A. A. Braga (eds.), *Police Innovation: Contrasting Perspectives*. New York: Cambridge University Press.

———, and A. A. Braga. (2003). "Measuring and Improving Police Performance: The Lessons of Compstat and its Progeny." *Policing: An International Journal of Police Strategies and Management* 26:439–53.

———, and A. A. Braga. (2004). "Police Performance Measurement: A Normative Framework." *Criminal Justice Ethics* 23:3–19.

Nagin, D. (1999). "Analyzing Developmental Trajectories: A Semiparametric, Group-Based Approach." *Psychological Methods* 4:139–57.

Nasar, J. L. (1981). "Environmental Factors and Commercial Burglary." *Journal of Environmental Systems* 11:49–56.

Nettler, G. (1978). *Explaining Crime*. 2nd ed. New York: McGraw-Hill.

Newman, O. (1972). *Defensible Space*. New York: Macmillan.

Nichols Jr., W. W. (1980). "Mental Maps, Social Characteristics, and Criminal Mobility." In: D. E. Georges-Abeyie and K. Harries (eds.). *Crime: A Spatial Perspective*. New York: Columbia University Press.

O'Connor Shelly, T., and Anne Grant (eds.). (1998). *Problem-Oriented Policing: Crime-Specific Problems, Critical Issues, and Making POP Work*. Washington, D.C.: Police Executive Research Forum.

Ohlin, L., and F. Remington (eds.) (1993). *Discretion in Criminal Justice: The Tension Between Individualization and Uniformity*. Albany: State University of New York Press.

Pate, A., R. Bowers, and R. Parks. (1976). *Three Approaches to Criminal Apprehension in Kansas City: An Evaluation Report*. Washington, D.C.: Police Foundation.

Pate, A., and W. Skogan. (1985). *Coordinated Community Policing: The Newark Experience*. Technical Report. Washington, D.C.: Police Foundation.

————, M. A. Wycoff, and L. Sherman. (1986). *Reducing Fear of Crime in Houston and Newark: A Summary Report.* Washington, D.C.: Police Foundation.

Paternoster, R., R. Brame, R. Bachman, and L. Sherman. (1997). "Do Fair Procedures Matter? The Effect of Procedural Justice on Spouse Assault." *Law & Society Review* 31:163–204.

Pawson, R., and N. Tilley. (1997). *Realistic Evaluation.* London: Sage.

Pease, K. (1991). "The Kirkholt Project: Preventing Burglary on a British Public Housing Estate." *Security Journal* 2:73–77.

————. (1998). *Repeat Victimization: Taking Stock.* Crime Detection and Prevention Series Paper 90. London: Home Office.

————, and G. Laycock. (1996). *Repeat Victimization: Reducing the Heat on Hot Victims.* Washington, D.C.: National Institute of Justice, U.S. Department of Justice.

Petersilia, J. (2003). *When Prisoners Come Home: Parole and Prisoner Reentry.* New York: Oxford University Press.

Petrosino, A., R. Boruch, H. Soydan, L. Duggan, and J. Sanchez-Meca. (2001). "Meeting the Challenge of Evidence-Based Policy: The Campbell Collaboration. *Annals of the American Academy of Political and Social Science* 578:14–34.

Phillips, P. D. (1980). "Characteristics and Typology of the Journey to Crime." In: D. E. Georges-Abeyie and K. Harries (eds.), *Crime: A Spatial Perspective.* New York: Columbia University Press.

Pierce, G. L., and W. Bowers. (1981). "The Bartley-Fox Gun Law's Short-Term Impact on Crime in Boston." *Annals of the American Academy of Political and Social Science* 455:120–37.

————, S. Spaar, and L. Briggs. (1988). *The Character of Police Work Strategic and Tactical Implications.* Boston, Mass.: Center for Applied Social Research.

Police Executive Research Forum. (2008). *Violent Crime in America: What We Know About Hot Spots Enforcement.* Washington, D.C.: Police Executive Research Forum.

Police Foundation. (1981). *The Newark Foot Patrol Experiment.* Washington, D.C.: Police Foundation.

Polvi, N., T. Looman, C. Humphries, and K. Pease. (1990). "Repeat Break-and-Enter Victimization: Time-Course and Crime Prevention Opportunity." *Journal of Police Science and Administration* 17:8–11.

Polvi, N., T. Looman, C. Humphries, and K. Pease. (1991). "The Time-Course of Repeat Burglary Victimization." *British Journal of Criminology* 31:411–14.

Poyner, B. (1988). "Video Cameras and Bus Vandalism." *Security Administration* 11:44–51.

Press, J. S. (1971). "Some Effects of an Increase in Police Manpower in the 20th Precinct of New York City." New York: Rand Institute.

Quetelet, A. J. (1842). *A Treatise of Man.* 1969 ed. Gainesville, Fla.: Scholar's Facsimiles and Reprints.

Raine, A. (1993). *The Psychopathy of Crime.* New York: Academic Press.

Rand, A. (1986). "Mobility Triangles." In: R. M. Figlio, S. Hakim, and G. F. Rengert (eds.), *Metropolitan Crime Patterns.* Monsey, N.Y.: Criminal Justice Press.

Read, T., and N. Tilley. (2000). *Not Rocket Science? Problem-Solving and Crime Reduction.* Crime Reduction Series Paper 6. London: Policing and Crime Reduction Unit, Home Office.

Ready, J., L. Green Mazerolle, and E. Revere. (1998). "Getting Evicted from Public Housing: An Analysis of the Factors Influencing Eviction Decisions in Six Public Housing Sites." In: L. Green Mazerolle and J. Roehl (eds.), *Civil Remedies and Crime Prevention.* Crime Prevention Studies 9. New York: Criminal Justice Press.

Reinier, G. H. (1977). *Crime Analysis in Support of Patrol.* National Evaluation Program: Phase I Report. Washington, D.C.: U.S. Government Printing Office.

Reiss, A. (1971). *The Police and the Public.* New Haven, Conn.: Yale University Press.

———. (1980). "Victim Proneness in Repeat Victimization by Type of Crime." In S. Fienberg and A. Reiss (eds.), *Indicators of Crime and Criminal Justice: Quantitative Studies.* Washington, D.C.: Bureau of Justice Statistics, U.S. Department of Justice.

———. (1995). "The Role of Police in Crime Prevention." In: P. O. Wikstrom, R. V. Clarke, and J. McCord (eds.), *Integrating Crime Prevention Strategies: Propensity and Opportunity.* Stockholm: National Council for Crime Prevention.

———, and J. Roth (eds.) (1993). *Understanding and Preventing Violence.* Washington, D.C.: U.S. National Academy Press.

Rengert, G. (1980). "Theory and Practice in Urban Police Response." In: D. Georges-Abeyie and K. Harries (eds.), *Crime: A Spatial Perspective.* New York: Columbia University Press.

———. (1981). "Burglary in Philadelphia: A Critique of an Opportunity Structure Model." In: P. J. Brantingham and P. L. Brantingham (eds.), *Environmental Criminology.* Beverly Hills, Calif.: Sage.

———, M. Mattson, and K. Henderson. (2001). *Campus Security: Situational Crime Prevention in High-Density Environments.* Monsey, N.Y.: Criminal Justice Press.

———, and J. Wasilchick. (1990). "Space, Time, and Crime: Ethnographic Insights into Residential Burglary." Report submitted to U.S. Department of Justice, National Institute of Justice.

Repetto, T. (1976). "Crime Prevention and the Displacement Phenomenon." *Crime & Delinquency* 22:166–77.

Rhodes, W., and C. Conley. (1981) "Crime and Mobility: An Empirical Study." In: P. J. Brantingham and P. L. Brantingham (eds.), *Environmental Criminology.* Newbury Park, Calif.: Sage.

Rich, J., and D. Stone. (1996). "The Experience of Violent Injury for Young African-American Men: The Meaning of Being a 'Sucker.'" *Journal of General Internal Medicine* 11:77–82.

Ritti, R., and S. D. Mastrofski. (2002). *The Institutionalization of Community Policing: A Study of the Presentation of the Concept in Two Law Enforcement Journals.* Final report to the U.S. National Institute of Justice. Manassas, Va.: George Mason University.

Robinson, J., B. Lawton, R. Taylor, and D. Perkins. (2003). "Multilevel Longitudinal Impacts of Incivilities: Fear of Crime, Expected Safety, and Block Satisfaction." *Journal of Quantitative Criminology* 19:237–74.

Roncek, D. (1981). "Dangerous Places: Crime and Residential Environment." *Social Forces* 60:74–96.

———, and R. Bell. (1981). "Bars, Blocks, and Crime." *Journal of Environmental Systems* 11:35–47.

———, and D. Faggiani. (1985). "High Schools and Crime." *Sociological Quarterly* 26:491–505.

———, and A. Lobosco. (1983). "The Effect of High Schools on Crime in Their Neighborhoods." *Social Science Quarterly* 64:598–613.

————, and P. Meier. (1991). "Bar Blocks and Crimes Revisited: Linking the Theory of Routine Activities to the Empiricism of 'Hot Spots.'" *Criminology* 29:725–55.

————, and M. Pravatiner. (1989). "Additional Evidence that Taverns Enhance Nearby Crime." *Sociology and Social Research* 73:185–88.

Rosenbaum, D. (1993). "Civil Liberties and Aggressive Enforcement." In: R. Davis, A. Lurigio, and D. Rosenbaum (eds.), *Drugs and the Community.* Springfield, Ill.: Charles C. Thomas.

————. (ed.) (1994). *The Challenge of Community Policing: Testing the Promises.* Thousand Oaks, Calif.: Sage.

————. (2002). "Evaluating Multi-Agency Anti-Crime Partnerships: Theory, Design, and Measurement Issues." *Crime Prevention Studies* 14:171–225.

————. (2006). "The Limits of Hot Spots Policing." In: D. L. Weisburd and A. A. Braga (eds.), *Police Innovation: Contrasting Perspectives.* New York: Cambridge University Press.

Roth, J., J. Ryan, S. Gaffigan, C. Koper, M. Moore, J. Roehl, C. Johnson, G. Moore, R. White, M. Buerger, E. Langston, and D. Thacher. (2000). *National Evaluation of the COPS Program—Title I of the 1994 Crime Act.* Washington, D.C.: National Institute of Justice, U.S. Department of Justice.

Sabol, W., H. Couture, and P. Harrison. (2007). *Prisoners in 2006.* Washington, D.C.: U.S. Department of Justice, Bureau of Justice Statistics.

Sacks, S. (2003). "Evaluation of Police Patrol Patterns." Working paper 2003–17, University of Connecticut, Department of Economics.

Sadd, S., and R. Grinc. (1994). "Innovative Neighborhood Oriented Policing: An Evaluation of Community Policing Programs in Eight Cities." In: D. Rosenbaum (ed.), *The Challenge of Community Policing: Testing the Promises.* Thousand Oaks, Calif.: Sage.

Sampson, A., and C. Philips. (1992). *Multiple Victimization: Racial Attacks on an East London Estate.* Home Office Crime Prevention Unit Paper 36. London: Home Office.

Sampson, R. (1985). "Neighborhood and Crime: The Structural Determinants of Personal Victimization." *Journal of Research in Crime and Delinquency* 22:7–40.

————. (1999). "What 'Community' Supplies." In R. Ferguson and W. T. Dickens (eds.), *Urban Problems and Community Development.* Washington, D.C.: Brookings Institution Press.

———. (2002). "The Community." In: J. Q. Wilson and J. Petersilia (eds.), *Crime*. Oakland, Calif.: ICS Press.

———, and D. J. Bartusch. (1998). "Legal Cynicism and (Subcultural?) Tolerance of Deviance: The Neighborhood Context of Racial Differences." *Law and Society Review* 32:777–804.

———, and W. B. Groves. (1989). "Community Structure and Crime: Testing Social Disorganization Theory." *American Journal of Sociology* 94:774–802.

———, and J. Laub. (1993). *Crime in the Making: Pathways and Turning Points through Life*. Cambridge, Mass.: Harvard University Press.

———, and J. Lauritsen. (1994). "Violent Victimization and Offending: Individual-, Situational-, and Community-Level Risk Factors." In: A. Reiss and J. Roth (eds.), *Understanding and Preventing Violence: Social Influences*, vol. 3. Washington, D.C.: U.S. National Academy Press.

———, and S. Raudenbush. (1999). "Systematic Social Observation of Public Spaces: A New Look at Disorder in Urban Neighborhoods." *American Journal of Sociology* 105:603–51.

———, S. Raudenbush, and F. Earls. (1997). "Neighborhoods and Violent Crime." *Science* 277:918–24.

Scherdin, M. J. (1992). "The Halo Effect: Psychological Deterrence of Electronic Security Systems." In: R. V. Clarke (ed.), *Situational Crime Prevention: Successful Case Studies*. Albany, N.Y.: Harrow and Heston.

Schnelle, J., R. Kirchner, J. Casey, P. Uselton, and P. McNees. (1977). "Patrol Evaluation Research: A Multiple-Baseline Analysis of Saturation Police Patrolling during Day and Night Hours." *Journal of Applied Behavior Analysis* 10:33–40.

Schumann, H., C. Steeh, L. Bobo, and M. Krysan. (1997). *Racial Attitudes in America*. Cambridge, Mass.: Harvard University Press.

Scott, M. (2000). *Problem-Oriented Policing: Reflections on the First 20 Years*. Washington, D.C.: Office of Community Oriented Policing Services, U.S. Department of Justice.

———. (2004a). *Burglary of Single Family Houses in Savannah, Georgia*. Final Report to the U.S. Department of Justice, Office of Community Oriented Policing Services.

———. (2004b). *The Benefits and Consequences of Police Crackdowns*. Problem-Oriented Guides for Police, Response Guides Series 1. Washington,

D.C.: U.S. Department of Justice, Office of Community Oriented Policing Services.

————, and R. V. Clarke. (2000). "A Review of Submission for the Herman Goldstein Excellence in Problem-Oriented Policing." In: C. Sole Brito and E. Gratto (eds.), *Problem Oriented Policing: Crime-Specific Problems, Critical Issues, and Making POP Work*, vol. 3. Washington, D.C.: Police Executive Research Forum.

Scott, R. (1987). *Organizations: Rational, Natural, and Open Systems*. 2nd ed. Englewood Cliffs, N.J.: Prentice Hall.

Sechrest, L. D., and A. Rosenblatt. (1987). "Research Methods." In: H. Quay (ed.), *Handbook of Juvenile Delinquency*. New York: Wiley.

Sechrest, L. D., S. White, and E. Brown. (1979). *The Rehabilitation of Criminal Offenders: Problems and Prospects*. Washington, D.C.: U.S. National Academy of Sciences Press.

Shaw, C., and H. McKay. (1942). *Juvenile Delinquency in Urban Areas*. Chicago: University of Chicago Press.

Shaw, C., and E. Myers. (1929). *The Juvenile Delinquent*. In: Illinois Crime Survey. Chicago: Illinois Association for Criminal Justice.

Shaw, J. (1995). "Community Policing against Guns: Public Opinion of the Kansas City Gun Experiment." *Justice Quarterly* 12:695–710.

Sherman, L. (1987). "Repeat Calls to Police in Minneapolis." *Crime Control Reports* 4. Washington, D.C.: Crime Control Institute.

————. (1990). "Police Crackdowns: Initial and Residual Deterrence." In: M. Tonry and N. Morris (eds.), *Crime and Justice: A Review of Research*, vol. 12. Chicago: University of Chicago Press.

————. (1991). "Herman Goldstein: Problem-Oriented Policing [book review]." *Journal of Criminal Law and Criminology* 82:693–702.

————. (1992a). *Policing Domestic Violence: Experiments and Dilemmas*. New York: Free Press.

————. (1992b). "Attacking Crime: Police and Crime Control." In: M. Tonry and N. Morris (eds.), *Modern Policing*. Crime and Justice Series 15. Chicago: University of Chicago Press.

————. (1995). "Hot Spots of Crime and Criminal Careers of Places." In: J. Eck and D. Weisburd (eds.), *Crime and Place*. Crime Prevention Studies 4. Monsey, N.Y.: Criminal Justice Press.

———. (1997). "Policing for Crime Prevention." In: L. Sherman, D. Gottfredson, D. L. MacKenzie, J. E. Eck, P. Reuter, and S. Bushway. (eds.), *Preventing Crime: What Works, What Doesn't, What's Promising*. Washington, D.C.: Office of Justice Programs, U.S. Department of Justice.

———. (1998). *Evidence-Based Policing*. Ideas in American Policing Series. Washington, D.C.: Police Foundation.

———. (2002). "Fair and Effective Policing." In: J. Wilson and J. Petersilia (eds.), *Crime*. Oakland, Calif.: ICS Press.

———, and R. Berk. (1984). "The Specific Deterrent Effects of Arrest for Domestic Assault." *American Sociological Review* 49:261–72.

———, M. Buerger, and P. Gartin. (1989). *Repeat Call Address Policing: The Minneapolis RECAP Experiment*. Final Report to the U.S. Department of Justice, National Institute of Justice. Washington, D.C.: Crime Control Institute.

———, and J. E. Eck. (2002). "Policing for Crime Prevention." In: L. Sherman, D. P. Farrington, B. Welsh, and D. L. MacKenzie (eds.), *Evidence-Based Crime Prevention*. New York: Routledge.

———, D. P. Farrington, B. Welsh, and D. L. MacKenzie. (2002). *Evidence-Based Crime Prevention*. New York: Routledge.

———, P. Gartin, and M. Buerger. (1989). "Hot Spots of Predatory Crime: Routine Activities and the Criminology of Place." *Criminology* 27:27–56.

———, D. Gottfredson, D. L. MacKenzie, J. E. Eck, P. Reuter, and S. Bushway. (1997). *Preventing Crime: What Works, What Doesn't, What's Promising*. Washington, D.C.: U.S. Department of Justice, National Institute of Justice.

———, and D. Rogan. (1995a). "Effects of Gun Seizures on Gun Violence: 'Hot Spots' Patrol in Kansas City." *Justice Quarterly* 12:673–94.

———, and D. Rogan. (1995b). "Deterrent Effects of Police Raids on Crack Houses: A Randomized Controlled Experiment." *Justice Quarterly* 12:755–82.

———, J. Schmidt, and R. Velke. (1992). *High Crime Taverns: A RECAP Project in Problem-Oriented Policing*. Final Report to the National Institute of Justice. Washington, D.C.: Crime Control Institute.

———, and D. Weisburd. (1995). "General Deterrent Effects of Police Patrol in Crime Hot Spots: A Randomized Controlled Trial." *Justice Quarterly* 12:625–48.

Silverman, E. B. (1999). *NYPD Battles Crime: Innovative Strategies in Policing.* Boston, Mass.: Northeastern University Press.

———. (2006). "Compstat's Innovation." In: D. L. Weisburd and A. A. Braga (eds.), *Police Innovation: Contrasting Perspectives.* New York: Cambridge University Press.

Skogan, W. (1990). *Disorder and Decline: Crime and the Spiral of Decay in American Neighborhoods.* New York: Free Press.

———. (2006). *Police and Community in Chicago: A Tale of Three Cities.* New York: Oxford University Press.

———, and G. Antunes. (1979). "Information, Apprehension, and Deterrence: Exploring the Limits of Police Productivity." *Journal of Criminal Justice* 7:217–42.

———, and K. Frydl (eds.) (2004). *Fairness and Effectiveness in Policing: The Evidence.* Committee to Review Research on Police Policy and Practices. Committee on Law and Justice, Division of Behavioral and Social Sciences and Education. Washington, D.C.: The National Academies Press.

———, and S. Hartnett. (1997). *Community Policing, Chicago Style.* New York: Oxford University Press.

———, S. Hartnett, J. DuBois, J. Comey, M. Kaiser, and J. Lovig. (1999). *On the Beat: Police and Community Problem Solving.* Boulder, Colo.: Westview.

———, and T. Meares. (2004). "Lawful Policing." *Annals of the American Academy of Political and Social Science* 593:66–83.

———, and L. Steiner. (2004). *CAPS at Ten: Community Policing in Chicago.* Chicago: Illinois Criminal Justice Information Authority.

Skolnick, J. H., and D. Bayley. (1986). *The New Blue Line: Police Innovations in American Cities.* New York: Free Press.

Skolnick, J. H., and J. J. Fyfe. (1993). *Above the Law.* New York: Free Press.

Sloan-Howitt, M. A., and G. L. Kelling. (1990). "Subway Graffiti in New York City: 'Getting Up' vs. 'Meanin' It and Cleanin' It'." *Security Journal* 1:131–36.

Smith, M. (2003). "Exploring Target Attractiveness in Vandalism: An Experimental Approach." In M. Smith and D. Cornish (eds.), *Theory for Practice in Situational Crime Prevention.* Crime Prevention Studies 16. Monsey, N.Y.: Criminal Justice Press.

Smith, W., S. Frazee, and E. Davison. (2000). "Furthering the Integration of Routine Activity and Social Disorganization Theories: Small Units of

Analysis and the Study of Street Robbery as a Diffusion Process." *Criminology* 38:489–523.

Sole Brito, C., and T. Allan (eds.) (1999). *Problem-Oriented Policing: Crime-Specific Problems, Critical Issues, and Making POP Work*, vol. 2. Washington, D.C.: Police Executive Research Forum.

———, and E. Gratto (eds.) (2000). *Problem-Oriented Policing: Crime-Specific Problems, Critical Issues, and Making POP Work*, vol. 3. Washington, D.C.: Police Executive Research Forum.

Sousa, W., and G. L. Kelling. (2006). "Of 'Broken Windows,' Criminology, and Criminal Justice." In: D. L. Weisburd and A. A. Braga (eds.), *Police Innovation: Contrasting Perspectives*. New York: Cambridge University Press.

Sparrow, M. (2008). *The Character of Harms*. New York: Cambridge University Press.

———, M. H. Moore, and D. M. Kennedy. (1990). *Beyond 911: A New Era for Policing*. New York: Basic Books.

Spelman, W. (1993). "Abandoned Buildings: Magnets for Crime?" *Journal of Criminal Justice* 21:481–95.

———. (1995). "Criminal Careers of Public Places." In: J. Eck and D. Weisburd (eds.), *Crime and Place*. Crime Prevention Studies 4. Monsey, N.Y.: Criminal Justice Press.

———, and D. Brown. (1984). *Calling the Police: Citizen Reporting of Serious Crime*. Washington, D.C.: U.S. Government Printing Office.

———, and J. E. Eck. (1989). "Sitting Ducks, Ravenous Wolves, and Helping Hands: New Approaches to Urban Policing." *Public Affairs Comment*, 35(2): 1–9.

St. Jean, P. K. B. (2007). *Pockets of Crime: Broken Windows, Collective Efficacy, and the Criminal Point of View*. Chicago: University of Chicago Press.

Sunshine, J., and T. R. Tyler. (2003). "The Role of Procedural Justice and Legitimacy in Shaping Public Support for Policing." *Law and Society Review* 37:555–89.

Sutherland, E. (1947). *Principals of Criminology*. Chicago: J. B. Lippincott Co.

Suttles, G. D. (1968). *The Social Order of the Slum: Ethnicity and Territory in the Inner City*. Chicago: University of Chicago Press.

Taylor, R. (1997). "Social Order and Disorder of Street-Blocks and Neighborhoods: Ecology, Micro-Ecology, and the Systematic Model of

Social Disorganization." *Journal of Research in Crime and Delinquency* 34:113–55.

———. (1999). "The Incivilities Thesis: Theory, Measurement, and Policy." In: R. Langworthy (ed.), *Measuring What Matters: Proceedings from the Policing Research Institute Meetings.* Washington, D.C.: National Institute of Justice, U.S. Department of Justice.

———. (2001). *Breaking Away from Broken Windows: Baltimore Neighborhoods and the Nationwide Fight against Crime, Grime, Fear, and Decline.* Boulder, Colo.: Westview Press.

———. (2006). "Incivilities Reduction Policing, Zero Tolerance, and the Retreat from Coproduction." In: D. L. Weisburd and A. A. Braga (eds.), *Police Innovation: Contrasting Perspectives.* New York: Cambridge University Press.

———, and S. Gottfredson. (1986). "Environment Design, Crime, and Prevention: An Examination of Community Dynamics." In: A. Reiss and M. Tonry (eds.), *Communities and Crime.* Crime and Justice Series 8. Chicago: University of Chicago Press.

———, S. D. Gottfredson, and S. Brower. (1984). "Block Crime and Fear: Defensible Space, Local Social Ties, and Territorial Functioning." *Journal of Research in Crime and Delinquency* 21:303–31.

Tonry, M. (1995). *Malign Neglect.* New York: Oxford University Press.

Townsley, M., R. Homel, and J. Chaseling. (2003). "Infectious Burglaries: A Test of the Near Repeat Hypothesis." *British Journal of Criminology* 43:615–33.

Tracy, P. E., and K. Kempf-Leonard. (1996). *Continuity and Discontinuity in Criminal Careers.* New York: Plenum.

Trasler, G. (1993). "Conscience, Opportunity, Rational Choice, and Crime." In: R. Clarke and M. Felson (eds.), *Routine Activity and Rational Choice.* Advances in Criminological Theory 5. New Brunswick, N.J.: Transaction Publishers.

Travis, J. (2005). *But They All Come Back: Facing the Challenges of Prisoner Reentry.* Washington, D.C.: Urban Institute.

Trojanowicz, R. (1983). "An Evaluation of a Neighborhood Foot Patrol Program." *Journal of Police Science and Administration* 11:410–19.

Tyler, T. R. (1990). *Why People Obey the Law: Procedural Justice, Legitimacy, and Compliance.* New Haven, Conn.: Yale University Press.

———. (1998). "Public Mistrust of the Law: A Political Perspective." *University of Cincinnati Law Review* 66:847–76.

———. (2000). "Social Justice: Outcomes and Procedures." *International Journal of Psychology* 35:117–25.

———. (2001). "Public Trust and Confidence in Legal Authorities: What Do Majority and Minority Groups Members Want from the Law and Legal Institutions?" *Behavioral Sciences and the Law* 19:215–35.

———. (2003). "Procedural Justice, Legitimacy, and the Effective Rule of Law." In: M. Tonry (ed.), *Crime and Justice: A Review of Research*, vol. 30. Chicago: University of Chicago Press.

———. (2004). "Enhancing Police Legitimacy." *Annals of the American Academy of Political and Social Science* 593:84–99.

———. (2005). "Policing in Black and White: Ethnic Group Differences in Trust and Confidence in the Police." *Police Quarterly* 8:322–42.

———. (2006). "Legitimacy and Legitimation." *Annual Review of Psychology* 57:375–400.

———, R. Boeckmann, H. J. Smith, and Y. J. Huo. (1997). *Social Justice in a Diverse Society*. Denver, Colo.: Westview.

———, A. A. Braga, J. Fagan, T. L. Meares, R. Sampson, and C. Winship. (2007). "Legitimacy and Criminal Justice." In: T. R. Tyler, A. A. Braga, J. Fagan, T. L. Meares, R. Sampson, and C. Winship (eds.), *Legitimacy and Criminal Justice: A Comparative Perspective*. New York: Russell Sage Foundation.

———, and J. Fagan. (2008). "Legitimacy and Cooperation: Why Do People Help the Police Fight Crime in Their Communities?" *Ohio State Journal of Criminal Law* 6:231–75.

———, and Y. J. Huo. (2002). *Trust in the Law: Encouraging Public Cooperation with the Police and Courts*. New York: Russell Sage Foundation.

———, and C. Wakslak. (2004). "Profiling and the Legitimacy of the Police: Procedural Justice, Attributions of Motive, and the Acceptance of Social Authority." *Criminology* 42:13–42.

U.S. Bureau of Justice Statistics. (1998). *Criminal Victimization and Perceptions of Community Safety in 12 Cities*. Washington, D.C.: Department of Justice.

———. (2001). *Community Policing in Local Police Departments, 1997 and 1999*. Washington, D.C.: Department of Justice.

U.S. National Advisory Commission on Civil Disorders. (1968). *Report of the National Advisory Commission on Civil Disorders*. Washington, D.C.: U.S. Government Printing Office.

U.S. President's Commission on Law Enforcement and Administration of Criminal Justice. (1967a). *The Challenge of Crime in a Free Society*. Washington, D.C.: U.S. Government Printing Office.

U.S. President's Commission on Law Enforcement and Administration of Criminal Justice. (1967b). *Task Force Report: The Police*. Washington, D.C.: U.S. Government Printing Office.

Visher, C., and D. L. Weisburd. (1998). "Identifying What Works: Recent Trends in Crime Prevention Strategies." *Crime, Law and Social Change* 28:223–42.

Vollmer, A. (1933). "Police Progress in the Past Twenty-Five Years." *Journal of Criminal Law and Criminology* 24:161–75.

Walker, S. (1992). *The Police in America*. 2nd ed. New York: McGraw-Hill.

Warner, B., and G. Pierce. (1993). "Reexamining Social Disorganization Theory Using Calls to the Police as a Measure of Crime." *Criminology* 31:493–518.

Webb, B., and G. Laycock. (1992). *Reducing Crime on the London Underground: An Evaluation of Three Pilot Projects*. London: Home Office.

Weisburd, D. L. (1993). "Design Sensitivity in Criminal Justice Experiments." In: M. Tonry (ed.), *Crime and Justice: A Review of Research*, vol. 17. Chicago: University of Chicago Press.

———. (2002). "From Criminals to Criminal Contexts: Reorienting Criminal Justice Research and Policy." *Advances in Criminological Theory* 10:197–216.

———. (2003). "Ethical Practice and Evaluation of Interventions in Crime and Justice: The Moral Imperative for Randomized Trials." *Evaluation Review* 27:336–54.

———. (2008). *Place-Based Policing*. Ideas in American Policing Series 9. Washington, D.C.: Police Foundation.

———, W. Bernasco, and G. Bruinsma (eds.) (2009). *Putting Crime in its Place: Units of Analysis in Geographic Criminology*. New York: Springer.

———, and A. A. Braga. (2003). "Hot Spots Policing." In: H. Kury and J. Obergfell-Fuchs (eds.), *Crime Prevention: New Approaches*. Mainz, Germany: Weisser Ring.

————, and A. A. Braga. (2006). "Hot Spots Policing as a Model for Police Innovation." In: D. L. Weisburd and A. A. Braga (eds.), *Police Innovation: Contrasting Perspectives*. New York: Cambridge University Press.

————, and C. Britt. (2007). *Statistics in Criminal Justice*. 3rd ed. New York: Springer-Verlag.

————, S. Bushway, C. Lum, and S. Yang. (2004). "Trajectories of Crime at Places: A Longitudinal Study of Street Segments in the City of Seattle." *Criminology* 42:283–322.

————, and J. Eck. (2004). "What Can Police Do to Reduce Crime, Disorder, and Fear?" *Annals of the American Academy of Political and Social Science* 593:42–65.

————, and L. Green. (1994). "Defining the Drug Market: The Case of the Jersey City DMAP System." In: D. L. MacKenzie and C. Uchida (eds.), *Drugs and Crime: Evaluating Public Policy Initiatives*. Newbury Park, Calif.: Sage.

————, and L. Green. (1995). "Policing Drug Hot Spots: The Jersey City DMA Experiment." *Justice Quarterly* 12(3): 711–36.

————, and L. Green (Mazerolle). (2000). "Crime and Disorder in Drug Hot Spots: Implications for Theory and Practice in Policing." *Police Quarterly* 3:331–49.

————, R. Greenspan, E. Hamilton, K. Bryant, and H. Williams. (2001). *The Abuse of Police Authority: A National Study of Police Officers' Attitudes*. Washington, D.C.: The Police Foundation.

————, and C. Lum. (2005). "The Diffusion of Computerized Crime Mapping Policing: Linking Research and Practice." *Police Practice and Research* 6:433–48.

————, C. Lum, and A. Petrosino. (2001). "Does Research Design Affect Study Outcomes in Criminal Justice?" *Annals of the American Academy of Political and Social Science* 578:50–70.

————, L. Maher, and L. Sherman. (1992). "Contrasting Crime General and Crime Specific Theory: The Case of Hot Spots of Crime." *Advances in Criminological Theory* 4:45–69.

————, S. Mastrofski, A. McNally, and R. Greenspan. (2001). *Compstat and Organizational Change*. Washington, D.C.: Police Foundation.

————, S. Mastrofski, A. M. McNally, R. Greenspan, and J. Willis. (2003). "Reforming to Preserve: Compstat and Strategic Problem Solving in American Policing." *Criminology and Public Policy* 2:421–57.

————, and J. McElroy. (1988). "Enacting the CPO Role: Findings from the New York City Pilot Program in Community Policing." In: J. Greene and S. Mastrofski (eds.), *Community Policing: Rhetoric or Reality?* New York: Praeger.

————, and J. T. McEwen (eds.) (1997). *Crime Mapping and Crime Prevention.* Crime Prevention Studies 8. Monsey, N.Y.: Criminal Justice Press.

————, N. Morris, and J. Ready. (2008). "Risk-Focused Policing at Places: An Experimental Evaluation." *Justice Quarterly* 25:163–200.

————, C. Telep, J. Hinkle, and J. E. Eck. (2010). "Is Problem-Oriented Policing Effective in Reducing Crime and Disorder? Findings from a Campbell Systematic Review." *Criminology and Public Policy* 9: 139–72.

————, and C. Uchida. (1993). "Raising Questions of Law and Order." In: D. Weisburd and C. Uchida (eds.), *Police Innovation and Control of the Police: Problems of Law, Order, and Community.* New York: Springer-Verlag.

————, and E. Waring (with E. Chayet). (2001). *White Collar Crime and Criminal Careers.* Cambridge: Cambridge University Press.

————, L. Wyckoff, J. Ready, J. Eck, J. Hinkle, and F. Gajewski. (2006). "Does Crime Just Move Around the Corner? A Controlled Study of Spatial Displacement and Diffusion of Crime Control Benefits." *Criminology* 44:549–92.

Weiss, A. (2001). "The Police and Road Safety." Paper prepared for the U.S. National Research Council Committee to Review Research on Police Policy and Practice.

Weitzer, R., and S. A. Tuch. (2006). *Race and Policing in America: Conflict and Reform.* New York: Cambridge University Press.

Welsh, B. C. (2006). "Evidence-Based Policing for Crime Prevention." In: D. L. Weisburd and A. A. Braga (eds.), *Police Innovation: Contrasting Perspectives.* New York: Cambridge University Press.

————, and D. Farrington. (2000). "Monetary Costs and Benefits of Crime Prevention Programs." In: M. Tonry (ed.), *Crime and Justice: A Review of Research*, vol. 27. Chicago: University of Chicago Press.

————, and D. Farrington. (2004). "Surveillance for Crime Prevention in Public Space: Results and Policy Choices in Britain and America." *Criminology and Public Policy* 3:497–526.

Western, B. (2006). *Punishment and Inequality in America.* New York: Russell Sage.

White, G. F. (1990). "Neighborhood Permeability and Burglary Rates." *Justice Quarterly* 7:57–67.

Whitehead, J. T., and S. Lab. (1989). "A Meta-Analysis of Juvenile Correctional Treatment." *Journal of Research in Crime and Delinquency* 26:276–95.

Wickersham Commission. (1931). "Wickersham Report on Police." *American Journal of Police Science* 2:337–48.

Wikstrom, P. H. (1995). "Preventing City Center Street Crimes." In: M. Tonry and D. P. Farrington (eds.), *Building a Safer Society: Strategic Approaches to Crime Prevention. Crime and Justice: A Review of Research*, vol. 19. Chicago: University of Chicago Press.

Willis, J. J., S. D. Mastrofski, and D. L. Weisburd. (2004). "Compstat and Bureaucracy: A Case Study of Challenges and Opportunities for Change." *Justice Quarterly* 21:463–96.

Willis, J. J., S. D. Mastrofski, and D. L. Weisburd. (2007). "Making Sense of Compstat: A Theory-Based Analysis of Organizational Change in Three Police Departments." *Law & Society Review* 41:147–88.

Wilson, D. B. (2001). "Meta-Analytical Methods for Criminology." *Annals of the American Academy of Political and Social Science* 578:71–89.

Wilson, J. Q., and G. Kelling. (1982). "Broken Windows: The Police and Neighborhood Safety." *Atlantic Monthly* (March): 29–38.

Wilson, J. V. (1990). *Gainesville Convenience Store Ordinance: Findings of Fact. Conclusions and Recommendations.* Washington, D.C.: Crime Control Research Corporation. (Photocopy.)

Wilson, O. W. (1950). *Police Administration.* New York: McGraw-Hill.

Wilson, O. W. (1963). *Police Administration.* 2nd ed. New York: McGraw-Hill.

Wilson, O. W., and R. McLaren. (1977). *Police Administration.* 4th ed. New York: McGraw-Hill.

Winship, C., and J. Berrien. (1999). "Boston Cops and Black Churches." *The Public Interest* (Summer): 52–68.

Wolfgang, M., and F. Ferracuti. (1967). *The Subculture of Violence: Toward an Integrated Theory in Criminology.* New York: Tavistock.

Wolfgang, M., R. Figlio, and T. Sellin. (1972). *Delinquency in a Birth Cohort.* Chicago: University of Chicago Press.

Wolfgang, M., T. Thornberry, and R. Figlio. (1987). *From Boy to Man, From Delinquency to Crime.* Chicago: University of Chicago Press.

Worden, R. E. (1995). "The 'Causes' of Police Brutality: Theory and Evidence on Police Use of Force." In: W. A. Geller and H. Toch (eds.), *And Justice for All: Understanding and Controlling Police Abuse of Force.* Washington, D.C.: Police Executive Research Forum.

Wycoff, M., and W. Skogan. (1986). "Storefront Police Offices: The Houston Field Test." In: D. Rosenbaum (ed.), *Community Crime Prevention: Does It Work?* Thousand Oaks, Calif.: Sage.

Zimring, F., and G. Hawkins. (1973). *Deterrence: The Legal Threat in Crime Control.* Chicago: University of Chicago Press.

INDEX

Abandoned residential homes, 83
American Housing Survey, 226

bars, 81–82, 170
Bayley, David, 43, 222
Block, Carolyn, 35
boost accounts, repeat victimization, 94
bounded rationality, 21
Bratton, William, 53
broken windows policing, 44, 47–49
broken windows thesis, 77–78
    physical incivilities, 77
    social incivilities, 77

Campbell Collaboration systematic review
    of crime and disorder effects,
        127–34
    of crime displacement, 134–35
    of crime prevention benefits, 141–42
    meta-analysis, meta-analysis of hot
        spots experiments
    overview, 115–16
    police crackdown programs, 118
    police enforcement efforts, 117–18
    search strategies, 119–20

selected studies, characteristics, 120–27
selection criteria, 116–18
CCTV. *See* closed-circuit television
    (CCTV) surveillance system
Challenge of Crime in a Free Society, 42
citizen involvement, 203–12
Clarke, Ronald V., 16, 57
closed-circuit television (CCTV)
    surveillance system, 169
commercial burglaries, 83
Committee to Review Research on Police
    Policy and Practices, 111–15
    crime displacement, 114
    problem-oriented policing, 113, 114
    tasks, 111
community policing, 46–47, 187
    citizen involvement, 203–12
    decentralization, 212–14
    problem-oriented policing, 214–17
Compstat system, 52–53
    crime mapping and, 53
    features, 240–42
    potential weaknesses of, 242–43
computerized crime mapping, 28–30
    Compstat and, 53

convenience stores, robberies at, 85–86, 143

Cordner, Gary, 155

crime concentrations, and hot spots, 23, 24–27
  Seattle study, 23, 25–26

crime deflection, and repeat victimization, 95

crime displacement, 14–22
  Campbell Collaboration systematic review of, 134–35
  concept, 6
  purported inevitability of, 142–47
  spatial displacement, 17–22

crime fighter model
  preventive patrol, 39
  rapid response, 39–40
  follow-up investigations, 40

crime hot spots. See hot spots

crime mapping, 27–30
  Compstat and, 53
  computerized, 28–30

crime opportunities, measures of, 80–81

crime pattern theory. See environmental criminology

crime place research, review of
  facilities, 80–84
  offender mobility, 88–91
  offender target selection, 91–92
  overview, 79
  site features, 85–88

crime places (see also crime place research, review of)
  "broken windows" thesis, 77–78
  environmental criminology, 75–77
  rational choice perspective, 67–72
  routine activity theory and, 72–75
  theoretical perspectives and, 67–78
  and theories, 66–67

crime prevention (see also hot spots policing; preventive patrol; problem-oriented policing)

hot spots as targets for, 23–27
  mechanism, 180–82

crime scripts, 72 (see also script analytic approach)

crime triangle, 73–74

criminal behavior, instability of, 225–26

criminal justice system, 41–43

criminal markets, 64

criminological theory
  "broken windows" thesis, 77–78
  communities and, 55–56
  crime concentrations and, 58–59
  crime opportunities and, 55–56
  crime rates and, 57
  environmental criminology, 75–77
  hot spots policing and, 55–59
  individual motivation in, 57
  rational choice, 67–72
  routine activity, 72–75
  situational crime prevention and, 57–58
  specific places and, 58
  traditional crime prevention, 56–57

crisis, in American policing, 36–54
  criminal justice system, failure, 41–43
  innovations, as response to, 44–54 (see also innovations, in response to policing crisis)
  professional policing (see professional policing)

Davis, Edward F., 187

decentralization, 212–14

defensible space theory, 85

deterrence, 37

diffusion of crime prevention benefits, 16

disorder-crime connection, 77–78

displacement. See crime displacement

distribution of crime, 58–9

domestic-violence, and repeat victimization, 95

drug dealing locations, 83

hot spots policing (*continued*)
  empirical evidence for. *See* empirical
    evidence, for hot spots policing
  Minneapolis study. *See* Minneapolis
    Hot Spots Patrol Experiment
  operational changes to, 230–32
  overview, 3–5
  repeat victimization and. *See* repeat
    victimization
  research and practice, 27–31

incapacitation, 37
innovations, in response to policing
    crisis, 44–54
  broken windows policing, 47–49
  community policing (*see* community
    policing)
  Compstat, 52–53
  hot spots policing (*see* hot spots
    policing)
  problem-oriented policing (*see*
    problem-oriented policing)
  third-party policing, 51–52

Jersey City Displacement and Diffusion
    Project, 17–22
  place in, 64, 65
Jersey City Drug Market Analysis, 15–16,
    114
Jersey City Problem-Oriented Policing
    in Violent Places experiment, 113,
    160–62

Kansas City Gun Project evaluation, 113–14
Kansas City Preventive Patrol
    Experiment, 5, 8–9
  design, 8
  findings, 8
Kelling, George L., 8
Kelly, Clarence, 8
Kerner Commission on Civil
    Disorders, 42–43

legitimacy, 189–90
  and behavior, 199–202
  minority communities, 188, 196–99
  prospects for, 227–30
Levine, James, 40
lifestyle theory, of repeat
    victimization, 93–94
Lowell Policing Crime and Disorder Hot
    Spots project, 162–63

Maple, Jack, 53
Martinson, Robert, 56
Mayland report. *See* University of
    Maryland report
Meta-analysis of hot spots
    experiment, 115–16, 135–40
Minneapolis Hot Spots Patrol
    Experiment, 5, 12–14, 27–28, 112–13
  place in, 64
minority communities (*see also*
    community policing)
  and criminal justice system, 41–43
  and legitimacy, 196–99
Moore, Mark, 223
Murphy, Patrick, 8

National Research Council report. *See*
    Committee to Review Research on
    Police Policy and Practices
near-repeat victimization, 96–97
Newark Foot Patrol Experiment, 45
non-experimental designs. *See*
    observational research designs

observational research designs
  defined, 104
  external validity, 105–7
  overview, 104–5
  statistical power, 107
offender-focused crime prevention
    efforts, 56–57
offender mobility, 88–91